Praise for *Rebel Mother*

"Thoroughly engrossing."

—*The New York Times Book Review*

"[Andreas's] life is rich with the gift of a woman who let herself truly be known by her son, warts and all. . . . *Rebel Mother* traces Carol Andreas's transformation from a traditional 1950s housewife into a Marxist traveling the globe in search of the revolution."

—*The Dallas Morning News*

"Moving . . . poignant . . . *Rebel Mother* makes the case for a mother-son bond powerful enough to transcend economic hardship, emotional missteps, intermittent absences, and, ultimately, differences in values and politics. . . . Compelling and unusual."

—*The Boston Globe*

"A remarkable memoir . . . *Rebel Mother* relates an incredible childhood of communes and coups across the U.S. and Latin America."

—*Vice*

"This is a riveting story, compellingly told by an accomplished writer. Peter had his own radical turn when, defying his mother, he moved away from radicalism. His academic work in political science and writing about Latin America, however, show he is still very much the son of his beloved mother."

—*The Baffler*

"A warm, tender tale of protective love and codependency in a mother-son pair living in extreme circumstances."

—*Foreign Affairs*

"*Rebel Mother* is highly compelling and a rewarding read—as well as a resonant reminder of what, for many, is one of life's most formative relationships."

—*Swarthmore College Bulletin*

"Enthralling . . . Writing with candor and sincerity, Andreas—now an international studies professor at Brown University—creates an unforgettable portrait of a remarkable woman. . . . *Rebel Mother* offers a sympathetic and fascinating glimpse into the life of a radical woman, a tumultuous era, and a sensitive young man's coming-of-age."

—*BookPage* (Top Pick in Nonfiction)

"[A] luminous memoir . . . vivid, picaresque . . . Andreas's exuberant but clear-eyed memoir paints an indelible portrait of his charismatic mother, the era's expansive pursuit of freedom and idealistic commitment, and the toll of exhausted dreams and frayed relationships the idealists left behind."

—*Publishers Weekly* (starred review)

"Those who enjoyed Jeannette Walls's *The Glass Castle* will find much to admire here. . . . This is both a story of a mother and son's fierce devotion to one another, and a fascinating portrait of a woman's life spent committed to radical ideas and politics, and how this affected her closest ally and confidant."

—*Booklist* (starred review)

"A profound and enlightening book that will open readers up to different ideas about love, acceptance, and the bond between mother and son."

—*Library Journal*

"An illuminating portrait of a childhood of excitement, adventure, and love positioned against the backdrop of 1970s-era South America. . . . Andreas fully immerses readers in his experiences."

—*Kirkus Reviews*

"An astonishing story of love and life within a family at war."

—Tim Weiner, author of *Legacy of Ashes* and *Enemies*

"Peter Andreas's memoir is a tender portrayal of a revolutionary era; of an infuriating, fascinating, contradictory, loving and much-beloved woman; and of a childhood like no other."

—Tina Rosenberg, author of
The Haunted Land and *Children of Cain*

"An incredible journey into bandit country—the heartbreaking terrain between mother and son. A gorgeous, bighearted book."

—Brando Skyhorse, author of
Take This Man and *The Madonnas of Echo Park*

"This is a beautiful book that recalls a radical period of Latin America history, written through the eyes of a child but with the perspective of a true scholar of international affairs."

—Ricardo Lagos, former president of Chile

"Just when we thought we had heard all the most amazing stories of American life during the wild 1960s and '70s, this astonishing memoir appears. It's the classic story of a boy's coming-of-age, but with a dazzling overlay of fleeing to South America and becoming caught up in a mother's radical dreams. Young Peter had a unique boyhood, and grown-up Peter Andreas tells his story with a compassion that places it among the most moving memoirs of that turbulent era."

—Stephen Kinzer, author of *The Brothers* and *Bitter Fruit*

"This is a truly captivating account of an extraordinary childhood on the run with an errant mother who preached free love and revolution from Colorado to Peru. A startlingly revealing memoir of one American family's torn-apart life, *Rebel Mother* is an unforgettable read."

—Jon Lee Anderson, author of *Che Guevara: A Revolutionary Life*

ALSO BY PETER ANDREAS

Smuggler Nation: How Illicit Trade Made America

Blue Helmets and Black Markets: The Business of Survival in the Siege of Sarajevo

Policing the Globe: Criminalization and Crime Control in International Relations (with Ethan Nadelmann)

Border Games: Policing the U.S.–Mexico Divide

REBEL MOTHER

*My Childhood Chasing
the Revolution*

Peter Andreas

Simon & Schuster Paperbacks

NEW YORK   LONDON   TORONTO   SYDNEY   NEW DELHI

Simon & Schuster Paperbacks
An Imprint of Simon & Schuster, Inc.
1230 Avenue of the Americas
New York, NY 10020

First Simon & Schuster paperback edition April 2018

SIMON & SCHUSTER PAPERBACKS and colophon are registered trademarks
of Simon & Schuster, Inc.

For information about special discounts for bulk purchases,
please contact Simon & Schuster Special Sales at 1-866-506-1949
or business@simonandschuster.com.

The Simon & Schuster Speakers Bureau can bring authors to your
live event. For more information or to book an event, contact the
Simon & Schuster Speakers Bureau at 1-866-248-3049
or visit our website at www.simonspeakers.com.

Interior design by Paul Dippolito

Manufactured in the United States of America

10 9 8 7 6 5 4 3 2 1

The Library of Congress has cataloged the hardcover edition as follows:

Names: Andreas, Peter, 1965– author.
Title: Rebel mother : my childhood chasing the revolution / Peter Andreas.
Other titles: My childhood chasing the revolution
Description: New York : Simon & Schuster, [2017]
Identifiers: LCCN 2016059214 (print) | LCCN 2017017085 (ebook) |
ISBN 9781501124457 (Ebook) | ISBN 9781501124396 (hardcover) |
ISBN 9781501124426 (trade pbk.) Subjects: LCSH: Andreas, Carol. | Feminists—
United States—Biography. | Women revolutionaries—United States—Biography. |
Andreas, Peter, 1965—Childhood and youth. | Mothers and sons—Biography. |
Women political activists—United States—Biography. |Americans—Peru—Biography. |
Americans—Chile—Biography. | College teachers—United States—Biography. |
Radicalism—United States—History—20th century.
Classification: LCC HQ1413.A48 (ebook) | LCC HQ1413.A48 A54 2017 (print) |
DDC 305.42092 [B]—dc23
LC record available at https://lccn.loc.gov/2016059214

ISBN 978-1-5011-2439-6
ISBN 978-1-5011-2442-6 (pbk)
ISBN 978-1-5011-2445-7 (ebook)

For Stella and Annika

With my mother in Lima, Peru, December 1973

Contents

V. RETURN TO PERU

VI. MILE-HIGH HIDEOUT

VII. TEEN YEARS

EPILOGUE

Author's Note

After my mother's sudden death, I found scattered through her tiny redbrick house more than a hundred diary notebooks. They covered three decades, beginning in the years when she and I had traveled South America together. She had used whatever was available, from spiral to legal pads and even my school notebooks from our time in Peru, when she'd switched back and forth between writing in English and Spanish. I always knew my mother kept a diary—I'd often watched her write in it when I was a little boy—but I had no idea she had kept them all. As we were clearing out her house together, my two older brothers had no interest in the notebooks, so I packed them up, along with my mother's half century of personal correspondence and other documents, and carried them home to Providence in duffel bags. I spent weeks reading through those dusty old diaries, a way of talking to my mother one last time, reliving my roller-coaster childhood by her side as we fled, time and again, across borders in search of her elusive revolution.

Now, more than a decade later, these diaries have helped me finally tell the story of those wild years with my Mennonite-turned-Marxist mother, a passionate, headstrong woman whose radicalism extended from the geopolitical down to her own domestic sphere. It's a story I've long struggled to decipher and come to terms with, now even more so with my late entry into the world of parenthood. In addition to relying on my own memories and interviews with friends and family members, I've re-created and extended dialogue and scenes described in my mother's diaries, notes, books, and personal correspondence. I do wonder, of course, what my mother would think of this book if she were still alive—though I could never have written it while she *was* alive. She would surely have enjoyed arguing with me about it, but I have no doubt she would be glad I wrote it. It is our story.

I.

LEAVING

Today,
I dance for hours alone in a beautiful world.
I dance with Peter, my little boy, who cannot live with me.
I dance because I never felt free to dance before.
And there is no one else in the world who is free enough
to dance with me.

—Opening lines of Carol Andreas,
Sex and Caste in America

Carol and Carl

MY MOTHER HAD always been the one to pick me up from nursery school, but one late June afternoon in 1969, a couple of weeks before my fourth birthday, my father arrived first and pushed me into the backseat of his gray Chevy Malibu. I could tell that something was not right by how tightly he gripped my hand and hurried me out of the school building to his car. Standing on my toes on the seat to look out the back window, I saw my mother's beige VW station wagon arrive behind us just as we started to pull away from the curb.

I waved at her. "Daddy, Daddy, Mommy's coming!"

"No, Mommy's leaving," my father grumbled, turning his head back briefly. "Now please, sit down." My father slammed the accelerator and the car jerked forward, tipping me off balance.

My mother, seeing that my father had already taken me, tailed us for as long as she could. She projected an air of calm, waving cheerfully at me from over the steering wheel, but she must have been anything but. Eventually, my father accelerated so fast that she became smaller and smaller, then disappeared into the distance. "Mommy's gone," I cried out, tears welling in my eyes.

"Yes, that's right, Peter, Mommy *is* gone. But don't worry, I'll take care of you."

That afternoon was my first memory. It marked the beginning of my parents' war over me. Earlier that day, while no one was home, my mother had quickly packed as much as she could into her car, mostly clothes and books but also a few of her favorite Pakistani pictures hanging in the living room, and moved out of the house for good. When my father got home from work and saw the empty closet, the first thing he'd done was rush to my preschool. Over the next six years, I would be kidnapped from school two more times—both times by my mother, who would carry me first across the country and then across continents. My father won that opening battle, but he would lose the war.

During her devoutly conservative childhood, my mother would have seemed like the last person to kidnap her own child. She was born in 1933 in North Newton, a tightly knit Mennonite community of a few thousand inhabitants in central Kansas, where Mennonite wheat farmers from Ukraine had originally settled in the 1870s. When my mother was a child, most people didn't venture out of North Newton much; if they did, they were usually visiting other Mennonite communities in rural Middle America. As a pacifist Christian sect closely related to the Amish—though unlike the Amish they don't reject the technologies of modern life—Mennonites mostly intermarried, spent Sundays at church, and kept to themselves.

My mother's parents, Willis Rich and Hulda Penner, had met while waiting in line their freshman year to enroll in classes at Bethel, the local college where most college-bound Mennonites in the area went to school and where Willis would eventually become director of public relations. Although they were devoutly religious—going to church, praying before meals, singing church hymns, dressing conservatively—they were also less strict than other Mennonite families in North Newton. As the PR man for the college, Willis made sure to bring interesting speakers from all over the world to campus, and Hulda would entertain them at their house a few blocks away. My mother and her three siblings served the guests at the table, which gave her an opportunity to pepper them with questions.

Perhaps it was partly due to such outside influences that, by the time my mother was a teenager, she had become enough of a skeptic to declare herself an agnostic, which I imagine must have rattled the rest of the community. Her parents, though, took it in stride. Mennonites did not dance ("that led to sex") and did not play cards ("that led to gambling"), but Willis and Hulda let their children do both—as long as it was out of sight, behind closed doors. So when the doorbell rang while the kids were playing cards, they quickly hid them under the table; and they could playfully dance around the house, but any kind of dancing in public, including at the high school dances organized for the non-Mennonites from the other side of town, was not allowed.

The Rich family differed from the rest of the community in other ways, too. They were Democrats in a Republican town. Willis's sister, Selma, whom my mother looked up to as a role model, was an early civil rights advocate and campaigned to integrate the local swimming pool and movie theater. Also unusual was that Willis had gone to Columbia University for a graduate degree in education, and his first job was as a teacher in the non-Mennonite town of Bentley, Kansas. Although there were plenty of Bibles scattered about the house, Willis spent more time reading Norman Vincent Peale's *The Power of Positive Thinking*—and enthusiastically quoting from it out loud to his kids—than he did Scripture. Willis was always upbeat and optimistic, which remained true even after he became afflicted with multiple sclerosis and was confined to a wheelchair.

During Christmas vacation, 1947, just a little more than a month after my mother turned fourteen, she and a friend had gone out sledding—or tried to, anyway, in the flat Kansas fields. She'd been allowed to exchange her plain skirt for a pair of pants for the sledding, and the curls of her fine, shoulder-length hair poked out of her wool winter cap. It was her smile and her beautiful green eyes that captivated my father, the handsome twenty-year-old Bethel College student who stopped by the side of the road that afternoon and offered to pull her sled behind his shiny black 1931 Ford Model A coupe. My mother asked my father if he played a sport and he replied, with a grin, "I play the radio." He was not the athletic type, but he did have a car, and it did have a radio.

My father, Carl Roland Andreas, started taking my mother, Carol Ruth Rich, out once a week, holding her hand at the drive-in or at the high school and college basketball games. Except for the nearly seven-year age gap, my father seemed like a perfect suitor—polite, responsible, hardworking, and from a good Mennonite family. His grandfather had even been a Mennonite minister married to the church organist.

Beyond her pretty face, my father was drawn to my mother's complex combination of innocence and maturity. My mother, in turn, was flattered by the attention of an older man, especially one who had resisted his mother's pressure to become a minister. And he seemed downright worldly compared to the other Newton boys; he had traveled to Cuba with his college roommate during a winter break, worked on the railroad in Colorado for a year after high school, and spent the last year of World War II as a conscientious objector in a Civilian Public Service camp in Mississippi, building latrines in poor rural communities. My mother admired those who defied the draft and had tasted life outside of Kansas. Her hero growing up was her cousin Dwight (Aunt Selma's son), who spent six months in county jail for refusing to register for the draft and then lived in India for four years before returning to teach at Bethel.

Two years after they met, my mother and father got engaged and kissed for the first time. A year after that they were married. My mother was seventeen; my father, twenty-four. Mennonite girls in North Newton often married young, but usually not *that* young, and usually not to someone *that* much older.

Yet, even as my father's college buddies teased him for robbing the cradle, most everyone seemed pleased with the match—except for the bride. My mother was already starting to have ideological doubts about traditional marriage as a concept itself. As my mother would later tell it, as she and my father arrived at their late-afternoon marriage ceremony on Bethel's Goerz House lawn, she turned suddenly and blurted: "You know what? It just occurred to me that I really don't know if I believe in monogamy." A bold thing to say in 1950s America, this was downright scandalous in a conservative religious community in central Kansas.

"Tootsie, what difference does it make?" my startled father replied, trying to stay calm. "Look over there. There must be five hundred people waiting for us. They all believe in monogamy. They can't all be wrong. And besides, you want to live with me, don't you? How else can we swing that?"

They went through with the ceremony and then moved into an upstairs apartment near campus on South College Avenue. While my father waited for my mother to get through school, he took

Carol and Carl Andreas, May 1951

a job as a bill collector and bookkeeper for the local Mennonite
Deaconess Hospital. Whatever my mother's hesitations, the truth
was my father was her ride out of North Newton. Originally from
Beatrice, Nebraska, a few hours' drive away, he had no plans to
stay in town after college. He and my mother both wanted to go to
graduate school, which meant not only leaving North Newton but
probably Kansas as well. Many others from my mother's generation,
including her siblings, would also end up moving away, but she was
more eager to grow up and get out to see the world than most. Always disciplined and studious, she skipped a grade at Newton High
and rushed through Bethel as fast as she could. "I was only nineteen
when I finished college," my mother always reminded me. "I did it
so I could be with your father."

As soon as she had her diploma, she and my father moved to
Minneapolis–Saint Paul to attend the University of Minnesota to-

My father and mother as a traditional 1950s married couple

gether, where my father earned an MA in hospital administration and my mother an MA in psychology. My mother got him through his course work by helping him write and type up his papers.

Soon they had two little boys, Joel and Ronald, a year and a half apart. My mother loved her children but grew restless under the expectations of a 1950s housewife, a role she'd never intended to play. With my mother's encouragement, my father signed up for a four-year stint as coordinator of a U.S. government–funded medical school program in Karachi, Pakistan. My father saw it as a good career move, but my mother, now in her mid-twenties, was mainly eager to experience life outside of America—and Pakistan happened to be the post that was open. She miscalculated. Instead of worldly adventure, she found herself in an even more insulated life, cooped up in charge of two rambunctious boys in a stifled and claustrophobic U.S. diplomatic community. My mother did her best to keep busy—she studied Urdu, scoured for antiques in Karachi's old bazaar, volunteered to teach English to Pakistani women—but was still restless and frustrated.

It didn't help matters that my father was a workaholic who, according to my mother, was reluctant to take a single day off work, not even a Saturday or Sunday. This was true even before the move to Pakistan; there were no family vacations except for the once- or twice-a-year cross-country drives to visit relatives back in Kansas. In Karachi, my father had little family time beyond an obligatory short daily walk with the kids at dusk—usually taking them to review progress on the city's brand-new sewage plant—while my mother, dripping sweat, struggled to have dinner on the table when they got home.

My father even resisted the weekend outings she tried to plan: when she insisted on going to the beach, he would reluctantly drive them there but would spend the day sitting in the car. My father could be maddeningly practical: from his perspective, what was the point of sitting on the ground or in a rickety beach chair if the

car seat was more shaded and comfortable? He did not share my
mother's interest in foreign cultures or in mingling with the locals;
he was just there for the job opportunity, a career stepping-stone,
and looked forward to returning to the States. He did everything he
could to avoid the spicy cuisine, even if it meant embarrassing my
mother by refusing to eat at neighbors' dinner parties (my father
was not a picky eater, but he preferred his food as bland as possible).
Even back home he had never liked to eat out, choosing cheap, over-
processed chain restaurants whenever possible. As my mother started
to experience the world outside of the American Midwest, she came
to see my father as frustratingly square and provincial. The only
dream that dominated my father's life was to save a million dollars
by the time he retired. She had no dream—not yet—but she had
become ashamed of the privileged lives of the diplomatic community
and local elites floating in a vast sea of poverty.

My mother also felt restless when she and the kids were cooped
up together in the air-conditioned bedrooms during the years before my brothers started school. More than anything, though, she
felt isolated. One of her favorite Karachi memories was of a homely
camel poking its head affectionately into her car window as she was
stopped at an intersection. She would later write, "I had an urge to
hug it and kiss it, as if we were two misfits in the world who had finally found each other—a fleeting recognition of my solitude during
a time when I didn't even know enough to keep a diary."

When the Karachi assignment came to an end in the early sixties,
my parents and brothers went right back to the Midwest, this time
settling down in Detroit, Michigan. My parents bought a downtown
townhouse in Lafayette Park, a middle-class "urban renewal" community. My father had accepted a job offer as business manager for
the Wayne State University School of Medicine, and a few years later,
he moved on to become a staff member of the United Automobile

Workers union, where he would spend the rest of his career, negoti-
ating Social Security and pension benefits.

Intellectually restless and physically exhausted from raising two
energetic boys, my mother decided to work on a PhD in sociology
at Wayne State, where she read works by Marx, Engels, and other
radical theorists for the first time. My father was supportive of my
mother getting a PhD as a sensible career move—he liked the idea
of two incomes—even though he didn't really understand why
anyone would be interested in sociological theory, and certainly
wasn't prepared for the ways in which her personal beliefs might
be affected. In the midst of writing her doctoral dissertation, a
critique of U.S. aid to Pakistan as a tool of political and economic
domination, she unexpectedly became pregnant—yet another boy.
"You were a mistake," my mother used to say, "but a happy one." I
arrived on July 8, 1965.

One of the black-and-white pictures my mother pasted in my
baby album is of our entire family—my mother, father, and two

Family photo, May 30, 1966

older brothers—gathered together on a lawn, me in the middle propped up on my father's knee, everyone posing for the camera. My father and mother are both beaming—he at the camera and she at the infant me—proud of the family they created. The caption under the photo, in my mother's neat, easy-flowing cursive handwriting, reads, "This picture, which was taken on May 30, 1966 (Mother and Daddy's 15th wedding anniversary), was sent to many family friends and illustrates the joy that reigned in Peter's family when he was a baby." I wonder if she knew then how fleeting it would be.

As happy a surprise as I might have been, I was nonetheless inconvenient. My arrival coincided with my mother's attempt to move beyond being a housewife, so she and my father hired a nanny, Mrs. Ruffie, to help take care of me during the day. My mother was preoccupied with her new life as a part-time professor (at Wayne State and at the University of Michigan in Ann Arbor) and a part-time activist—which to her were the same thing. As the civil rights, women's rights, and antiwar movements were exploding across the country, with college campuses at the epicenter, my mother saw her job in the classroom as a way to mobilize students to join the cause and clamor for social justice. I went to my first antiwar demonstration before I was eating solid foods. At age three, I rode a "flower power" tricycle sporting a peace sign in a parade.

My mother's passion for political activism in the mid-sixties found its first outlet in a campaign against the war toys in her sons' toy box. It was the perfect cause for a mother with pacifist Mennonite roots; G.I. Joe never met a more formidable adversary. In my mother's view, war toys—an evil marriage of American militarism and consumer capitalism—were part of the Pentagon's pro-war propaganda machine targeting impressionable children. She fired off letters to all the major toy companies, berating them for contributing to the "war mania" her sons were exposed to. She gave them a long list of toys they could be making instead of plastic guns and soldiers.

My mother proudly called me the
"flower-power trike rider"

She pleaded, how about "fire-fighting and forest ranger sets?" She even offered her help: "I promise to work actively to promote the sale of such new toys if you will openly declare a policy of responsible action in eliminating war toys from your inventory." They replied that their military toys were simply a response to consumer demand; that the toys promoted patriotism and offered a healthy outlet for children's hostilities.

My mother was undeterred. She wrote letters to the newspapers and organized petitions, going door-to-door in our neighborhood, collecting hundreds of signatures to pressure area stores to stop carrying war toys. A local drugstore and a supermarket reluctantly agreed to replace their war toys on display with shovels, buckets, garden tools, and other toy kits and games. My mother's crusade was written up in a front-page story in the *Detroit Free Press*, with the headline "One Mother Opens Fire on War Toys for Kids." Meanwhile, my older brothers, tired of simple toys like the wooden building blocks our father had made for them, sneaked away to play with toy soldiers at their friends' houses.

But by the end of the decade, though she'd lost none of her strident moral righteousness, my mother stopped preaching pacifism and began embracing the anger that she felt was essential for radical change. As was true for so many activists at the time, the escalating war in Vietnam became the turning point in my mother's sympathies. She and my pacifist father both marched against Washington's military involvement in Vietnam, but unlike my father, my mother began to root for the other side—Ho Chi Minh and the Vietcong, whom she viewed as heroic anti-imperialists defiantly fending off foreign military aggression. As she came to see it, how could anyone expect them to defend themselves by simply sitting on their hands? Privileged Western observers far from the villages being carpet bombed by U.S. warplanes, she argued, were in no position to tell the North Vietnamese to simply lay down their arms. But as my father insistently kept trying to remind my mother, their Mennonite upbringing told them to be against *all* wars, *all* violence, and not take sides. A rift was growing between my parents.

Another fault line in their marriage was the idea of monogamy, which my mother came to see as a source of male oppression that perpetuated a patriarchal society. When my mother confessed to my father that she'd had a fling with a man from California named Burt while attending a War Resisters League meeting in Golden, Colorado, he angrily demanded Burt's California address. Over the next several months, he kept sending Burt letters demanding not only that he apologize to our family, but that he cease having affairs with anyone:

I am increasingly disturbed by the realization that you
were able to behave in such an irresponsible fashion with
my wife last September in Golden, Colorado. You were

*aware of the fact that she was a married woman with
three fine boys, and I believe that you owe her family an
apology. It will make it possible for me to establish a finer
relationship with Carol if I know that you will be more
careful in the future of such involvements with others.*

When my father didn't get a reply, he sent another letter: "Please refer to my letter to you regarding your relations with my wife in Golden, Colorado, last September. You may not appreciate the great anxiety you have created in this family. Carol comes from a very fine home with high moral standards. I likewise come from a fine and stable home where the kind of behavior you exhibit is unheard of." He concluded, "I expect to hear from you soon."

The reply my father eventually received was not what he had asked for:

Dear Mr. Andreas,

*Yes, I was aware of the fact that Carol was a married
woman with children, and I can understand and maybe
even feel some of the anxiety that our relationship created
there. But Carol is also an adult human being, capable
of approaching the world as an individual and of
evoking a response as an individual.*

*I cannot make a Satan out of myself for you. That
would be both dishonest to myself and terribly insulting
to Carol. I don't use people lightly. And while my
morality is different than yours it is a morality, and quite
a strict one. It is based on a response to the individual in
the situation and on their worth as autonomous human
beings, rather than on static rules.*

*Finally, I can't make any promises about my future
involvement with others. This is so, first, because, as I
said, I don't approach people with a set of static rules.*

More importantly, though, I can't make any such promise
because the request for it doesn't make any sense. When
you ask that, you are saying that the relationship between
A and B (you and Carol) is dependent on C's (Burt's)
pledge of future conduct with D, E, and F (unknown,
unmet other). The relationship between you and Carol
depends only on you and Carol. The attempt to create
a Satan to serve as a parking place for your unresolved
questions is doomed to failure.

    You and your family have my sincere best wishes for
the new year.

Burt's response left my father feeling even more indignant. His hardwired 1950s sensibilities were banging up against the loosening morals of the 1960s. Peace never really returned to the family after that affair. From then on, my parents argued in their bedroom late at night in angry, hushed voices. My mother arranged for them to see a marriage counselor, but after going once my father refused to go again.

Meanwhile, my mother had become a full-blown political activist in a city consumed by activism. Detroit was in flames. The July 1967 riots left fires burning around Lafayette Park, where we lived, and the governor sent in National Guard troop carriers to major intersections nearby. President Johnson deployed army troops. Forty-three people died, over one thousand were injured, more than seven thousand arrested, and over two thousand buildings destroyed. Yet, in the midst of this chaos, my mother cheerfully sent a letter to family and friends, urging them to visit: "This year there should be an added incentive to visit the city that leads the nation in promoting rebellion among its alienated minorities."

To show her solidarity and join the cause, she became a member of People Against Racism, which worked in tandem with the Black Panthers and the Dodge Revolutionary Union Movement. As a coordinator of the Detroit Committee to End the War Now, she helped organize massive antiwar demonstrations and started hanging out with Maoists, Trotskyists, members of the Communist Party USA, and black nationalists of the Republic of New Africa. My mother became a spokesperson for the Union of Radical Sociologists at American Sociological Association meetings, and was a founder of the journal *The Insurgent Sociologist*, meant to provide a voice and publishing outlet for left-wing activist sociologists.

My mother also led the way in uniting disparate feminist groups in the Michigan Women's Liberation Coalition. Male reporters were banned from the press conference announcing the coalition, which itself became the lead story in the press coverage. "Feminist Groups Oust Newsmen; Form Council" ran the headline in the *Detroit Free Press*; "Feminist Meeting Clears Out Men" reported the *Detroit News*. It was a calculated move; my mother told the *Free Press*, "We felt we had to make this point to them, that part of the oppression of women stems from the fact that the media is largely controlled by men." The *Detroit News* quoted her as saying that the ban would continue "until we're satisfied enough women have been hired in radio and television." Male camera operators, however, were allowed into the press conference "just this one time," she said. Of course, they had to let them in: otherwise, with no women camera operators present, there would be no media coverage of the press conference.

In the wake of all of this, the classroom was simply another opportunity for my mother to engage in political organizing and her vague but lofty-sounding "consciousness raising." She taught a course at the University of Michigan on the Sociology of Sex, and it inspired her to write a book, *Sex and Caste in America*. The book was a manifesto of sorts for women's liberation, in which she declared that the nuclear family should be abolished: "The family maintains the economic structures that thrive on sexism (as well as on racism and imperialism)." I was much too young to understand at the time, but I can only imagine how my father, the straitlaced, traditional American family man, felt about her declaration.

During this time, my mother's appearance changed radically along with her politics. She disposed of the heels, mascara, and hair spray that had defined her look as a 1950s housewife, and later, as a prim and proper young professional. She stopped putting her hair up or curling it, and instead let it hang straight down. Razors were out, unshaved legs and armpits were in. Pants replaced dresses. She tossed out all her bras, and would not put one on again for years. She avoided curling irons and makeup for the rest of her life. Her favorite pair of shoes, brown leather Pakistani sandals with thin straps, soon were pretty much all that remained from her old shoe collection. Cool and casual replaced proper and conventional. There was only one thing left for my mother to do to complete her transformation and leave the last remnants of her housewife identity behind.

My mother and father in June 1969, the month they separated

Separation

BY THE TIME my parents were racing to each be the first to kidnap me from preschool that June day in 1969—the same day my mother left my father—their life goals were catapulting in wildly opposite directions. My father wanted to move to the suburbs, provide a stable home, and save money for the kids' college trust funds and for a comfortable and secure retirement like a good, responsible family man does. Other than having Mennonite pacifist values, the last thing in the world my ultra-pragmatic father wanted was to be seen as a rebel or a troublemaker. He spent more of his time preoccupied with the minutiae of pensions and health benefits in contracts (the UAW had hired him for his technical knowledge in this area rather than for any background or interest in labor organizing) and navigating his daily commute to his downtown office than thinking about how the system was rigged by the rich to exploit the poor. But my mother had come to believe that the evils of the system had to be destroyed by any means necessary—which meant people like my father, who wanted to work within the system, were themselves part of the problem, not the solution. She thought they pacified workers by softening capitalism's sharper edges. She didn't want a conformist raising her children; her boys were going to be radicals.

For a year and a half before the divorce hearing, we all lived in limbo. I was four years old at the start of it. Much to my father's relief, the judge gave him temporary custody of me; my two older brothers insisted on living with my mother, and so they all moved to a two-bedroom rental near Lafayette Park. Back and forth my brothers and I went, in what our parents called a "trading arrangement": I would go stay with our mother for the weekend while my brothers went to stay with our father. The only constant in my life was the indisputable fact that my father and mother were always angry with each other.

When I was at my mother's, my father would call to check that there were no "other men" around. "I wouldn't want little Peter exposed to that."

"Oh, Carl, for once, try to be human, not male," my mother would yell, slamming the receiver down. When my father called back, my mother would let it ring and ring. When I'd ask her why she wasn't answering the phone, her casual answer would be that "it's just your father harassing us again." She'd then yank the cord from the wall.

My mother was both impulsive and stubborn; once she decided to leave my father, there was no going back. My father nevertheless persisted in believing she'd return to the fold. He held out hope, even after she sent him a sharply worded letter explaining, "I have no intention of becoming a wife again, although I am secure in the knowledge that I can be a good mother."

Yet, in complete denial, my father busily continued to oversee the building of a modern four-bedroom suburban home near my mother's first tenure-track job at Oakland University, outside of Detroit. Construction on the two-level house was not complete when my mother picked up and left. But he kept at it, convinced that a bigger and better roof over our heads might somehow keep us all together and magically transform us back into the happy family from that long-ago photo. Months after she moved out, he wrote my mother: "I would like to remind you that I am willing and able to support our family in our home and that I have no intention of terminating our long and faithful, at least on my part, relationship." He added a PS: "Let me know if I can assist you with your 1969 income tax return."

My mother could not be coaxed back, but my father would not give up. He was offended by my mother's divorce petition and vowed to fight it; said he didn't believe in divorce. "There hasn't been a divorce in our family in five hundred years," he snarled. In 1969, the state of Michigan still didn't have no-fault divorce laws, which meant that accepting my mother's divorce petition would imply that he had been culpable for the problems in the marriage. My father was a proud man, and in many ways just as stubborn and self-righteous as my mother. "I'll appeal this case all the way to the Supreme Court if I have to," he insisted to anyone who would listen. He was convinced that he had done everything right as a husband and father and that my mother was fully to blame for her own unhappiness.

My father took out his frustrations on my mother's parents: "With an attitude such as Carol's, she will not be compatible with any sane male (one who has some standards and wants to make a suitable home for his family)." He went on: "Carol wishes to engage in pleasurable activities, including sex, with others. She does not want to be committed to any one or any thing. She wants to be free to pursue whatever she, at the moment, wants to pursue." My father complained that he had been left home to take care of the boys "while Carol was engaging in mutually pleasurable activities on a mountain side with a hippie by the name of Burt. Also, she is having a ball of a time now that she is not confined to the care of a preschooler. She is a real 'swinger' (we used to use the term tramp). The only question is, where does all this leave my three sons whom I would like to see grow up to be solid citizens and good and faithful husbands."

I'm sure my mother's activities must have been unsettling for her parents, but they were not about to turn against their own daughter and take my father's side. Though my mother had long distanced herself from her Kansas Mennonite roots, through it all she and her parents were careful to maintain a respectful and even supportive relationship, and they weren't going to jeopardize that now.

My father also sought sympathy and validation by writing a more

politely worded letter to the minister at the Bethel College Mennonite Church back in Kansas:

> *Carol has separated herself altogether from the church*
> *and her ties with her family are nebulous. She has*
> *been greatly influenced by her readings in sociology*
> *and by her teaching associates. Her concepts of love,*
> *marriage, morality, responsibility, freedom, have all*
> *taken on new meanings. Our definitions of these terms*
> *are "old fashioned" and should be discarded. She has an*
> *entirely new set of standards which she claims are more*
> *compatible with our modern society.*

My outraged father then went public with his complaints, sending a letter to the editor that was published in the *Detroit News* in
May 1970:

> *To the editor,*
>   *After sharing 18 years of baby-sitting, making beds,*
> *washing dishes and other household chores, my liberated*
> *wife now wants a divorce. She has been given equal*
> *opportunity to attend school and obtain three university*
> *degrees since marriage and currently is a full-time*
> *university professor, earning as much as I. She wants our*
> *three children, our home, and half my salary! When will*
> *men obtain equal rights in our divorce courts?*

I have no idea what my father hoped to accomplish with this
letter. I imagine he was simply feeling powerless and needed to feel
he had "done something" to try to fix it.

My father became even angrier when the court informed him that
he had to pay my mother support payments. Appalled, he wrote the
court that she should actually pay support payments to him, that if

she does not find this to her liking that the kids were welcome to live with him in the new family home, and that "my wife is also welcome to share our home if she properly behaves herself."

Soon after my father got temporary custody of me he flew in his mother, Frieda, from Kansas to help take care of me, and to do all the cooking and other household chores that my mother had always done. The three of us moved into the empty new house in the suburbs once it was ready. I was happy to have Grandma there, but it made my mother furious, not because she was being replaced but because she thought my father should learn how to handle such things on his own. Grandma Andreas didn't seem to agree. A cheerful seventy-something, with curly, neatly cut short silver hair and thick glasses, she took on my mother's old domestic tasks without complaint.

Perhaps the greatest benefit of Grandma Andreas' presence was that she kept us all to a predictable routine, with each meal served as close as possible to the same exact time every day of the week, just the way my father liked it. Few things could throw him off as much as disrupting his eating schedule. Grandma even handled the phone communication with my mother about coordinating my and my brothers' visits. No matter how unpleasant the phone call was, Grandma invariably closed with "Carol, I pray for you every day." And my mother would retort, "You know, Carl will never learn how to be a responsible single parent with you there as his crutch."

At one point, my mother sent my father an angry note about Grandma:

She has succumbed to your way of thinking and is no longer helping Peter to adjust, but is trying to use him as a way of getting to me. You have never had a very warm

*relationship with your mother, and it is clear to me
that you are using her shamelessly and that each of you
is bringing out the worst in the other. Can you blame
Peter for wanting to escape such a setting and come to
live with me?*

I don't know what I'd said to my mother. I have no recollection of wanting to escape. I wanted to live with *both* of my parents. My father was safety and stability; I could count on him to walk in the door every evening before dinnertime. My mother was warmth and affection; I relied on her for long hugs and loving smiles. I wanted all these things. What child wouldn't?

Once I started kindergarten when I was five, Grandma Andreas gently held my hand and walked me slowly to the bottom of the hill every morning to the bus that would take me to Meadowbrook Elementary School; and I knew I could depend on her being there waiting for me every afternoon at the same stop, bundled up in her gray wool coat and matching scarf. She would have dinner ready by the time we heard the sound of the garage door and my father driving in after his thirty-mile commute. When he walked in he'd holler, "How's my little boy Peter?" and I'd run to greet him. He liked to call me a "chip off the old block." Not understanding, I would complain, "I'm not a chip!" I'd rarely heard my father laugh, but I remember this would always make him smile.

Meanwhile, my older brothers, living with our mother, went to Miller Junior High in downtown Detroit, two of only a handful of white students at the school, which made my mother proud. A year and a half apart in age, Joel and Ronald were inseparable, and almost indistinguishable. Back then, in the midst of race riots and the antiwar protests, even junior high kids were turning into political activists, but few were as radical and outspoken as my brothers. As before, they still liked to play with toy soldiers, but now instead of pretending they were American soldiers, they pretended they were Vietnamese guerrillas shooting at the Americans.

With my mother cheering them on, Joel and Ronald refused to say the Pledge of Allegiance at their school and campaigned to rename the school Angela Davis Junior High, in honor of the black activist and Communist Party leader. When they failed, Joel angrily wrote the principal, "Miller has a pig for a principal and a pig for its name [named after a white former police commissioner]. I think that both should be changed." Some of the black kids at school admiringly nicknamed my brothers "White Panthers." They organized school debates about the war and led student walkouts as an antiwar protest. Joel and Ronald even made a Vietcong flag and ran it up the flagpole at their old elementary school late at night as a politically inspired prank. In November 1969, at ages eleven and thirteen, they traveled on their own by bus to Washington, D.C., to participate in a massive antiwar demonstration. My father tried to stop them from boarding the bus, telling them they were too young to go on their own, but they told him our mother had given them permission.

By that time, Joel and Ronald wore tie-dyed T-shirts, grew their hair long, and had become vegetarians. My mother was proud of them; my father was horrified. Being against the Vietnam War was one thing; it simply marked you as a good pacifist Mennonite. But promoting revolution was quite another.

When my brothers took my mother's side against my father in disputes both political and personal, my father desperately clung to me, since I was still young enough to be malleable. I was his last hope for his dream of a traditional family life. Ultimately, there would be no contest between my parents over my brothers' loyalties, but the war over me was just getting started.

Berkeley

WHEN THE DIVORCE hearing finally arrived on November 20, 1970, my mother lost. Judge George T. Martin looked down at my mother and told her that she had no grounds for divorce: "These two shall be married . . . until death do them part. Case dismissed." My father was relieved; he felt vindicated that the family's dignity and reputation would remain intact. Now, he thought, with divorce off the table, my mother would finally come to her senses and give up what he called "all that women's lib crap." In my father's eyes, my mother had left him at the same time that she had become a feminist, so feminism was to blame for the destruction of his family.

My father couldn't have misread the situation more profoundly. Instead of giving up, my mother decided to take matters into her own hands.

One late November day, she showed up at my school, removed me from my kindergarten class, and whisked me away to a friend's home across town where my father could not find me. This was a year and a half after the first time I had been kidnapped, and it would not be the last.

"Where are we going, Mommy?" I asked as we left the classroom and headed for her car, double-parked in front of the building.

"We're taking a time-out from school," my mother replied. "Don't worry. It's only for a little while." And we drove away. I hoped I'd be back at school soon, but I had no idea whether a time-out meant an hour, a day, or more. I also had no idea that this would turn out to be the first of many such time-outs in the years ahead.

When the school called my father to tell him that my mother had taken me out of class, he immediately retaliated by rushing over to Miller Junior High and taking Joel out of school. He brought fourteen-year-old Joel to his house, telling him that he wouldn't let him go until our mother returned me, in some desperate plan to swap sons. But Joel ruined the scheme by escaping, running down the street with my father frantically chasing after him. My father drove all over the neighborhood, searching everywhere, but Joel had gotten away and somehow managed to find his way back to my mother, who already had Ronald and me with her.

Within days, my mother had quit her tenure-track university job without notice, before classes had even ended, and was moving her three boys across the country with a U-Haul trailer attached to the back of her car. She also took the family dog, Sunny, a beagle–basset hound mix we had adopted from the pound.

"Is the time-out over?" I asked my mother as we began our secretive cross-country move. "Am I going back to school now?"

"No, not yet. But when it's over, you'll go to a new school."

"Will my friends be there?"

"You'll make new friends."

"And Daddy?"

"Don't worry about Daddy. Mommy will take care of you."

Our destination was Berkeley, California, a counterculture mecca with liberal divorce laws. My father had no idea where we were until months later, in early 1971, when Alameda County Judge William M. McGuiness sent him a notice that my mother had been granted not only a divorce but also custody of all three kids.

My father's strategy to hang on to his family by refusing my mother a divorce had completely backfired. All his life he had followed the rules, the recipe for success: marrying a nice Mennonite girl from his college town, starting a family, saving for a big house in the suburbs, setting up trust funds for his three boys' college educations. And now he'd lost it all. My father, a simple, conventional 1950s man, had been blindsided by the '60s revolution. He never quite figured out what had hit him. He was left bitter and disoriented, and never fully recovered. And this was the only version of my father I would ever know.

My father began sending angry letters to Judge McGuiness, warning him of the disasters he'd wrought and the woman they were both dealing with: "If it were under her power, she would overthrow our American political system. Her conviction is that the family structure, as we know it, only perpetuates the capitalistic system and therefore needs to be destroyed. You, Mr. Judge, have helped Dr. Andreas destroy our family."

My father still held out hope that he could somehow get me back. He wrote to me in early May 1971:

> *Hi Peter!*
>
> *I have good news for you. Today I saw my lawyer and he is going to help you come back home. We are going to have Judge Martin give orders that your mother will have to let you go. This will take some time but you should be home in time to go to Meadowbrook School this fall. Tell Joel and Ronald that they can also come. Bring Sunny also. Please have Joel or Ronald help you write me a card sometime. You can also draw a picture. I found a very good tree in our yard to make a tree house. We shall start on this as soon as you return. When I see Jimmy, Martha, and your other friends, I shall tell them about our good news, all hope that you will soon be able to come home. Say hello to Joel and Ronald.*
>
> *Love,*
> *Your daddy*

But the birthday letter he sent me two months later was much more somber:

> *Dear Peter,*
>
> *On this sixth birthday of yours, we are torn apart by a woman who has no feelings for human relationships. You are too young to understand the consequences of this fact and unfortunately not given the opportunity to express your discontent. Please be patient for only by being patient and long-suffering can we win out in this conflict. Let me assure you, Peter, that I am doing all that is humanly possible to obtain your early release. Until then, and only then, can we rejoice in your attainment of your sixth birthday.*
>
> *With love,*
> *Your daddy*

Reading these letters now—my father kept copies of them along with everything else—it seems clear that they were actually directed at my mother. After all, I didn't know how to read yet, and so surely my father realized that my mother would have to read them to me. She never showed me the letters at all; I didn't even know they existed until a few years ago.

While my father stewed in Michigan, my mother, Joel, Ronald, and I moved into a large, cream-colored stucco house on Walnut Street in North Berkeley.

"We're going to turn this into a commune," my mother declared.

"What's a commune?" I asked.

"It's a big home where everyone lives together."

"Oh, like a family?"

"Yes, exactly. Just like a big family," she replied. "But even better, because everyone is equal." This sounded appealing.

My mother got the commune started by simply posting a notice on the bulletin board at the food co-op on Shattuck Avenue a few blocks away. The house had seven bedrooms and we converted the living room into an eighth. A sizable yard and garden were out back. I spent many afternoons out on the wide porch while Sunny kept lazy guard by my side. Sometimes Sunny and I wandered around the neighborhood together. No one noticed our absence, but as a curious yet cautious kid I was not going to stray too far. We lived in a hip part of town, with the original Peet's coffee shop around the corner and a French café called Chez Panisse behind the house. Live Oak Park was just up the street.

Usually there were eight to ten people living in the house at any one time. Communal living meant carefully divvying up the chores and cooking. Each week, everyone in the house contributed seven dollars toward food. We found creative ways to save money, includ-

Hanging out with Sunny in Berkeley

ing mixing powdered milk with real milk. My task was to make the orange juice every morning from the frozen can of concentrate. On the floor, sitting cross-legged at a long, low dining table, we all ate dinner together—typically some bland concoction with noodles or rice, not always easily identifiable but always vegetarian. At all times of day, that common room was full of people smoking cigarettes and caught up in loud and intense conversations.

My mother had been right: it *was* like a big family—except that those who left never came back, and new people were always arriving. And apart from my brothers, who were in their early teens but thought of themselves as adults and insisted that my mother and everyone else treat them that way, I was the only kid in the commune. I didn't mind. I got plenty of attention. My mother was by default the mother of the house, though she didn't really like that role because it included picking up after everyone else, and no one else seemed to care if the place was a mess. It also bothered my mother that no one else looked after her little boy. She complained about it in a letter to her father, whom she wrote to regularly: "I had a dream in which Peter and [his friend] Garrett took off accidentally in a horse and carriage that was soon out of control and nobody seemed concerned about it in the least except me. I guess I'm feeling like people here in the house aren't as responsible as I think they should be." To her dismay, communal living didn't mean communal parenting.

Mostly, though, my mother was pleased with how the commune was working out. She later described the place in a diary entry:

> House meetings about every other night. People are feeling good. . . . Main thing I feel here is that people are very accepting of each other—there is no trashing, no sneaking around to avoid each other, no nosiness, no pushiness. There are frequent celebrations, acceptance of outsiders, people are basically good to each other. I am surprised at myself for how non-judgmental I am (people don't do their jobs as

*they should but jobs do get done). The house is never locked,
Sunny gets fed, the plants get watered, people do get to bed
eventually, neighbor kids wander in and out.*

I lived with my mother and Joel in the main part of the house,
while Ronald took over the semifinished basement, a dark dungeon
with tiny windows. Though Ronald and Joel had once been close,
Ronald's relationship to the family began to change during this
period. From the very start, he wanted nothing to do with the rest
of the commune. We saw him less and less, and he seemed content
that way. So we mostly left him alone. Joel, the oldest, was the most
outgoing of us three boys. He liked to be in the thick of things and
he was always active and sociable. Ronald, the middle child, was
much more aloof, always suspicious and judgmental of others. His
signature laugh—short, nervous, high-pitched—matched his subtle
sneer. So while Joel was the earnest activist and aspiring revolutionary, Ronald was in some ways the more rebellious one. Whereas Joel

Ronald and Joel in Berkeley in the early seventies

dressed like a sloppy hippie—so proud of his own indifference to clothing that he wasn't the least bit upset when his laundry was stolen at the Laundromat—Ronald always appeared carefully put together in his cowboy boots, cowboy shirts, bell-bottom pants, and wide-rimmed brown leather hat. A thick strand of his long light-brown hair hung down over his right eye. He viewed collective activities like cooking and cleaning with disdain. So while Ronald was the best cook in the house and was rightly proud of his vegetarian dishes, he only cooked for himself.

Nosy little brother that I was, I sometimes sneaked down to the basement to take a peek at what Ronald was up to, and when he caught me there, he would bark, "Get outta here, get back upstairs." With the basement all to himself, Ronald could smoke pot as much as he wanted. He earned extra cash by selling dope to his friends and acquaintances who dropped by.

I can't imagine that my mother didn't know: I remember the distinct sweet smell of marijuana smoke rising up through the cracks in the basement door and into the kitchen. I recognized that same smell in other rooms, too. When I finally asked Joel what it was, he said, "Oh, that's just someone smokin' weed." People smoked weeds? That didn't sound like much fun, and Joel didn't seem particularly interested, yet it was obviously one of Ronald's favorite activities. My mother, meanwhile, didn't smoke anything. Whether it was a habit carried over from a culturally conservative childhood or an offshoot of her later ideological purity, I'm not sure, but the fact was that, for all her rebelliousness and unconventional ways, she never touched drugs.

The commune housed an eclectic mix of characters, employed and unemployed, students and dropouts, almost all young, long-haired hippies, though people's commitments to political causes varied quite a lot. It was of course a given that everyone opposed the draft and the war. At one point, a Vietcong flag hung out a front window. The biggest political insult was to call someone a pig. Macho men were "sexist pigs," rich people were "capitalist pigs," President Nixon was an "imperialist pig," and cops were simply "pigs." When I asked my mother why everyone seemed to hate pigs, she laughed. "It's nothing personal against pigs," she reassured me, pointing out that most everyone in the house except us was a vegetarian and opposed killing animals.

One thirty-something activist in the house named Paul spent almost all of his time organizing demonstrations and protests on nearby Telegraph Avenue. He spent so little time at home that eventually the housemates called him out for shirking his chores. He insisted that his revolutionary calling did not leave time for such trivial matters and then moved out in a huff.

Soon, three young people—Peter, Toni, and Linda, all dressed in brightly colored shirts, bandanas, bead necklaces, and faded bell-bottom blue jeans—moved into the vacated room. They had a baby with them named Chalali. Peter was the baby's father, Toni was the mother, and Linda was the father's ex-girlfriend. They'd come from a commune in Vermont, looking for sunnier weather and a more urban environment. Right after they moved in, Linda got involved with another member of the commune named Steve, whose ponytail reached all the way down his back. Steve's inclusion didn't seem to change the dynamic with Peter and Toni at all; it was unconventional, but perfectly harmonious.

For a while the commune also had a resident crazy old lady named Margaret, who got crazier and crazier. One day, she snapped, convinced that Ronald was holding her daughters hostage in the basement. She did have two adult daughters, but they had never been to the house. "They're down there! They're down there! He's holding my girls down there!" she screamed over and over again, her eyes panicked. "Please, please help me free them!" No matter how much everyone tried to calm her down, she insisted that Ronald was imprisoning her daughters, yet she refused to go below to see for herself. Eventually, she was hospitalized in a mental institution in Napa Valley. Some months later, she killed herself.

My mother didn't have a regular job but managed to land part-time teaching opportunities at various community colleges in nearby Oakland that were also hubs of political activism. However, these teaching stints didn't provide health insurance for her or us three kids. So my mother came up with what she thought was a perfectly sensible solution: write to my father and ask him to keep us all on his health insurance. After all, from her perspective, it was entirely my father's fault that she had to leave Michigan and give up her old tenure-track job with benefits. When he didn't reply, my mother then wrote directly to his employer, asking for health coverage. This got my father's attention and provoked a response:

> *Dear Carol Andreas,*
>   *Since you are a well-educated female, in good physical health, experienced, sexy, intelligent, liberated, and youthful, I suggest that you go out and buck the job market like your male counterparts must do. If you associate yourself with a reputable firm, your employer will provide prescription drug, sickness and accident, extended disability, accidental death and dismemberment insurance to mention just a few. . . . The UAW has an excellent employee benefit program. However, due to the recent period of economic adjustment, we are all doing our share to save the union from unnecessary expenses. I therefore discontinued the coverage for all dependents except for Peter. I thought you had obtained custody of Joel and Ronald and were now assuming responsibility for their care. As you know, the UAW is part of the "Establishment." I am sure you would not want to compromise your position and accept a handout from one of those "evil" institutions.*

My mother's next move was to try to get the California courts to order my father to pay child support for the three of us. In his reply to the Oakland County prosecuting attorney, my father wrote that he would not support our care in a "hippie commune," that he would be happy to provide a home for us in a "Christian environment" in Michigan, that the Wayne County Circuit Court had dismissed the divorce filed by Dr. Andreas, and that Dr. Andreas then "absconded with my three children and has been living in sin in a commune in Berkeley, California." He concluded, "Your assistance in recovering my children from Dr. Andreas and returning them to their home will be greatly appreciated."

My mother then tried to put the Michigan house up for sale that my father was still living in: "FOR SALE: Contemporary house on wooded hillside in faculty subdivision—2970 Heidelberg. Post and beam construction, beautiful natural woods throughout, four bedrooms, three baths, study, large recreation room or studio, screened porch, deck, double garage, several fireplaces, undyed wool carpeting. Price, $50,000. Available—August 15." My mother should have realized, though, that this move would be easy for my father to block, since he would need to sign off on any sale.

My mother was stuck. Though she finally had all three kids and the divorce she had long wanted, she was still tied to my father through their joint property. And my father would never agree to a property settlement unless my mother returned me to him, which she wouldn't consider. In early 1972, my mother's father, Grandpa Rich, tried to play the role of intermediary. He told my father, "If President Nixon and Chou En-lai [Chinese leader] can meet in an amiable way without belligerence, the same thing should certainly be possible with Carol and Carl." Apparently, though, Nixon and Chou En-lai were more flexible than my parents; Grandpa Rich soon gave up. He wrote my father: "For a blundering old man to attempt to mediate a conflict between a practiced and skilled UAW official and a leader in women's liberation seems foolhardy."

Just as my mother had promised, my "time-out" from school eventually ended and she enrolled me in Berkeley's Whittier Elementary School. Joel and Ronald also returned to school, but going to class was the last thing on their minds. Joel's real passion was a polemical comic book about the Rockefeller family and its exploitative billions that he had begun drawing the summer after ninth grade. For my brother, the Rockefellers personified all the evils of capitalism and American imperialism that he and my mother were fighting so fiercely against. Draft pages were scattered all across his room, where he sat cross-legged on the floor, hunched over, drawing for hours every day with Rapidograph pens. Sunny kept him company, sprawled out on top of the pages, but Joel didn't seem to mind. What he did mind was my interrupting, so I would only go into his room to try to coax Sunny out to play. Ronald was less respectful of the project; once, during one of their huge fights, Ronald grabbed the book and threatened to destroy it.

Luckily, the comic book survived and went on to become a hit—in reality, a spectacular hit, given that my brother wrote it when he was only fifteen, with no help other than encouragement from our mother. *The Incredible Rocky vs. The Power of the People! Featuring America's Richest Family* was published in 1973 by the left-wing group NACLA (North American Congress on Latin America) and sold more than one hundred thousand copies in multiple editions. The title was a parody of superhero comics, with the cover drawing depicting Nelson Rockefeller in a Superman outfit, cape and all, holding a huge gun with oil gushing out of it. The radical group Weather Underground even sent Joel a fan letter praising the comic book, along with a copy of their own book, *Prairie Fire*, which Joel said was "very revolutionary inspiring," and proclaimed that he had "never felt more completely oriented toward the revolution than at that moment."

Cover of *The Incredible Rocky*

Joel and some of his friends spent much of their time organizing what they called Berkeley Young People's Liberation, headquartered in the small, overstuffed mildew-smelling garage next to the house. By their logic, if women could have a liberation movement, why couldn't kids? They insisted that ageism—in this case, prejudice against empowering and trusting young people to make their own decisions—was a leading source of oppression in society. They spent hours deliberating over their positions and platforms on kids' rights, held weekly strategizing meetings to plot how to take over the Berkeley schools, and passed out flyers encouraging young people to stand up for and liberate themselves: "We are here especially for young people who are leaving their parents' homes, either legally or illegally."

One thing Joel and Ronald still had in common was that they hardly ever mentioned our father. It was almost as if he no longer existed and that life started when we moved to Berkeley. Joel and Ronald also did their best to pretend I didn't exist. Neither of them wanted to play the protective older brother role or spend time with me. It had begun in Detroit, when my parents' marriage broke apart, and both Joel and Ronald seemed to have considered that a kind of severing of our basic family ties. They immediately started calling our parents by their first names, and spending time away from home, on their own projects, from young ages. Neither of them wanted a baby brother tagging along.

Of course I craved more brotherly attention, but I focused on Joel, who at least didn't dislike me. Ronald always seemed to resent my existence and wish our mother had left me behind in Michigan. Then again, Ronald didn't seem to really like anybody all that much. He became my anti–role model: I was determined to become everything I thought he was not—sociable, likable, agreeable.

My own life in the commune and at school was far less complicated than my brothers'. I had many of the basic trappings of an all-American childhood—a steady supply of Cap'n Crunch and Hostess Ding Dongs and Saturday-morning cartoons. I was hooked on *Speed Racer*. My mother didn't seem to care; maybe it was her way of recognizing that I needed a few conventional things in my life. I spent most afternoons out on the streets with the other neighborhood kids, including my best friends, Fritz and Garrett. We played tag and hide-and-seek, climbed trees and walls, played kickball and dodgeball. I excelled at the last two, which I was sure marked me as a star athlete.

Even though my mother was busy with teaching, running the house, antiwar protests, teach-ins, and other political activist stuff, she found time for me. On weekends, she would take me on outings to Tilden Park, a short drive from Berkeley, where we ambled along the narrow dirt paths among the towering redwood trees. A few nights a week, even though I had no specified bedtime, we still had a soothing little ritual. My mother would tuck me in as she softly sang, "There was a boy, a very, very special boy . . ." while gently tracing her finger across my forehead, around my eyes, and down my cheeks, over and over again. Even today, when I try to remember the sound of my mother's voice, the first thing I hear in my head is her singing that dreamy childhood song. And I can still even feel her finger lightly caressing my face.

When I turned seven, in July of 1972, my mother mobilized the entire commune to throw me the best birthday party a little boy could ever imagine: everyone in the house played a role in an elaborate treasure hunt, including one exceptionally tall housemate with long dark hair and an almost equally long beard who dressed up as Blackbeard and guarded a treasure of chocolate coins hidden in the garage. For Easter, we colored Easter eggs and invited all the neighborhood kids to an egg hunt in our backyard. With someone always in the house, I was never home alone.

The only thing missing in my life was my father, with whom I had virtually no contact. I still missed him and thought about him often, along with some of my school friends back in Michigan, and wondered if I'd ever return. But otherwise, I was doing fine at school, and my teachers liked me, and I liked them—just like in Michigan. Life was, overall, relatively normal, even as I grew up in a commune. But that was about to change.

II.

CHILE

I think your concerns about my fate in Latin America are exaggerated. I have good contacts there. I am not an aggressive man-hating type and although men are often afraid of personal involvement with me they are usually willing to listen to what I have to say. . . . I do feel that motherhood contains my energies too much, and this will be especially true with such an ambitious undertaking—but I am adventurous for Peter, too. I think he will gain confidence from traveling and learning Spanish.

—Carol Andreas, letter to her father, summer 1972

From Guayaquil to Santiago

IN EARLY SEPTEMBER 1972, less than two years into our stay in California, my mother announced that we were moving to South America.

"Is this another time-out from school?" I had just settled into second grade at Whittier Elementary.

"No, it's much bigger than that," she replied, her eyes shining. "We're going to be part of a revolution. It will be the biggest adventure of your life."

The next several years would prove her right.

No longer a polite and proper Mennonite teenager, by her late thirties my mother had learned to thrive on conflict and action. Berkeley was too hip and hippie-saturated, a cozy little city with permanently pleasant weather that in no way resembled the front lines of the revolution. We had moved west to get away from my father and find a sympathetic judge, but my mother was growing politically restless. Compared to gritty Detroit, where she'd thrived as a leader of the antiwar and feminist movements, my mother felt lost in the groovy Berkeley crowd. What was the point of being into antiwar activism if everyone in town already opposed the war? More generally, my mother had less and less patience or tolerance for "feel-good American bourgeois liberalism." She was especially fed up with the liberal brand of feminism that had come to dominate the women's movement, which she considered too reformist: the goal was to create more equality and opportunity for women within the system rather than to overthrow it.

One night, my mother attended a local bookstore reading about social change in Chile, where two years earlier, in 1970, a socialist had been democratically elected president. President Salvador Allende's victory had been celebrated by leftists worldwide, and he was implementing a radical agenda. The speaker at the bookstore was a twenty-five-year-old Stanford grad student named Richard Feinberg. His stories of life in Chile as a peace corps volunteer seduced my mother, as did his accounts of the transformations underway in Chile. She was quickly hooked—not only on Feinberg, who became her lover, but on Chile itself. She jumped on the Allende bandwagon, eager to write a book about the role of women in the new, revolutionary Chile. "We're joining the revolution," I told all my friends at school. "My mother says it'll be fun."

Her hope was to take all three of us boys. But Joel was engrossed in his Berkeley activism and finishing his Rockefeller comic book. He wanted to remain in the commune on his own, and my mother agreed, even though he was just turning sixteen. While we were gone, he would survive on food stamps and a stack of $100 checks that my mother left him—one for each month of the year. On the other hand, fourteen-year-old Ronald liked the idea of going to South America, but as always, he wanted to do his own thing and had no intention of tagging along with my mother and me. Of course, my brothers were too young to be on their own, but at that point my mother had given up playing a traditional parental role with them. She had long ago lost any real control over their lives and simply accepted their declarations of independence. But she still wanted to take her little seven-year-old with her. She didn't see another option, anyway: sending me back to my father was out of the question, and she certainly wasn't going to leave me behind in the commune with Joel.

Some of my mother's relatives urged her to let my father have me. "Peter will have a more stable home with his father," Grandpa

Rich advised in his letters and phone calls from Kansas. "It will be better for him and easier for you." Grandpa Rich, who had recently lost his wife to cancer, worried about our safety in South America. But knowing he could not talk his daughter out of going to Chile, he still tried to convince her it would be best to leave me behind.

"Nonsense," my mother shot back. "The best thing for Peter is to be part of history, not against it, to be with the people, not against them." She was convinced that American parenting's emphasis on security, comfort, and stability was merely part of the mythology about the superiority of the traditional nuclear family. A child needed to be exposed to the world, and she wanted me to share in the thrill of real revolutionary change. In her mind, her embrace of revolution and rejection of the conventional definition of "good" mothering was in itself proof that she was a good mother.

My mother, Ronald, and I flew off to South America, connecting through Miami, in September of 1972. She and I each had a knapsack and a duffel bag swung over our shoulders, while Ronald brought his backpack. Sensing how nervous I was to be leaving behind my world of Cap'n Crunch cereal and Saturday-morning cartoons, my mother tried to comfort me, in her own way.

"Just remember how lucky you are," she murmured as she adjusted the airplane seat belt for me. She reminded me that we were going to be participants in a "real revolution," that all those spoiled, sheltered American kids will never get to experience anything like that, and that's why it was good I was with her rather than with my father.

I nodded.

"Look, I know it's hard to leave, but I promise you'll understand someday and be glad. We can't just sit around and expect the revolution to come to us." She squeezed my hand and I finally smiled. Her confidence made me feel special. It was a privilege that my mother was taking *me* to join her on her quest.

Content that she'd laid my concerns to rest, my mother gave me a pat on the head and then turned to the book she had brought to read on the flight, a collection of speeches by anarchist activist Emma Goldman. If she had any worries of her own about what was in store for us, or reservations about leaving, she hid them well.

Our ultimate destination was Santiago, the Chilean capital. But first, we stopped in Guayaquil, Ecuador, where we visited Walter Franco, a former student of my mother's. She planned for the three of us to learn some Spanish in Ecuador and to get our bearings before heading farther south to Chile. But soon after we arrived, Ronald took off traveling on his own. I was relieved. Ronald had been a lot easier to deal with in Berkeley, where he mostly kept to himself in the basement and we had left each other alone. Once we got to Ecuador, though, he turned on me, telling me that our mother should have left me behind. I would angrily defend myself, yelling at him to leave me alone and stop criticizing me all the time. My mother commented in her diary: "Ronald is constantly making snide remarks to or about Peter, and Peter fights back, so we have a ways to go there—a ways to go, but I don't know where to." We didn't go anywhere with Ronald; he went traveling on south without us, telling us he'd meet up with us later in Chile. My mother couldn't really stop him even if she had wanted to, and part of her may have actually been as glad as I was to see him go. Things would be simpler and easier with just the two of us.

We spent a month in Ecuador. After a short stay with Walter Franco's family, my mother decided she wanted to live "with the people," and so we rented a small home in a Guayaquil slum along the river. Only the main street was paved, with the side streets full of garbage and sewage. The grayness of the neighborhood was only interrupted by the occasional cluster of carefully tended plants or a tree.

My mother and I slept together in a creaky, lumpy bed, protected from mosquitoes by a carefully repaired tent of netting overhead. Roosters woke us every morning, soon followed by the sounds of street vendors, oversized trucks lumbering by, babies crying, and radios being turned on to music or the morning news. My mother would hurry to the nearby bakery for fresh rolls before it closed at 8:00 a.m., and often brought home fresh fruit for breakfast. A bag of six bananas or tangerines only cost five cents.

Unlike many other homes in the area, we were lucky to have running water (even if no hot water), including a shower and a toilet. Perhaps my mother decided to pay a little extra rent for these things because she was not quite ready to give them up. There was a place in back to wash laundry by hand. There was not a lot of room, but we had it all to ourselves. All around us, homes of the same size each housed a dozen or more people.

Many of our neighbors lived in bamboo shacks propped precariously on stilts above the mud and sewage, where thousands of tiny clams grew. The shacks were connected by narrow, single-slat bridges, and I loved running across them, as a challenge and an adventure. Somewhere in my seven-year-old id, I even secretly hoped to fall into the black muck below, purely out of curiosity. After one morning spent digging up clams, I slipped and did fall in, right as we were leaving. I was blackened from head to foot. It took my mother an hour to clean the sludge off me.

For a little gringo boy accustomed to the comforts of America, Guayaquil was a rude introduction to our new life. As my mother wrote in her diary when we arrived, "I'll have to bribe Peter with a Pepsi every day or something like that to get him to want to live primitively. I'm excited about it." It's not as if my mother was adjusting any more easily than I was, though. A few days later she added to her diary: "It amazes me that anyone survives living like this. Dogs and other animals are not protected from rabies, for instance, and most of them (the dogs) seem half mad to me. The trucks race down the street and people nonchalantly jump aside. We were going to walk into the really poor areas today. I don't need it."

In the tropical heat, everything felt dirty and sticky. Giant flying cockroaches rose up through the sewer system and infiltrated our home, crawling through the drain when I showered, appearing somehow inside the toilet bowl while I was sitting on it. They were utterly fearless and refused to scatter when lights came on. Usually it took at least two stomps to crunch them, forcing me to quickly overcome my squeamishness. I was both impressed and intimidated by their boldness. And then there were the spiders. As my mother pointed out in her diary: "It's a good thing Peter and I are enamored of Charlotte, the spider who is E. B. White's heroine. We have enormous spiders living with us."

One late September afternoon, I got lost for hours wandering around the streets of our neighborhood, looking for an ice cream cone. Every block looked pretty much the same, and I soon became disoriented. Eventually, a round elderly man, who had been slowly nursing a beer in front of his house, called out to me the third or fourth time I wandered past. It must have been clear that I had no idea where I was. He gave me a warm, knowing look and put me in the back of his rusty old pickup truck. We drove slowly up and down each street, block after block, until I finally spotted our home and pounded on the top of the cabin for him to stop.

My mother barely glanced up from her reading when I walked in. "Where've you been?" she said casually. "I was starting to get a little worried."

As much as I had craved her help and comfort while I was lost, I wanted her to be proud of me for finding my way home without tears. I told her the whole story with as much bravado as I could muster—including the ice cream I never found.

She took it all in stride, not even commenting on my ride from the old man. "Well, next time you wander off, just don't forget our address again. Now, let's go find you some ice cream; sounds like you deserve it."

Soon after we moved into our neighborhood, my mother tried to enroll me in the local school, but I only lasted a couple of days. I hardly knew any Spanish, and I felt intensely uncomfortable among the other students, as if I were some sort of exotic new creature on display at the zoo. I was probably the only gringo they'd ever seen in class. Their constant attention bothered me so much at first that my mother shook me out of a nightmare one night after I had been screaming, "Stop staring at me!"

I was also upset that the teacher disciplined me by smacking my hands with her ruler when I wasn't paying attention or sitting up straight. "That's not how my old teachers treated me," I complained. "I don't want to go back there, ever."

My mother could have just told me to toughen up, but she took my side, and chose to keep me out of school.

I was starting to pick up Spanish faster on the street than in the classroom, anyway—talking to neighbors, playing with kids, chatting with vendors, listening to conversations. But even though I was learning Spanish, being out of school I certainly wasn't becoming literate, in Spanish or English. As my mother noted in her diary, "I wonder if Peter will ever learn to read and write—he really doesn't want to study, and I guess he has his hands full."

Otherwise, the street was better than the classroom in every way. I found a new favorite game, *fútbol* (soccer). Everywhere and anywhere—streets, alleys, dirt roads—boys of all ages kicked around a beat-up plastic or leather soccer ball, using makeshift goalposts. They let me join their games, and were impressed I could kick equally well with my right and left feet, but that didn't stop them from teasing me about my long hair.

My mother refused to let me cut my hair short like theirs. "That's how they cut hair in the military. You don't want to look like an American soldier, do you?"

It was the haircut my brothers had had as little boys. My father would mow their hair down to a few millimeters from their scalps with his big, white electric razor; it was simple and fast and he didn't have to pay a barber. Regretting her own compromises as a 1950s housewife, my mother was determined to raise me differently, in every possible way.

Near the end of our month in Guayaquil, the neighbors started to call me Pedrito and my mother Carolina, which pleased her enormously. She liked it so much that she referred to me as Pedrito in her letters to Grandpa Rich, and at the bottom of the letters she signed her name as Carolina.

I spent our last days in Guayaquil in a hospital bed, hooked up to an IV bag. It all started with a bad case of diarrhea, which my mother tried to treat with some pills she picked up at the local drugstore. I had immediately swallowed the pills with a gulp of water as she'd instructed and then felt worse. Much worse.

It turned out that my mother had misread the Spanish label and accidentally fed me a laxative. Luckily, Walter Franco's father happened to run a local hospital clinic. The main thing I remember about my three-day hospital stay was how luxuriously clean and neat the place was compared to where we lived. I could order grilled cheese sandwiches anytime, day or night, and the nurses pampered me. Other than the uncomfortable IV needle stuck in my arm, which left me with a lifelong needle phobia, I didn't want to leave. My mother stayed in the hospital room with me, and we took turns telling each other stories about the animals and insects in our house, including the rat that lived under our bed, as well as a dead spider I found under there attached to her egg sac. I think my mother must have been as struck as I was by the contrast between the hospital and the conditions in which we'd been living. She confessed to her diary what she'd never have said to me: "I feel kind of guilty for exposing him to such hazards, but if he gets through OK he'll have some understandings that he may be glad for later. We have been living in one of the largest slums in South America."

The crisp, cool weather in Santiago was a welcome relief after tropical Guayaquil. It was also, apart from the smog, a lot less dirty. We knew no one in the Chilean capital when we arrived there by plane in late October 1972. All my mother had was a little notebook with a scribbled list of contacts whom she hoped might help with her research on women in Allende's socialist Chile.

My mother was excited to finally be in Chile, to be part of the Allende revolution. Allende was taking on the rich landowners and the foreign companies that owned Chile's copper-mining industry. He nationalized the copper mines and many of the country's other major industries, took over large agricultural estates to distribute land to the campesinos, raised workers' wages, and established relations with Cuba and China. These radical moves prompted the Nixon administration to retaliate by supporting Allende's opponents and squeezing the country economically. The CIA had already tried but failed to covertly block Allende from taking power after he won the election.

We arrived in Santiago in the midst of a major crisis—a strike by all the forces opposed to the Allende government—which meant that most stores were shut down, there were food shortages, some schools were closed, and people were in the streets calling for the return of ex-presidents Frei or Alessandri. The army was everywhere. Clouds of tear gas made Santiago's already polluted air even harder on the eyes and nostrils.

In response to the anti-Allende protests, thousands of supporters of Allende and his political party, Unidad Popular, also took to the streets, rolling up newspapers and lighting them to make torches. Allende's supporters blamed hoarders and the government's right-wing opponents for the country's severe shortage of basic necessities, from food to cloth to toilet paper. One pro-Allende demonstrator carried a sign that read NOW THAT THERE ISN'T ANY TOILET PAPER, *EL MERCURIO* (a right-wing newspaper) IS THE BEST, NO? The marchers chanted, "*Ya van a ver, ya van a ver, cuando los obreros se toman el poder*" (They're going to see, they're going to see, when the workers take power).

In the first letter from Chile that my mother sent to her father, whom she wrote to often to reassure him that we were fine, she was ecstatic: "One can see clearly that the underdogs have come to power. This is a little preview of what revolution might look like in the USA 20 years from now." She later wrote in her diary: "Witnessing the complex political and economic processes that go into making (or killing) a revolution in a small relatively underdeveloped country like Chile, my mind boggles to think what is ahead for the USA."

We settled into an upper-level room in an old downtown hotel. From our window we watched police forcing grocery stores to open their doors rather than hoarding supplies. When I asked my mother what was going on, she said, "The government is finally getting the right-wingers to start sharing." I had always been told that "sharing" was a good thing, so I smiled and nodded.

During those first couple of weeks in Santiago, we ate our meals at the public cafeteria on the ground floor of the newly built cultural center downtown. On the second floor, a conference on Latin American women was getting underway, organized by Chilean communists. Students we had met at the cafeteria took turns entertaining me while my mother attended the weeklong conference. My mother's aura of optimism inspired people to trust her and open up. It was easy for her to make friends, which came in handy when she needed free impromptu childcare. It also helped that Chilean supporters of Allende tended to welcome foreigners like my mother who came to show solidarity and join the cause. And she was especially intriguing as an older single mother, since this did not match the profile of the typical leftist foreigner visiting Chile.

My mother at a conference on Latin American women,
Santiago, October 1972

My mother tried again to enroll me in a local public school a few weeks after we arrived in Santiago. One morning she blithely put me on a public bus and sent me off to school on my own, with five escudos in my pocket to bring myself home at the end of the day. As she wrote in her diary that night, "Peter was late getting home and described his trip excitedly—is a bit scared to do it again tomorrow, but I think he will." I'm not sure how my mother expected me to navigate a foreign city by myself so soon after arriving and barely able to speak the language, but I do know that I didn't last long at that school. My Spanish was still not good enough to follow along in class, leaving me frustrated and confused.

My mother then tried another school, this time a small private one close to downtown with partial English instruction. That worked out fine until my mother decided that she didn't want me surrounded by privileged upper-class kids, many of whose parents probably opposed Allende. I didn't complain; the schools were shut down a lot anyway due to strikes or political unrest. My mother wasn't particularly concerned. I was busy learning, even if it wasn't in the classroom. As she wrote in her diary, "I have resolved my dilemma regarding his education by deciding that he is getting a whole lot of education and working quite hard at it—and will ask me to teach him how to read when he's ready."

Part of my out-of-the-classroom education was picking up all the revolutionary lingo, and I also began drawing colorful pictures with revolutionary slogans like *Venceremos*. Without any real understanding of what it all meant, I started to mimic my mother, talking constantly about being for "the people," "the masses," "the working class," and being against "the system," "the ruling class," "the dominant elite," "the bourgeoisie," and the "capitalists" and "imperialists." We called Chilean conservatives who opposed Allende *momios* (mummies) for being stuck in the past. I could tell my mother was proud of how politically sophisticated her little boy sounded. I even started to differentiate between socialists and communists. One day my mother asked me to go get her a pen so she could jot something down in her diary. I found the pen, and as I handed it to her I said, "You're clearly a socialist and not a communist."

"Oh, really, why's that?"

"Well, everyone knows the communists are the hardest workers and the socialists are the hardest talkers. If you were a communist you would have looked for the pen yourself instead of asking me to do it."

She laughed. "Maybe you're right, Peter. Maybe out of a humble recognition of the fact that I am more of a talker than a worker, I am about to ask for admission to Allende's socialist party."

We eventually found an old *pension* to rent with two young Uruguayan political exiles who had been granted asylum in Chile. Different as they seemed—Roberto was short, round, and flamboyant, and Carlos was tall, bony, and soft-spoken—they shared a passion for radical politics and an ability to laugh at pretty much anything. My mother and I took an immediate liking to them, though that did not always mean harmonious living.

The house had seven bedrooms, a spacious open hallway/living room in the middle with walls covered in political posters, and an expansive backyard with a garden with grapevines and a big fig tree that I liked to climb to peer over the wall into the neighbor's property. My mother, Roberto, and Carlos decided to rent out the other rooms to the foreigners who, since Allende's election, had been making a pilgrimage to Chile to witness the transformation and be part of history. More than a dozen people lived in the extra bedrooms at different times—Americans, a Canadian, an Ecuadorian, an Australian, a Frenchman, and a handful of Chileans. We called our new home a "commune of exiles."

At night, after dinner, my mother sometimes lit candles and gathered us all in the living room to hold hands and sing "The Internationale"—the anthem of the international communist movement—squeezing and raising our hands together in celebration at the end. It was fun to sing along, though I had only a vague idea what the words meant. Thinking back to those nights of singing about revolution, I can't remember the verses, but I do remember that it felt like we were part of something, something important, something that was changing the world for the better. That feeling would not last, but none of us knew that then.

The Santiago commune was not a true commune, not like Berkeley, where most everything was done collectively. A lot of the work fell to my mother, which made her angry. As Roberto put it, "I want no part in the domestic revolution"—by which he meant more egalitarian distribution of work inside the home.

Roberto and the other men in the house tried to hire a housecleaner, but my mother put her foot down: "Revolutions are never easy." She wanted the men in the house to learn how to clean up after themselves.

Roberto countered, "Peaceful coexistence isn't any easier."

My mother continued to hound them about housework and lecture them about the importance of men sharing domestic respon-

sibilities with women. One evening, as a sort of peace offering to the
men in the house, my mother made an enormous pizza and brought
slices of it along with a glass of wine to each of them in their rooms.
For the time being, anyway, that peace gesture put an end to the
arguments about women's liberation. Still, the men often teased my
mother by calling her *gringa* or *flaca* (skinny). They also complained
that I always forgot to lock the front door. Our most communal
activity was trying to house-train a boxer puppy, which I named
Pepe. Since I had been the one pushing for the dog, because I'd been
missing Sunny (our old beagle–basset hound we had left with Joel in
Berkeley), my domestic chore was cleaning up Pepe's messes. But I
was seven years old, which meant the house soon smelled of messes
I'd missed. No one seemed particularly bothered.

Even as my mother and Roberto fought over how to run the
house, they made peace behind closed doors. Once, while I was

Playing with Pepe in the backyard of our Santiago home

With neighborhood kids in front of our
Santiago home, 1973

climbing up the bars on the front windows, I peered into my
mother's bedroom and saw her naked in bed with Roberto, chatting
casually. At least this time she was being private about it: during the
weeks of sharing a room with her in the downtown Santiago hotel,
I occasionally awoke in the middle of the night to the sounds of my
mother screaming, whimpering, and moaning, only to realize when
the sun came up that someone was sharing her bed. At first, it terrified me: I thought she was being beaten, but in the morning she
never had bruises. In time, I learned to cover my head with a pillow
to try to block it all out, then lie frozen in the morning, feigning
sleep, until our overnight guest had left the room. My mother and I

never spoke about it. I have no idea if she ever realized I knew; perhaps she felt better thinking I was sound asleep. Now that we had left the hotel and rented a house, I was relieved to have my own room.

One afternoon, our landlady suddenly stormed in with her brother, her son, and three young thugs armed with knives. They ransacked the place and tried to forcibly evict us. "Get out, you goddamn communists," she screamed over and over again. "Go back to wherever you came from. I don't want to rent to any goddamn communists."

My mother refused to budge. "You can't come in here and force us out like that," she told the landlady slowly, in broken Spanish, with a calm, firm voice, clenching a long stick in her hand by her side. "We're not scared of you. We're not leaving."

She and the landlady just stood there, glaring at each other. The landlady was upset that we had reported the excessive rent she charged to a government price-control office and planned to start making lower payments at the official rate. The police finally arrived to sort things out and determined that we could continue living there until a court date was set to settle the matter. The landlady and her accomplices finally gave up and left—but not before she and her son took with them the stash of cigarette cartons and other black-market items they had secretly stored in the back of the house without our knowledge.

Almost every weekend my mother and I joined volunteer work brigades in the countryside, a short bus ride from Santiago, and sometimes managed to coax some of our housemates to join us. I always looked forward to these weekend outings, getting out of the polluted city and being part of a group activity alongside my mother. The front page of the November 13, 1972, Chilean leftist newspaper *El Siglo* included a picture of my smiling mother proudly holding a bundle of sticks, with the caption "*Yo trabajo por Chile*" (I work for Chile). The story read: "An urban North American, recently arrived in the country, worked yesterday alongside the militants . . . planting vine sticks." She told *El Siglo*, "I want to be part of the struggle."

During our first weekend doing *trabajo voluntario*, we boarded buses and traveled eighty-five kilometers south to a small town called Graneros to load bags of flour and bring them back to the city. When we unloaded the flour at bakeries, people in the neighborhood brought us food and told us about their problems getting supplies amid widespread hoarding and black marketeering. On our way back to Santiago at the end of the day we stopped for water at a farmhouse and sat around on the grass for about an hour while members of the work brigade sang revolutionary songs and made political speeches.

One of the work brigades we joined was part of an organization called the Women's Patriotic Front; others were recruited from schools and from Communist Youth and Socialist Youth groups. I was proud to be working alongside the adults weeding fields and planting grapevines and fruit trees. Though I was only seven, I felt like I was actually participating in this revolution.

One day as the morning's work began, I picked up a bundle of the reeds that a small group of us were using to tie grapevines. A brigade leader who had not been there on other days stopped me, thinking I wanted to play with the reeds. "Those are for grown-ups. Put them down," she told me sternly, staring at me and wagging her skinny finger.

"No." I gripped my bundle of reeds tightly.

She called to a man nearby, asking him to cut the cord that held my bundle together, to force me to drop it. My Spanish wasn't yet good enough for me to know what she'd asked. When the man drew his knife and loomed closer, I was terrified and did the only thing my instincts had taught me: I reached into my back pocket and brought out my own pocketknife, opened the blade, and waved it at him to stay away. I don't know if I would have actually used the knife—I would not have even had a knife back in the U.S., let alone had the guts to threaten to use one—but fortunately I didn't have to find out. Startled by my defiance, the man stopped and looked at the woman for guidance. She huffed loudly and ran off to find my mother. "Foreigners and children are not welcome in the Women's Front," she told us after my mother defended me instead of apologizing.

We didn't go back to the work brigades for a long time after that incident. By the time we did return, the woman had resigned, and the fields were now dotted with foreigners and children who had come in solidarity. My mother and I felt triumphant. *If this is joining the revolution*, I thought, *then I am all for it.*

Around this time, my mother wrote a poem about me, which I would discover years later, hidden away in her diary:

Fragile child
Far from innocent
The other side of me—angry, selfish, curious, insistent.
You are my world—everything I am fighting for, everything I
    am fighting against.
Pockets full of candy, eyes full of tears.
Don't give up, don't give up.
You know more than anyone
The size and shape of the enemy
Your father and your mother in mortal conflict.
Pedrito, my son, don't forget your mama.

Renaico

WE NEED TO experience the real life of the Chilean campesino," my mother announced one day. The weekend stints with the voluntary work brigades were just not enough. As she had in Berkeley, she was getting politically restless living in Santiago, and was itching to see how the rest of the country was changing under Allende. Real revolutions, she liked to say, were made in the countryside, not just in the cities. "Let's find a revolutionary collective farm where the old landowners are no longer in charge and the peasants are being empowered. You'll like it better than Santiago," my mother assured me as I ran around the backyard, playing with the puppy.

All I cared about were the animals, which she promised in abundance: "Pigs and cows and sheep and horses. And they're owned by the people, not some rich landlord who exploits everyone like before."

We packed our duffel bags and headed south in the Chilean summer of January 1973. It was our first time hitchhiking, and it took us two days on the road. Although having me by her side made things more complicated for my mother, it also made it easier to get people to offer help. We slept outdoors, rode with truck drivers, and got a ride with a schoolteacher who gave me a straw hat. As she placed it on my head she ruffled my messy, unwashed hair, saying, "Here, this will help launch your career as a compañero." It was at moments like these that I felt like I was finally starting to belong.

The next day we stopped for directions at a farm near the small town of Renaico. My mother tried to explain to the farmers what type of collective farm she was looking for. Her Spanish was still pretty basic but good enough to get by, and they nodded and seemed to understand what she meant. They took us by horse cart to the nearby Centro Reforma Agraria Che Guevara. The dozen or so peasant families there had claimed the land in late 1971. Under Chile's new laws, the Allende government allocated each family a piece of land closest to their house and brought in electricity to the homes.

We passed between the long rows of tall eucalyptus trees that marked the wide entrance to Che Guevara and soon stopped to talk to a stocky middle-aged woman standing by the side of the road. Her name was Rosa. She spoke quickly in staccato and was especially hard to understand because she had no upper teeth. She seemed flattered that we were so interested in the farm. Rosa gestured for us to come into her home and meet her family—her husband, Mauricio, and their three boys, Sebastian (six), Octavio (fourteen), and Pedro (eighteen). Since it was getting late, Rosa invited us to spend the night. We all slept in the same room, two to each single bed, and covered ourselves with odd assortments of threadbare sheets, blankets, and old clothes. My mother and I spent the whole night fighting off fleas, but no one else seemed bothered by them. Fleabites aside, the sleeping arrangement made me feel like we were in the midst of a wonderful adventure.

The next morning we got up early and joined the dozen or so men clearing weeds from a field of beans. Like at the weekends of *trabajo voluntario*, I was always eager to participate in a group outdoor activity of mostly adults. Without hoes we couldn't help much—and the men hardly seemed to notice our presence—but we tried to show our commitment by doggedly pulling weeds by hand. Finally, my mother started chatting them up, telling them she'd grown up in Kansas farm country, and that "Che Guevara is the most beautiful farm I've ever seen." She left out the fact that she had never actually done any farming. As usual, her charm and sincerity had an immediate effect: a couple of the men headed off to find hoes for us.

One of the men we impressed with our enthusiasm for farm work was Rosa's eighteen-year-old son, Pedro. As we arrived home from the field that evening, Pedro asked, "Why don't you stay here? Maybe you can live with us?"

Rosa nodded enthusiastically, even though there was really no room for us in their tiny house. I looked to my mother, who, to my surprise, agreed.

Rosa was always first to rise, and she blared the news on the radio as a sort of alarm clock to rouse the rest of us. Pedro was always the last out of bed, and once he was up, I eagerly joined him to check on the animals. I loved helping him tend to all the chickens and pigs and cows and horses, and unlike my own brothers, he didn't mind my tagging along. Pedro, more than twice my age and almost twice my size, was my hero. He could do pretty much anything—fix fences, lasso a cow, hunt birds and rabbits, make a slingshot out of a twig and a piece of rubber. I followed him every-

On the farm in Chile. Pedro is in the middle, and I'm standing to his left.

where, and tried to walk and talk confidently like him. We even had the same name. Pedro called me Pedrito, which pleased my mother even more than me.

My mother helped Rosa around the house, cleaning and making breakfast, though she struggled at chopping wood and milking the cow. Her only complaints were that Rosa hung everyone's washed clothes on barbed wire that left tear marks and insisted on emptying the chamber pot in the vegetable garden—where much of our food, including tomatoes, corn, beans, and potatoes, came from—instead of in the outhouse. After a long day in the fields, our reward was a cleansing swim in the river, which everyone, young and old, enjoyed.

The main meal of the day was lunch, with only bread and milk typically served in the evening. The kitchen was always the center of activity. On the walls hung a peculiar mix of pictures—Che, Allende, Frank Sinatra, JFK. The only thing these famous male faces had in common was that they were Rosa's idols. There was also a blond pinup girl calendar that belonged to Pedro, which no one other than my mother seemed to mind. There were huge bags of dried corn and beans on the dirt floor, firewood was neatly stacked head-high along one wall, and onions were strung from the rafters. Two chickens roosted above the firewood, and the family's pig, Guerrillero, lived in a box in the corner but spent much of his time foraging for food under the kitchen table. He would inevitably bump into someone's legs and be sent back to his box—from which he would appear again a few minutes later.

Rosa's husband, Mauricio, a tall, big-boned man with a hunched back and only a few strands of hair left on his leathery head, always drank heavily at the end of the day. Once, after a trip into town to deliver a gift to the church for All Saints' Day, he got so drunk that he lost a suitcase full of groceries and necessities for the house. Rosa and my mother ran back to town, and they spent hours checking the bars for the missing suitcase, to no avail. Mauricio managed to find it somewhere the next day, and the crisis was averted, but I couldn't believe that someone would deliberately do that to himself. Despite all of my adventures so far with my mother, I'd never before seen anyone drunk and was terrified by the sight of him stumbling around and mumbling unintelligibly, and forgetting where he had been or what he had done.

Though I'd never witnessed my father take even a sip of alcohol, something about Mauricio reminded me of him. From our cozy spot on the farm, my father felt so far away, as if Michigan were an entirely different planet. I wondered what he would think of our new life. Would he be alarmed by our primitive living conditions, or impressed by how well I was handling it all? After dinner one evening, I dictated to my mother a short note to him, a description of my daily life, as if my father and I were chatting on the phone:

> *Dear Daddy,*
>
>   *I miss you. I am riding on lots of horses and playing futbol and swimming in the river. We are living up in the country. We hitchhiked to Renaico. I work in the fields. Yesterday afternoon I caught a cow with a rope. I was on a horse. I helped feed the calf. We make coffee out of wheat and then we mix it with warm milk and then we drink it. We pick beans every day. We make soup out of beans. Day before yesterday I rounded up cows with a stick. There are fleas in the bed. They itch me. We eat lots of corn. We have a puppy. I feed the chickens. After we live in Chile I might visit you. I am learning the language here. Please write.*
>
>   *Love,*
>   *Peter*

I was seven and a half years old but still didn't know how to read or write, though that was true of everyone at Rosa's house. The family relied exclusively on their little radio for all their news. There were no newspapers, and the communist party magazines, which someone had brought as a gift, were used as toilet paper.

A few weeks later, my mother and I returned to Santiago, where she had work to do on her book about women in Allende's Chile. I didn't want to leave Pedro or the animals, and would have gladly traded the relative comforts of the city for the crowded, flea-bitten nights at Rosa's. But my mother promised we'd return. When we left the farm, Rosa and her entire family accompanied us along the dirt road to the crowded train station in town, pressing gifts of hard-boiled eggs into our hands for the journey.

Just Passing Through

RONALD SUDDENLY SHOWED up at our Santiago house one night, not long after we had returned from the farm. We had not heard from him in months. He looked rugged, handsome, and healthy. His Berkeley-style long hair was now short, and both he and his backpack looked like they had been around the world several times. Though he'd known little Spanish when we'd first arrived in Guayaquil back in September, now he chatted easily with our housemates. He was barely fifteen.

The tensions that had run so high the last time we'd seen him evaporated as he shared the stories of his adventures. I was mesmerized.

Ronald told us in detail how, more than six months earlier, he first set off from Guayaquil to explore the Ecuadorian Amazon, then hitchhiked to Peru and Bolivia, and then went on to Chile and Argentina. He mostly caught rides with truck drivers or jumped freight trains. He had traveled all the water routes in the south—the Strait of Magellan, Tierra del Fuego, Cape Horn, Drake's Pass. He made it all the way down to Antarctica—he'd managed to get hired as a kitchen helper cleaning pots and pans on a ship after befriending the captain's daughter.

Ronald had traveled through Patagonia, a remote area as large as Alaska that was mostly inhabited by ranchers. He explained that, with few roads for hundreds of miles, he'd had to travel through one of the most remote stretches of southern Chile by horseback, buying a horse from some sheepherders for eighteen dollars. It took him two months to make the journey between Puerto Aysén and

Puerto Montt, riding seventy miles a day and letting the horse rest one day a week. As he described it, there were no towns, no roads, no electricity—nothing but giant mountain glaciers and deep blue mountain lakes. Ronald said he mostly traveled alone but at times tagged along with gauchos. He remained a vegetarian, living mostly on bread, cheese, and wine. He cut his hair short in order not to look like a hippie and to avoid being hassled by the police. He boasted, "I've crossed lots of borders and hung around with lots of pigs and never once been searched or arrested." I was especially thrilled to hear about all the animals Ronald had encountered along the way—eagles, ostriches, condors, swans, mountain lions and other wild cats.

Ronald could tell we were both completely captivated by his every word. One of our housemates walked into the room and asked Ronald about his travels, and so he told the story all over again, every detail, and we sat there and listened again, just as intently as the first time.

As he launched into a lecture on how we all needed to get out of Santiago, which he described as a "pocket of cement" where everyone thinks they're the center of the world, it was clear that he was still the same old Ronald, with the same sense of superiority. This time, though, it felt earned. My mother seemed proud of him; I was in awe.

When we tried to tell him about our time in Renaico and the farm, he was dismissive. "Too bad you didn't stay there longer. You should have stayed, or traveled more, instead of coming back to this concrete hellhole."

My mother began addressing him as an equal, asking his opinion of the coastal city of Valparaiso, where she planned to conduct some interviews for her book. Ronald told her he hated the place; that he had only gone there to try to get on a ship. Then, without even glancing at me, he said, "Carol, I'm sure Peter is slowing you down these days, and he can be so demanding. Why don't you leave him with some neighbors here so you can travel around and get out of Santiago?" *Ah, yes*, I thought to myself, *this is the brother I remember, always treating me like a nuisance and wanting me out of the way.* I bit my lip and didn't say anything.

Things went downhill from there. A few days after he arrived, my mother walked into the kitchen in her nightgown while Ronald was eating breakfast. He shot her a disgusted look, as if she'd personally insulted him. "Look at you," he sneered, "you haven't even washed your face, combed your hair, or brushed your teeth. How American." She tried to laugh it off but could not hide the pained look on her face.

Then they started arguing about politics and Chile. "I hate rich bourgeois people, and I hate ignorant, drunkard workers, and Chile is afflicted by both," Ronald declared between bites. "The only real enemies in Chile are the piggy rich and the lazy poor."

My mother countered, "Well, Allende is trying to take from the rich to help the poor, and the poor are mostly hardworking people, not lazy at all. And it's the men who get drunk—there will be a lot less of that as women become more empowered."

"Allende, Allende, I'm tired of hearing about Allende. Mostly he's just created a lot of bureaucracy. Carol, you're so naive."

I jumped in to defend my mother, hoping it would impress her. "Allende is fighting for the people; those against Allende are living off the people. Don't you see that?"

"Peter, you stay out of this," Ronald barked. "You don't know anything about Chilean politics anyway." I left the table.

"I am holding off with writing about my feelings toward Ronald," my mother wrote in her diary that week. "Just feel there is a huge mountain between us. He can't relate to bourgeois existence, but neither could he relate to building a community with working-class people." She continued: "He is a distant observer of everything around him, amused, critical, looking for something that will be worthy of his support. In the meantime, he won't do any work in the house or treat other people considerately, or so it seems to me. He holds me personally responsible for all the problems of the revolution—for his disillusionment."

My mother also wrote several letters to Joel back in Berkeley late that April, which included confessing her mounting frustrations about Ronald:

> *Ronald has a big hurt somewhere, I think, that his*
> *travels haven't cured. He sneers at Chile and has no*
> *interest in working except to earn money or gain*
> *something for himself. He can't get inspired by any kind*
> *of struggle except an isolated struggle against nature (I'd*
> *feel better if he'd settle for that and stay out of politics*
> *and judging other people. He has no sense of history or*
> *of economics—thinks the government here just plunked*
> *a lot of programs on the people three years ago). Ronald*
> *doesn't like to be categorized, but it's easy for people to*
> *categorize him as a typical American hippie. I have*
> *serious work to do here and get bogged down when I*
> *have to defend him or defend myself against him. I'd*
> *hate to see you sucked into the hypercritical aloofness that*
> *I see in him.*

Ronald was just passing through, and we were not unhappy to see him go. As he was taking off again, this time for Easter Island—a tiny spot of Chilean territory in the middle of the Pacific, thousands of miles from anywhere, which he would explore before returning to the mainland and hitchhiking all the way back to the States—my mother gave him some money, along with a poem she had written about the two of them:

> *One woman, one young man*
> *United by memories good and bad*
> *In a family old and new*
> *How absurd are our conversations*
> *And how important they are*

We want friendship but can't create it
We wait too long
We are actually enemies
I hear your voice in the corridor
Pontificating at my friends
I cover my head
I can't believe what I hear
You hear my voice in the kitchen
Telling stories of your childhood
And you enter the room full of fury and hatred
We are actually enemies
We embrace between battles
But the war continues
And will continue
Until death

Ronald scanned the poem quickly and then handed it back to her, saying only, "I don't relate to this. It's not my thing." And then he turned, threw his backpack over his shoulder, and was gone. We would not see him again for almost two years.

Back to the Farm

MY MOTHER KEPT our promise to return to the farm, some six months later. We made it back in July, right after my eighth birthday. It was wintertime in Chile. This time we traveled to Renaico by train, arriving on a Sunday morning after trying to sleep all night piled on the cold floor of the train car. At the farm, Rosa welcomed us back as if we were part of her family. The place was even more picturesque than we had remembered it—beautiful sky, tall eucalyptus and pine trees everywhere, snowcapped peaks in the distance overlooking half-plowed fields, piles of freshly cut firewood, and piglets, chickens, dogs, and cats racing in and out of the house. The winter rains had massaged the dust into the dirt road.

Beautiful as it was, winter was still harder on the farm. The cold made it difficult to convince yourself out of bed in the morning. My mother wore three pairs of socks to bed to try to keep her feet warm, and often left them on when she got up. I sometimes wore double socks, too. One morning, I was surprised to see Rosa's son, Octavio, sewing the tops of his shoes to the bottoms—he had no socks at all. I looked away. I felt bad for him—guilty about my own warm feet—but not enough to give him a pair of my socks. I was wearing the only pairs I had brought with me from Santiago. I wondered if Octavio noticed that I had two pairs on and if he resented me for it. The moment was an awkward reminder that I was still a privileged outsider even as I was trying hard to fit in.

The water pump would freeze up at night, so we had to thaw it out every morning with hot water in order to wash up and get the day started. As soon as I was ready, Pedro and I headed out on horse-back to check on the animals.

Despite the bone-chilling weather, I was elated. We planned only a short visit, but I ended up staying on with Rosa and her family while my mother traveled around Chile doing research for her book. It took no convincing to get me to stay. And they were more than happy to take care of me. I didn't want my mother to go, but I also didn't want to leave the farm, and she assured me everything would be okay and that she'd be back soon—though it was not entirely clear what soon meant. Everyone, including me, seemed to think it was a perfectly normal arrangement for her to leave me there.

As my mother was leaving, I told her, "I want to live here on the farm for years and years." At that moment, there was nowhere else on earth I wanted to be more, even if that meant trading in my closeness with my mother.

"Let's just see how things go for a few months, okay? And if we want to stay longer after that maybe we could buy an extra bed."

My mother seemed pleased that I was so eager to live there. I kissed her good-bye as I headed off for the hills with Pedro to shoot birds with slingshots.

Although I much preferred farmwork to school, Rosa ignored my protests and convinced the nuns who taught her youngest son, Se-bastian, at the local Catholic school to admit me. The school in Re-naico was more than a two-mile walk each way, which I didn't mind. On lucky days, Sebastian and I caught a ride in an oxcart, dangling our feet off the back, as it was on its way to sell produce at the town market. Octavio sometimes came with us on his way to sell beans at the market. Some kids, like Octavio, never went to school because their families needed them to work in the fields. At lunchtime, no one ever complained about the school food, which was mostly rice and beans, since it was one of the only schools around that had a free lunch.

But even as I dutifully went to school and tried to learn how to read and write, I always wanted to be on the farm. That's where I felt I belonged, that's where the fun was, and what I was learning at school didn't seem all that useful—to me, or to any of the other kids. I had none of the luxuries of my old life in America, no Saturday-morning cartoons, but I didn't miss them yet. Pedro, Sebastian, and I shared a twin bed, keeping each other warm through the winter nights. The only thing I dreaded, especially in the middle of winter, was taking a shower—which meant Rosa pouring buckets of cold water over my head. But that was only once a week. I fit right in; I was just a grubby little kid playing and working on the farm. I was the happiest I'd ever been, in those months before the coup.

El Golpe

JUST AFTER 9:00 A.M. on September 11, 1973, Rosa, Pedro, and I huddled around the radio in the kitchen, listening intently as President Salvador Allende broadcast what were to be his last publicly spoken words. Pedro and I had just gotten back from our first round of tending to the cows, horses, and other animals when Rosa yelled out for us to hurry in to listen to the radio. La Moneda, the presidential palace in Santiago, was being bombed; the military was staging a coup with the support of the country's disgruntled wealthy elite and the covert encouragement of the United States, which saw Allende as part of a growing communist threat in the region. Allende vowed never to give in to the military. He would be dead within hours; the junta that was taking over would claim he'd committed suicide with an AK-47 assault rifle given to him by Fidel Castro. Allende's voice on the radio was solemn yet defiant:

> My friends,
>
> Surely this will be the last opportunity for me to address you. The Air Force has bombed the towers of Radio Portales and Radio Corporacion.
>
> My words do not have bitterness but disappointment. May they be a moral punishment for those who have betrayed their oath. . . .
>
> I will pay for loyalty to the people with my life. And I say to them that I am certain that the seed which we have planted in the good conscience of thousands and thousands of Chileans will not be shriveled forever. . . .

Workers of my country: I want to thank you for the loyalty that you always had, the confidence that you deposited in a man who was only an interpreter of great yearnings for justice. . . . I address, above all, the modest woman of our land, the campesina who believed in us, the worker who labored more, the mother who knew our concern for children. . . . I address the youth, those who sang and gave us their joy and their spirit of struggle. I address the man of Chile, the worker, the farmer, the intellectual, those who will be persecuted. . . .

Workers of my country, I have faith in Chile and its destiny. Other men will overcome this dark and bitter moment when treason seeks to prevail. Go forward knowing that, sooner rather than later, the great avenues will open again where free men will walk to build a better society.

Long live Chile! Long live the people! Long live the workers!

These are my last words, and I am certain that my sacrifice will not be in vain. I am certain that, at the very least, it will be a moral lesson that will punish felony, cowardice, and treason.

When the radio went silent, I could think only of my mother. Where was she? Was she safe? Would I ever see her again? Barely eight, I didn't fully comprehend the political situation, but I was fluent enough in Spanish at this point to understand Allende's words—and knew enough to recognize that my mother could be in danger. After all, she was an active supporter of the leftist government that had just been violently overthrown. Indeed, her complaint about Allende was that he hadn't been leftist *enough*. Her sympathies were actually with the more radical Chilean MIR—Movimiento de Izquierda Revolucionaria, or Revolutionary Left Movement. She thought Allende should have distributed arms to the workers in preparation for a possible military coup. I had not seen or heard from her in more than a month. I also had no idea how to reach my father or anyone else. At that moment I felt more alone, more cut off, than at any other time in my life. I had been happy living on the farm, but now it suddenly seemed as if I was marooned there in the midst of a political hurricane.

Allende's voice was gone forever. Rosa and Pedro sat staring at the radio in stunned silence. Rosa glanced over at me, forcing a tepid smile, perhaps trying to comfort me, but I could see the fear in her dark eyes.

And so, after El Golpe, the right-wing military coup led by General Augusto Pinochet—the man who would rule Chile for the next seventeen years—I anxiously waited for my mother's return.

Days and then a week passed. I lay awake in the middle of the night, wondering where my mother was, wondering when she'd return for me, wondering if she was even still alive. Radio broadcasts by the new military government were blaming "foreign extremists" for Chile's ill-fated turn to the left. Sensing my worry, Rosa and her family did everything they could to reassure me. Finally, Rosa reached across the table for my hand early one morning at breakfast. A worry line bisected her eyebrows and her lips trembled slightly. She said, "Peter, if something has happened to your mother, you can stay here with us and be part of our family."

I nodded but said nothing. I hated to think what "something" meant. My mind raced with scary possibilities. Was my mother imprisoned? Tortured? In a morgue? Maybe in an unmarked grave, never to be found? And then I wondered what it would be like if I stayed there with Rosa's family. Would I end up with no socks like Octavio, sewing the tops and bottoms of my shoes together to keep them from falling apart? Or would my father somehow find me and take me to the safety of Michigan? That thought was comforting but also disturbing—it would mean my mother had never come back.

Unexpected anger began to build up inside of me, questions ric-
ocheting in my brain. How could my mother have left me there by
myself? Why hadn't she taken me with her, as she always had before?
Should I have tried to convince her to stay? How could she have put
herself in such danger knowing how much I needed her? How could
she care more about her book than about me?

A couple of weeks after the coup, as Rosa's family and I sat down
at the kitchen table for lunch, my mother suddenly appeared at the
door. I jumped up and ran to hug her, consumed by relief. Any angry
feelings I'd had instantly vanished. Rosa and the rest of the family
greeted her warmly and quickly made space for her next to me at the
table. She dropped her duffel bag by the door and sat down. She had
hitchhiked from Valparaiso, a day's drive to the north. "I had no way
of getting a message to you," she explained in a tired voice, putting
her left arm around my shoulders while taking bites of food with her
right hand. As my mother ate, Rosa kept filling her plate with more
rice and beans and potatoes.

Rosa said, "I told Peter not to worry about you, that you'd return—but if not, he planned to stay here as part of our family."

My mother looked at me admiringly, and I nodded. I could tell
she was pleased to hear this, for it meant I had chosen Chile over
my father. Truth was, I had no idea how to find my father or how
he would find me, so I was simply trying to adjust to the situation
as best I could. As much as I loved Rosa's family and the farm, I had
no doubt I would have gone back with my father if he'd come to get
me. But I didn't say that.

Between bites, my mother told us what she'd gone through since
the coup: hurriedly burning letters and papers expressing leftist
sympathies that might give cause for detention in the case of a search;
witnessing a battle scene between pro-Allende and pro-coup forces in
downtown Concepción (an industrial city in the middle of the country); helping a friend burn incriminating papers and hide weapons
in her backyard; the ordeal of hitchhiking to Renaico by catching

rides with rich sympathizers of the new military regime and telling them elaborate false stories about why she was in Chile (married to a Ford Foundation representative) and where she was going (to meet up with her husband and child). I was barely listening at that point, clinging on to the hand draped across my left shoulder. My mother was safe and we were together again.

My mother looked exhausted but relieved to have made her way back to the farm. "We need to leave, we need to get out of the country."

Reunited with my mother at last, I turned my grief to the thought of leaving Chile, the farm, Pedro, Rosa and her family—a family I feared I would never see again. Suddenly, the last thing in the world I cared about was having enough pairs of socks.

Twin calves were born to the family cow right before my mother and I left Renaico. I was captivated by the sloppy mess as Pedro reached deep into the birth canal with his bare hands to attach ropes to the calf's legs. We then all grabbed part of the rope and pulled hard, and out came the slimy calf. We repeated the process for the second one. One of the calves had to have its legs straightened with splints before it could try to walk. Everyone cheered in celebration of the birth—it was the only thing to celebrate. It gave us all a feeling of life amid an overwhelming sense of death.

The next day, my mother and I made our way back to Santiago by train. Whereas the last time we had said good-bye to Rosa and her family everyone was in a festive mood, this time could not have been more different. Unexpectedly, it was Mauricio who cried the most when we said good-bye at the entrance to the farm. I had never seen him shed tears while sober. He suddenly appeared far more frail and vulnerable than he ever had in a drunken stupor. Rosa hugged and kissed us. Octavio thanked me for the pair of socks I left him as a parting gift. Pedro just shook my hand and mumbled something about how he would have a hard time getting up in the morning not having me along to check on the animals. "Pedrito," he yelled out to me as my mother and I turned to go, "next time you come, we can hunt birds with the new rifle, not just our slingshots."

No one came with us into town to the train station, which we had to make sure to get to before the evening curfew began. No one risked violating it—a teenager had been gunned down recently while rushing home from the town plaza only a few minutes late. I sobbed silently for more than an hour after our train left Renaico, clutching my mother's side with both hands and burying my face in her sweater.

Back in the capital, some five hundred kilometers to the north, we headed straight to the downtown hotel where we'd stayed when we had first arrived almost a year earlier. There was nowhere better to turn: our old house—the "commune of exiles"—had been abandoned. We ran into an Australian on the street who had lived there and he told us everyone had fled when the landlady denounced them to the authorities right after the coup. Up the block, soldiers had stormed a house in a hail of bullets a few days earlier. On the afternoon of the coup, everyone in our old house began to frantically burn anything the new military government might consider "Marxist literature and propaganda."

The burning frenzy taking place across Chile included all of my mother's notes and research materials for her book, which she had left with friends in a Santiago shantytown. "I lost everything," she told me when she found out. My mother stood staring out the hotel window as she spoke, looking down at the eerily quiet street below. Although I felt helpless to do anything about her lost book materials, all I really cared about was that I had not lost *her*. My mother would still end up writing a book about Chile, but one that was more of a personal account.

Worse still, we found out, was that the landlady had reported to the police the two Uruguayans in our house—Carlos and my mother's lover, Roberto. They had been given political asylum under Allende and could now be deported. They tried to seek refuge in the Argentine embassy but were intercepted by soldiers right before they reached the entrance gate. They were sent to Santiago's National Stadium, which was turned into a giant prison for tens of thousands of people. Somehow they managed to get out after being granted political asylum in Europe. Two of the other foreigners in the house also ended up in the National Stadium but were later released into the custody of their governments.

Many others were not so lucky: thousands of the prisoners in the stadium were tortured, killed, or simply "disappeared." One American, Frank Teruggi, was detained at the National Stadium and was identified ten days later in the morgue. Earlier that year in Santiago, my mother and I had sat near him and his girlfriend at a public screening of a Czech film about the horrors of German occupation. They stayed for only the first minutes, saying it was more than they could take. Much later we heard that the body of another missing American, Charles Horman, had turned up in the morgue. His story would eventually be featured in the Costa-Gavras film *Missing*.

Friends told us that the American embassy had officially listed us as "missing." When my mother heard this she laughed. "And I'm sure the embassy wouldn't mind if we permanently disappeared." I didn't like the sound of that word. It sounded worse than death. And I wondered if my father thought we had "disappeared" and was looking for me. I wanted to get a message to him, but that would have to wait until we got out.

Washington had covertly backed the Chilean opposition to the Allende government, including funding an anti-Allende propaganda campaign. As Secretary of State Henry Kissinger said after Allende was elected in 1970, "I don't see why we need to stand by and watch a country go communist because of the irresponsibility of its own people." The violent overthrow of Allende and its brutal aftermath would become a powerful symbol for the international human rights movement and the struggle for social justice in Latin America for decades. It would also leave my mother with less faith than ever about the possibility of peaceful social change through elections, and more committed than ever to the belief that the capitalist system had to be overthrown by any means necessary. As she saw it, Chile's workers and peasants had been duped into believing in the electoral process and were robbed of their revolution, and the lesson was that workers and peasants everywhere should now trust in nothing but revolution through armed struggle.

Even if it had been safe for us to stay in Chile—the actual level of danger was never entirely clear in the midst of all the uncertainty and chaos right after the coup—the bitter truth was that there was nothing left for my mother to fight for in post-Allende Chile. There was certainly no emerging resistance movement. Allende and his revolution were both dead, and it left my mother feeling politically lost and disoriented.

To Buenos Aires

NOT LONG AFTER we returned to Santiago, my mother and I boarded a bus that was crossing the high Andes, headed for Buenos Aires. It was a two-day trip, including a five-hour stop at a remote mountain border checkpoint, where we had to get off the bus to be searched by Chilean soldiers. As we watched them frisk passengers ahead of us, sift through luggage, and check documents, my mother and I grew increasingly nervous.

We not only wanted to get out of Chile safely but also hoped our duffel bags would not be inspected too carefully. Tucked inside the cover of one of my notebooks, buried under my clothes, was a small black, white, and red poster that said CONSEJOS COMUNALES: UNI-DAD Y PARTICIPACION CAMPESINAS. It depicted a crowd of farm-workers demonstrating their militancy with raised pitchforks, sticks, banners, and clenched fists. The *consejos* (councils) were becoming organs of political power only in the final days of the Allende government. Gambling that the soldiers would focus on the adults and overlook the innocent-looking eight-year-old gringo boy at her side, my mother hid this poster in my belongings. She was determined to smuggle this political memento out of the country, right under the noses of the Chilean soldiers, as a last little act of defiance.

I did my best not to look nervous. While the soldiers patted my mother down and rifled through her luggage, I held my breath, avoided eye contact, and stared at my feet, hoping they wouldn't pay attention to me. They seemed bored and simply waved me through. I had no idea what they would have done if they had caught me, maybe just confiscate the material, but I was glad to not find out.

When we made it across the border into Argentina, my mother smiled approvingly at her little accomplice. "Well done, Peter!"

Once we arrived in Buenos Aires, more than a 1,500-kilometer drive from Santiago, my mother called Grandpa Rich collect to tell him we were safe. No one had heard from us since the coup. Newton was such a small place that the call made the local paper. "Newtonian's daughter safe" ran the headline in the *Newton Kansan* the next day. After Grandpa Rich had been assured we were safely out of Chile, I sat down to write a note to my own father and gave it to my mother to mail:

> *Dear Daddy,*
> *I'm very fyne.*
> *I wount to stay in soyth America with mammy.*
> *We will be in Buenos Aires for a little while.*
> *Bye daddy,*
> *Peter*

As it turned out, immediately after the coup, my father *had* been trying to track me down and bring me to Michigan. He had sent me a one-way airplane ticket to the American embassy in Santiago, but the embassy could not locate us. My father had also called his congressman in Washington, William Broomfield, to see if he could help find me in Chile and get me out. In his October 24 response letter to my father, Broomfield wrote, "The State Department has informed me that your son, Peter, is safe with his mother in Buenos Aires, Argentina." I'm sure my father was relieved to hear I'd gotten out of Chile, but I imagine he didn't think I was actually "safe" with my mother.

Buenos Aires, spread out on the southern shore of the Río de la Plata, looked like a sparkling, sophisticated first-world city—it made us feel like we had actually left South America, or at least the South

America we had known so far. At the time, Argentina was more stable than Chile, though the political situation was still tumultuous.
Juan Perón had just returned from exile in Spain—my first memory
of Buenos Aires was seeing posters of him plastered on walls all over
the city—and was about to start his third term as president.

Although we didn't plan to stay long in Argentina—my mother
didn't think it had enough revolutionary potential—we ended up
sharing an old downtown apartment with an ever-changing mix of
Chilean exiles. The only thing we had in common was that we had
all hurriedly left Chile and had no intention of staying in Argentina.

It was never clear to me who exactly was or wasn't living in the
apartment. On average, there were maybe seven or eight of us,
mostly single men or couples in their twenties or thirties. Someone
always ended up crashing in the living room. One day, a young
Chilean couple moved in with their infant; my mother and I woke
up the next morning to diapers drying in our window. A woman
named Carmen, whom we had met on the bus ride to Buenos Aires,
had a broken leg in a long plaster cast. She was almost always around,
sprawled out in the living room, puffing cigarettes and killing time.
She and her lover, Luis, made handicrafts to sell in the park on
weekends. Sometimes I would tag along to serve as an interpreter for
North American tourists. When Luis got a job on a boat to Australia
he made me a small leather pouch before he left. Gaston, a welder
from Santiago, had the clearest plans for the next stage of his life:
he was waiting for a passport to go to Mexico, where he hoped to
meet up with Heather, his American girlfriend with whom he had
been living in Chile before the coup, and then move to Los Angeles
together. In the meantime, he spent his days borrowing my mother's
little typewriter to write letters to Heather in Mexico City and making a daily batch of crepes for everyone in the house.

The kitchen and bathroom were always a mess, which no one
bothered to clean because the mess would immediately return. Almost as soon as someone brought any food into the kitchen it would

disappear. My mother bought three cartons of milk one night, and by morning one of them was left burned on the stove and the other two had vanished. No one did much cooking beyond Gaston's steady supply of crepes. Without regular jobs, it wasn't clear where anyone was getting money for anything, but one thing that everyone seemed to have enough money for was cigarettes. My mother and I were the only ones who didn't smoke.

My favorite housemate was Freddie, a musician with long dark hair who used to play with a Chilean musical group called Los Jaivas. Freddie slept on and off at all hours of the day, and sang and played his flute or guitar between naps at all hours of the night. He had little money and didn't help out much around the apartment, but no one seemed to mind. His contribution was to entertain the rest of us. Late one night, Freddie coaxed me into singing spontaneously about Chile, switched on his tape recorder, and then played along, going back and forth between his flute and guitar. I waxed poetic about Allende, the tragic end of his revolution, the beauty of the Chilean countryside, and all the animals I had taken care of on the farm. We stayed up late into the night. My mother was so proud of that tape that she sent a copy to Grandpa Rich in Kansas, and another copy to Joel and Ronald in California. A Bay Area public radio station, KPFA, would end up playing it as part of a story they produced about Chile and the coup. I tearfully begged my mother not to mail it, telling her that "Ronald will think I'm showing off, will make fun of me, and then everybody will hate it." My mother mailed it anyway.

Besides us, the only other non-Chilean in the apartment was my mother's lover Jean-Pierre, a lanky Frenchman with thick, wavy black hair and a bushy beard. My mother first met Jean-Pierre in Chile during one of our weekend stints with the volunteer work brigades in the countryside. Jean-Pierre returned to Paris shortly after that, but he and my mother kept writing long love letters to each other, and he came to join us in Buenos Aires a month or so after we got there.

With my mother and Jean-Pierre

Jean-Pierre had discovered he was bisexual while back in Paris, and told my mother about it the first night after he arrived in Buenos Aires. Before Jean-Pierre came, my mother and I had been sharing a single bed on the floor, but I ceded my spot on the mattress, and moved a sleeping bag to the other side of the small room. As I was trying to fall asleep that first night, I overheard Jean-Pierre and my mother talking in hushed voices.

"I have to tell you something, Carol. I slept with Madeleine in Paris."

"Oh. Who's Madeleine?" My mother didn't seem all that disturbed by this news.

"She's a friend, a good friend." Jean-Pierre paused for a few seconds. "And then I slept with Jean-Jacques."

"Huh? Jean-Jacques? That's a man?"

"Yes. He's another good friend."

Silence.

My mother and Jean-Pierre hanging out with
some of our Buenos Aires housemates

Jean-Pierre continued. "And then Jean-Jacques, Madeleine, and
I all slept together."

Silence.

"And now Jean-Jacques and Madeleine are sleeping together."

My mother sighed. "Well, I guess everyone is happy, then. You're
here with me. They're together in Paris."

"Exactly!" Jean-Pierre's relief was palpable. "So you're okay with
me being bisexual?"

"Sure." My mother laughed. "Well, just as long as you like women
as much as men."

But my mother wasn't as carefree about the confession as she'd
sounded that night. As she noted in her diary, "I know that his capac-
ity to live this way is part of what I like in him, part of what makes
it possible for us to relate together so well. Yet it is clear that I am
insecure enough at this point in my life to want all of him to myself."
Beneath my mother's stated ideological opposition to monogamy,
her instincts were more conservative than she let on.

Over breakfast the next morning I casually asked my mother, "What's a bisexual?"

My mother put her coffee cup down and looked at me intently. "Well, it's when a woman is attracted to both women and men, or when a man is attracted to both men and women. There's nothing wrong with that, it liberates people from the confines of traditionally defined sex roles."

"Like Jean-Pierre?"

She sighed. "Yes, Peter, it seems so."

"So, are *you* bisexual?"

"No, unfortunately not." My mother chuckled.

"And my father?"

"Oh, definitely not. But it would probably be good for him if he was." And then she added, with a wink, "Now, Peter, you're going to need to catch up on your sleep tonight."

Meanwhile, safely out of Chile, we were finally able to get back in contact with Joel and Ronald in Berkeley. Sounding disappointed that we had left Chile after the coup, Joel wrote to my mother, "Did you ever think about resisting, fighting? I guess it would be pretty hard for Peter to fight a guerrilla war." He also reported that he was as energized as ever about liberating kids: "Sunday's Young People's Liberation meeting was beautiful. We're united as communists and revolutionaries and young people and everybody feels really good about everyone else and the group. Revolutionary feeling is vibrating the marrow of my bones again." Joel enthusiastically predicted, "The revolution is building, soon it seems like an earthquake is due—really—the apoliticalness that started to set in 2 years ago has been blown away by all the heavy political things that are happening now. Watergate, gasoline rationing, Chile coup, Mideast war, oil company lies, Nixon finances, dirty deals . . . I swear the country is rising and fascism-modernity is falling."

Ronald also sent a couple of short letters—one of them mailed on my mother's birthday without mentioning her birthday—in which he proudly confessed that he had used fake documents to get a year of high school credit for the time he'd been traveling around South America. Ronald's follow-up letter a month or so later reported that he had been kicked out of high school for making fun of his biology teacher by writing a sarcastic make-believe love note to her that was copied and passed around to the students in the class. As he explained it, "I think it must have really humiliated her (she's the power-tripper teacher type)." Perhaps feeling like a protective older brother, Joel sent the principal an angry letter protesting Ronald's expulsion, accusing the principal of running the school in a very "ageist" and "anti-student" way, and warning that "kids liberation is coming." After he was kicked out of school, Ronald wrote us that he had lined up several part-time jobs, one cleaning buses and the other working at Steve's Sandwich Cart: "The afternoon work is pretty bad but being stoned helps." My teenage brothers were clearly managing their Berkeley lives in my mother's absence, each in their own way.

I didn't hear from my father—he had no way of contacting me—but I heard about him through Joel's letters to my mother. Joel complained that "Carl sent a really nasty letter, about how he didn't want Peter to follow in my footsteps (unsaid: you're fucking up)." Our father had been pestering him to see his report card, which Joel found offensive: "I wrote Carl an angry letter when he told me to send my report card—I think that's amazingly ageist using school evaluations of my progress." Joel complained, "Carl just don't understand where my life is at. I hope he sends money. I have $90 now, and my expenses here are $110 a month. I just realized how poor I am—no shoes! I never wear shoes, but now I've been suspended from school for not wearing them and I have no money to buy them."

Joel then wrote to say he wanted to hitchhike to South America to visit us and was trying to come up with a clever scheme to get school credit for it, like Ronald had. He hoped that might even allow him to graduate. Joel asked our mother to write a letter to Berkeley High "affirming that I am going to school down there for 1 semester taking the required courses." I have no idea if she ever ended up writing that letter, but I do know that Joel never graduated.

Argentina turned out to be only a two-month stopover for us, a place to figure out our next move and for my mother to hurriedly type up her Chile recollections (later published as a book, *Nothing Is as It Should Be: A North American Woman in Chile*). With Allende's social-ist Chile destroyed, my mother decided Peru now had the greatest promise for revolutionary foment.

III.

PERU

Wondering who will read this diary besides me. Wondering whether I will live a long time, wondering whether I'll live to see the revolution either here or in the USA, whether I will have a little part in it, a big part, whether I will die fighting.

—Carol Andreas, 1974

Jauja

EVERYONE AROUND ME screamed. A few days before Christmas 1973, my mother, Jean-Pierre, and I were on our way from Lima to Huancayo, a medium-sized city in Peru's central highlands. Our overstuffed train was winding along the highest tracks in the world, hugging the side of a mountain on the western slopes of the Andes, when it hit a boulder. It jumped the tracks, stuttered wildly, and then came to a screeching halt, barely avoiding a long, disastrous tumble down the mountain.

In those terrifying seconds after the impact, all my eight-year-old brain could think of was the order of French fries I had just placed. I screeched, "*Ay caramba, mis papas fritas!*" and our whole car burst into laughter.

During the chilly hours that we patiently waited by the side of the tracks for another train to come, my mother and I struck up a conversation with Angelica, a teenage girl with thick, long, braided black hair. She was maybe sixteen, and said she came from Jauja, the first capital of Spanish Peru and the cultural capital of the central highlands. A small town of mostly Indian inhabitants, it was only a short bus ride from Huancayo, and Angelica made us promise to visit her and her family.

Now that her Spanish was passable, my mother's plan was to try to get a job teaching sociology at the Universidad Nacional del Centro in Huancayo once the semester started in April. That way, she hoped, she could embed herself in the community and get involved in local political struggles. But that was still months away, and so we

With my mother by the side of our derailed train crossing the
Peruvian Andes, December 1973

decided to visit Jauja. Before boarding the bus we shopped at Huancayo's Sunday market. My mother bought me a beautiful white,
brown, and black alpaca sweater, and Jean-Pierre bought me a wood
flute and a little pouch as a good-bye gift. He would be returning to
Lima. My mother had lost interest in him, perhaps because he was
ultimately more into taking photos than talking politics. I would
miss Jean-Pierre and his fancy Nikon, especially since we didn't have
a camera of our own, though I would not miss having him in the
room with my mother and me at night.

Once again I had my mother all to myself, at least for the time
being. Things were less complicated when it was only the two of us.
She didn't ask me what I thought about Jean-Pierre or his leaving—
she never asked me about any of the boyfriends who came and
went—but maybe she could sense that I liked it best when we were
taking care of each other on our own.

With my new gifts after visiting
Huancayo's Sunday market,
December 1973

In Jauja, nestled in Peru's Mantaro Valley almost two miles above
sea level, all the buildings wore red-tile roofs and most were made
of adobe. Only part of the town had electricity, and even there the
current was unstable. Banners in the streets decried the electricity
problem. Cultivated hills, some dotted with crumbling Inca ruins,
surrounded the town.

We checked into a small hotel close to the town plaza and were
given a narrow room with one small bed. The hotel had no heat or
hot water, but our room was clean and cheap. It was the day before

With my mother near Jauja, January 1974

Christmas. I spent hours playing soccer in front of the hotel with
other neighborhood kids, and at night lit firecrackers with the hotel
owner's son. Most of the kids were friendly enough, except for the
bully who teased me and called me *gringa* because of my long hair.
My mother was still refusing to let me cut it.

On Christmas Day, drunken men, young and old, were dancing
in the streets. They reminded me of Rosa's husband, Mauricio, back
on the farm in Chile. I hoped he and Rosa and the family were safe.
And I couldn't help thinking of my own, assuredly sober father, so far
away, who was no doubt having a very different kind of Christmas
celebration. I imagined he would want me there with him, acting out
his dream of the happy family.

Angelica's home turned out to be only a few blocks from our
hotel, above a little restaurant her family owned on Junin Street.
There were only maybe half a dozen small tables, and the mostly

male customers seemed to come to drink Pilsen as much as to order food. My mother and I introduced ourselves to her family the day after Christmas and then came back every day thereafter. We ate all our meals there, usually the daily soup with garlic, potatoes, and rice. There was no menu; one simply ate whatever Angelica's mother, Emma, cooked that day.

I quickly became friends with Angelica and enjoyed hanging out at the restaurant. A week later, my mother and I moved in with Angelica's family; it was cheaper than staying at the hotel, and they had plenty of room for us. Hildo, Angelica's older brother, had just left to join the army, so we rented his room, its large windows looking over neighboring rooftops. Pigs, chickens, and rabbits lived in the muddy backyard. We had a table and an electric lamp, so my mother had a place to write in her diary or type away on her little manual Olivetti. My mother paid the family seven hundred soles a week for room and board. We still had some of the savings she had brought with us from Berkeley over a year earlier, but we were apparently close to broke, though she never shared her money concerns with me.

While we lived with Angelica and her family, my mother tried to work with me on my reading and writing, but I stubbornly resisted and was easily distracted by all of the people coming and going from the restaurant. I joined the neighborhood kids in water-balloon fights on the streets, trips to the outdoor market, and of course kicking a soccer ball around. I learned to pester foreign tourists, hoping to earn some spare change; I would offer to translate for them when bartering with vendors. Jauja became my playground, a world with no real rules or parental oversight. As my mother jotted down in one of her diary entries from January of 1974, "Peter drove by in a truck with a bunch of strangers. What's he up to?! Wonder if we're going to a party tonight?"

As I made friends across town, though, my focus was always on Angelica. I missed Pedro on the farm in Chile, but in Jauja, Angelica was my world. I was devoted to her, despite the fact that she had a boyfriend, Daniel. She, in turn, was happy to play big sister, something I'd never had. Angelica adored me and I adored her. She saved some of her most radiant smiles for me. She took me everywhere with her and had more luck than my mother did getting me to work on reading and writing lessons.

Angelica even managed to cure me of *sarna*. I had not been able to stop itching. My mother called it "the itch" because at first we had no idea what it was. I had blisters, redness, and intense itching on my fingers, with the webbed areas between my fingers oozing a clear pus. Turns out I had become a breeding ground for tiny mites. The local doctor told us I had something called *sarna* and gave us a white powder to put on it. We looked up *sarna* in our Spanish-English dictionary: scabies, otherwise known as mange. It was contagious, but my mother somehow managed not to get it from me. The mites were completely attached to me as their host. I was miserable. We tried new lotions and soaps. "The itch" still wouldn't go away. Then Angelica rubbed chili peppers into the soft skin between my fingers. That did the trick, and I was finally cured.

With Angelica in Jauja, January 1974

Angelica always took me with her to the movies on the weekend, but that was mostly an excuse to meet up with Daniel. There was only one movie theater in town, on the corner of the town's central plaza, and there was little logic to what it played—an old Western, a kung fu flick, a sappy romance. I didn't care. When Angelica was grounded for sneaking out to see Daniel, I chose to stay home with her and skip the shows. When Daniel tried to visit Angelica, her father kicked him and screamed at him and chased him away from the house. He didn't want any man near his daughter. Daniel, tall, muscular, and handsome, was twice the size of Angelica's pudgy and potbellied middle-aged father, but he always respectfully backed off. Sometimes Angelica gave me a love note to secretly pass on to Daniel, and it made me feel important that she trusted me to be their accomplice. I'd smuggle the note out the front door past Angelica's oblivious father, dart around the corner and hand it to Daniel waiting a block away, and then bring a note back to Angelica, who would give me a warm thank-you kiss on my forehead before disappearing to her room to read it. When she then reappeared with a new note, I'd slip back off to Daniel. Angelica's father never caught on.

One afternoon, Angelica took me to the church and cemetery for a funeral. When I came back, I ran to my mother, promising her that when she died I would keep fresh flowers on her grave. "Mommy, you should have seen all those graves with all those flowers. You like flowers, so I'll make sure to put flowers on your grave, too."

My mother paused, startled. "Oh, Peter, I appreciate the sentiment, but hopefully that won't be for a while yet. Besides, I want my body to be cremated—you know, burned to ashes—so I won't need to have a grave at all."

"But then where will I put the flowers?" I asked, disappointed.

My mother laughed. "Let's not worry about that right now. But in the meantime you can give me flowers whenever you want."

Ever since my mother was missing for those weeks after the military coup in Chile, I'd been worried that she was going to get herself killed. "Sometimes you have to die for a good cause," my mother had said to me when explaining Allende's death, which didn't help. Seeing my alarm, she continued: "Oh, don't worry, I'm not going to die like Allende anytime soon. It's possible, I suppose, but I'm not planning on it." Perhaps she never realized how terrified I was that she would suffer a violent death, but this was just one more example of her parenting philosophy. My mother never really treated me or spoke to me like a child. I liked that equality, that responsibility, that respect, even as I craved reassurance. And we did take care of each other, especially when sick, though she got sick a lot more than I did. One Jauja diary entry read, "Sick in bed today with diarrhea like I've never had before. . . . Peter is bringing me things I need and even dumped my shit pan, with a hanky tied to his nose."

By the middle of January, the town was gearing up for the annual Tunantada festival, when they celebrated the patron saints San Sebastián and San Fabian. Caught up in the excitement, my mother and I watched as the crowds gathered. Prominent men from the community, called *chutos*, began to clear the streets of people to make way for the bands. The *chutos* wore small rounded black hats with brightly colored cloth strips around the base, white shirts with matching scarves, elaborately embroidered vests, and knee-length pants. But most distinctive were their painted masks of animal skin and fur. I was captivated by their masked faces. The *chutos* were not smiling; they never smiled. There was something solemn and serious about them even as they danced about. They danced in high leather boots, almost bouncing along the ground, for hours, only stopping for the occasional drink of *chicha* or beer at one of the many street stalls set up for the occasion.

Among those who joined the festivities were dozens of men

With the *chutos* in Jauja, January 1974

dressed in elegant dark-colored Spanish-colonial costumes, wearing masks of paper with painted-blue eyes. Half were dressed up as women. At first this confused me—I thought they really were women and didn't entirely believe my mother when she insisted they were actually men. How weird, I thought, that men would impersonate women. When I asked her why these were not real women, she explained that women were not allowed and that this showed how sexist the society was.

There was also a band playing, with its members outfitted in neat, dark business suits, all the same material and color. They played brass instruments and huge wooden harps. The music was penetrating, complicated in its rhythm and melancholy in its mood. The musicians paused to eat and drink as the day went on, but seemed tireless as they walked along solemnly in a group until late at night. By this time, the streets were heavy with the smell of alcohol and urine, and drunken men slept in doorways.

On the second day of the celebration, an enormous crowd gathered in the Plaza de Yauyos. My mother and I watched the spectacle, seated in stands with Angelica and her family. *Chutos*, mounted on donkeys, prepared to show their strength in a gruesome duck-beheading contest. I didn't realize what was happening until two ducks were strung up by their feet on a wooden beam. I watched in horror as the *chutos*, riding underneath, took turns pulling at the ducks' heads. The frantic ducks somehow managed to elude death for a long time. I was horrified, but also mesmerized, and could not turn away and stop watching. The victorious *chuto*—the first one to successfully pull off a duck's head—removed his mask to receive the applause of the crowd. He then proudly presented the duck head, dripping with blood, to his wife, who held it up high as she emerged from the crowd to dance with him. The whole grotesque scene suddenly made me much less enamored of *chutos*. We left before finding out the fate of the second duck.

That night, my mother, as unsettled by the duck-beheading scene as I was, returned with me to our room, where we curled up to read a book together. Lying there with her as she read to me from the Spanish edition of *Tom Sawyer* we had picked up in Lima, I clung to her. We both needed an escape, just the two of us, even if only for a little while. We had joined the festivities to feel part of the community, but at the end of the day we felt more than ever like outsiders. We were the only ones who seemed at all disturbed by the gruesome contest.

Over the past few weeks my mother and I had settled in with Angelica's family but didn't feel entirely comfortable in Jauja. The real problem was that it wasn't clear how this layover in Jauja fit into my mother's larger search for the revolution—a search that had been suddenly thrown way off course by the military coup in Chile, leaving her drifting in political limbo. She hoped there might be revolutionary potential in the Peruvian highlands, where the large indigenous population remained marginalized and impoverished, with centuries-old grievances dating back to the Spanish conquest. But at the moment, there was no revolutionary rebellion. Still, even if my mother couldn't find the revolution, it didn't take her long to find a revolutionary.

Ocopilla

ONE EARLY AFTERNOON in late January, a young man came by the restaurant while we were eating lunch. Raul was short, trim, and stocky with thick dark hair. He wore a fake black leather jacket and black plastic-framed glasses with tape wrapped around the edges to keep the stems in place. One lens was chipped and cracked in the corner. Raul's father had, long ago, been married to Angelica's mother. Raul was a first-year chemistry student at the Universidad del Centro in Huancayo, and earned his living doing street theater. He came to the restaurant because he had his eye on young Angelica, but he became distracted by the *gringa* writing away in her diary at a corner table. My mother lifted her head, noticed Raul's stare, and smiled. That's all it took to prompt him to walk over and introduce himself. They were instantly attracted to each other. Raul hardly knew a word of English, but my mother's Spanish was by now good enough to keep up a conversation. He was twenty-one, though he told my mother he was twenty-five. She was forty-one, almost twice his age.

The two of them spent the entire day strolling through the streets of Jauja. She came home so late that night that I was crying when she walked through the door.

"What's wrong?" she asked.

"Where were you? It's the middle of the night. I thought you might have been arrested or robbed or something." I was angry, but mostly relieved.

"Oh, Peter, don't worry so much about me, and don't be so rigid and authoritarian like your father. Let your mother enjoy herself a little bit, okay?"

Raul came over the next day. He helped my mother translate her résumé into Spanish and wrote poetry on her little typewriter. Wary but curious, I watched him intently. Raul caught me looking at him while he typed and gave me a wink. "Your mother is a truly extraordinary woman, and you're an extraordinarily lucky boy to have her as your mother," he said.

I felt like replying, *Yeah, and you're lucky she's so into you, I'm sure it won't last,* but I didn't say anything. Besides, Raul seemed to be more into making declarations than having any sort of conversation. And I wasn't all that eager to talk to him, either.

The next day, Raul and my mother took a leisurely hike around the picturesque lake nearby, Laguna de Paca. She had promised to take me there but ended up going with Raul instead. Raul kept showing up, day after day. The family said nothing, but Angelica leaned over and whispered in my ear at breakfast one morning, "You should know, Raul is a little crazy and dangerous." I cringed but didn't know how to reply. How could I warn my mother, when she had fallen so deeply and easily for him? She wouldn't even be able to hear me. Her eyes held a glazed intensity.

Raul was a charmer. He was always joking and full of laughter; he was both romantic and politically intense, an irresistible combination for my mother, who wrote endless pages about him in her diary. He told her that he had left home at the age of fifteen to work in the mines, had organized workers, had been the messenger boy for Luis de la Puente Uceda (the martyred activist, politician, and guerrilla of the 1960s), and had even fought alongside Che Guevara in Bolivia. He showed her an old tattered book about Che Guevara that had a grainy black-and-white photo of Che sitting around a campfire with an "unidentified Peruvian," who Raul insisted was him. And she could not believe her good fortune when Raul told her he didn't smoke or drink, unlike nearly every other Peruvian man.

My mother was enchanted by Raul's life stories—about his childhood as the oldest of five, learning to survive on the streets of Lima selling food and newspapers and collecting bottles. Raul's family, like so many others, had migrated to Lima from the highlands. His mother spent three months in jail for spitting in the face of an abusive government official. His drunkard father refused to teach his sons how to drive because he didn't want them to be able to borrow his old pickup truck, which he used to haul junk for a living. When his mother didn't make enough money to feed them, Raul said, he pickpocketed tourists and put the money surreptitiously in her purse. If she caught him, he got a whipping.

Raul also told her gruesome details about taking part in a massacre of forty policemen when he was a teenager, and about being the sole survivor of a five-person guerrilla unit that hid in the jungle for six months. These dramatic tales of bravery and danger, which my mother was so eager to believe that she accepted them as entirely truthful (Raul would later confess to her that he made much of it up to impress her), left her feeling both awestruck and humbled. She admitted to Raul that they made her deeply question her preparedness for guerrilla warfare.

My mother was even more captivated by Raul's poetry and singing. He wrote poems about her every day, long and short, handwritten and typed. He even sang love songs to her while they took long walks together through the streets of Jauja. "Wish I could record all the poems and songs Raul makes up for me," she wrote. "When we walk together at night he sings and sings and sings, often making up words as he goes along."

My mother had found her dream man in a small village in the middle of Peru. Raul was everything my father was not: funny, spontaneous, affectionate, romantic, charismatic, passionate, and intoxicatingly political.

Within a week of meeting my mother, Raul told her that he wanted us to come live with him in Huancayo. Giddy with excitement, my mother talked to me incessantly about Raul and his wondrous plans for their life together filled with romance and revolution. She said she could never stomach being with the son of a "bourgeois Peruvian family," but Raul came from the slums, had fought against oppression and injustice his entire life, and was a proven revolutionary.

"You're dreaming, Mommy," I said to her, rolling my eyes and shaking my head. I then added, "You know, Angelica says he's trouble, that he's a little crazy."

As I'd predicted, my mother didn't want to hear me. All she said was "You should go to sleep now, Peter," and then tucked me in with a quick kiss on my forehead.

My mother had a look about her that I had never seen before. She had been involved with many men since she'd left my father; some lasted no more than a few days, some a week or two, a few stuck around for several months. I hadn't met all of them, and others I wouldn't learn about until reading through her diaries decades later, but this felt different. She seemed reckless, out of control. I worried that all this talk of fighting for the revolution with Raul could lead her into a situation as bad, or worse, than the one we'd just escaped in Chile.

But all my worrying got me no closer to a solution. A week later, in early February, we left Angelica's family and moved in with Raul in Ocopilla, a poor barrio up a long dirt road on a hill on the outskirts of Huancayo. My mother didn't discuss it with me ahead of time. She was so elated, so sure of her choices, that she assumed the three of us would be happy together.

I didn't realize her plan until we arrived at Raul's place, a tiny square room on the second floor of an old blue-green adobe house occupied by a family of fourteen. Besides the bedroom, Raul had use of the shared bathroom across the hall. He grinned as he opened the door to the bedroom, gesturing grandly as if the space were palatial. "We can all live here together," he said.

"Maybe we should get a place with two rooms?" my mother ventured. "I'm not sure we'll be able to fit a second bed."

"No, no, no, it'll be fine, you'll see." Raul pushed the window open, as if to prove the vastness of the space.

"But maybe Peter should have a separate room?"

"Nonsense," Raul said, locking his arm around my shoulders. "Peter needs the security of being with us. Isn't that right, Peter?"

I looked at my mother and opened my mouth.

"Good," Raul said, smashing me closer to him. "It's settled. We'll all be nice and cozy here together."

We quickly arranged the room in two parts, with a desk and table in between the beds. I took Raul's old bed, and he and my mother headed to the local market to buy a second twin mattress. They carried it home together over their shoulders and plopped it on the floor.

"Don't worry, Peter," my mother said as she slipped into her nightgown that first night at Raul's, "we'll only make love when you're asleep."

"And we'll try not to make too much noise," added Raul, chuckling, as he tossed his clothes to the side. Raul always slept naked, regardless of how hot or cold it was outside.

"Sure," I said with a sigh.

The next day we returned to the local market for a hot plate, some dishes, and a dustpan. Apparently Raul had never made a meal in the room before; he always ate at the market or grabbed a bite from street vendors or cheap restaurants. Our new hot plate would be on almost all the time—used both to boil water and to heat the room—under the single bare bulb that lit the room. We washed dishes in the shared bathroom across the hall, and washed our clothes and burned our trash in the backyard.

I dutifully did my part to help out, which my mother most appreciated when she was sick. One diary entry from those first months in Ocopilla read:

Raul is off to look for a doctor. I have much confidence in
Peter. He is a little man who is very playful and a little mis-
chievous, but always goes and buys our basic necessities. He
handles life well and is honest with his feelings—he is sane
and alive. He made a big effort to prepare breakfast—boiled
eggs with bread and tea, and an orange after. Now I'm going
back to sleep.

To wash our bodies, we either took a quick cold bath or committed to the long process of heating up enough water on the hot
plate to take a warm but shallow bath. Or, as a special treat, we went
downtown and paid for a little plastic tube of shampoo, a fresh towel,
and a hot shower at the public baths, which we ended up doing every
couple of weeks. To save money we all showered together in one stall.
I got used to the ritual and didn't really mind; I was just happy that
the water was hot.

The bathroom belonged to everyone in the house, but being
right next to it we had the advantage of proximity. Nobody took
responsibility for cleaning it; it was always a stinking, filthy mess,
and either the faucet or the toilet usually leaked. Someone from
the family downstairs tried to creatively deal with the toilet leak by
using dirt from outside to channel it to the drain in the floor, but
this only ended up making the bathroom floor muddy and clogged
the drain. When someone in the house broke the sink faucet without
taking responsibility for it, a huge commotion erupted in the house
over who would get a plumber and pay for the fix, which my mother
eventually did when she realized that it would otherwise never get
taken care of.

Soon after we moved in, Raul drew a picture of my mother and
me on the wall, perhaps to try to make us feel more at home in his
cramped room. We appreciated that creative gesture even though
Raul wasn't much of an artist and we only vaguely resembled the
drawing. Raul enjoyed drawing on the walls. They were painted light

With my mother and Raul in Huancayo, 1974

blue, but he drew pictures and made other scribble marks all over them in other colors.

I hadn't forgotten Angelica's warnings and remained suspicious of Raul, but even so, I was warming to him. Unlike some of the other men, he didn't ignore me. He seemed to think of me as an inseparable part of my mother rather than as an inconvenience or an annoyance. I didn't know if he actually liked me or simply hoped to impress my mother by his acceptance of me. My mother thought of me as a full part of their relationship: "Peter is very much in the middle," she wrote in her diary, "a positive force between us."

Our room also had some uninvited guests. When we discovered a mouse sneaking into the room through a small hole near the floor, Raul drew a house and trees around the hole where the mouse lived, and we put food in front of the hole to make him part of our "family." Over time, that mouse turned into an ever-growing family of mice that brazenly took over the room every night when we turned out the light. Eventually, my mother got so fed up that she decided to leave the light on, but all that accomplished was that none of us slept. Other houseguests included dozens of flies that clung to the ceiling, mostly without moving, as if drunk or asleep, until one of Raul's periodic fly-killing rampages. The fly population would immediately start to replenish; there was no screen on the single window in the room that overlooked the dusty street in front of the house.

"Try to treat Raul as your new father," my mother had said to me the day we moved in with him. "It will be easier for everyone that way, okay?"

I'd nodded. This was yet more evidence of how hard my mother had fallen for Raul; she'd never asked me to think of any of her other boyfriends as my father, so this was a big deal. It felt weird, and made me uncomfortable because it seemed like I was betraying my father, but I would give it a try.

From then on, Raul proudly introduced my mother and me as his wife and son to everyone we met, including the family that lived downstairs. My local ID card included Raul's last name. That looked

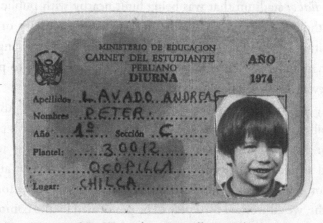

My ID card in Ocopilla, 1974

all wrong to me when I first saw the ID and read the name. And besides, I didn't really think of Raul as my father, despite my mother's and Raul's hopes, and I missed my real father. I often thought about how completely different he was from Raul; like a rock compared to sand. But I was willing to play along: it was sort of fun pretending to be a family, and I hoped it would help me fit in. I was obviously a gringo boy—despite my tanned skin and brown hair and eyes, there was no chance I could pass as a local—but I figured it couldn't hurt to claim a Peruvian father. And by now my Spanish was convincing and accentless.

The Catholic chapel in Ocopilla was a small adobe structure standing at the top of Cerro de la Libertad, which a few neighbors had built years earlier. Priests and nuns rarely visited it. Someone had given a key to my mother and Raul, and they—while devoutly antireligious—had no qualms about using the chapel for meetings with young people to discuss politics. They often brought me along. The group talked about how to block the logging that a private developer was doing on communal forestland; they complained about the industrial pollution and garbage that was fouling the creek, about the fancy *fútbol* stadium that was being built nearby with public funds even though many in the community had no electricity or other amenities. They wrote songs about these issues and also sang "The Internationale." Often, adults came to listen, or kneeled to pray in the pews while we talked politics in the atrium.

My mother and Raul called their new organization Juventud Ocopillana Progresista. We had light blue membership cards printed up for everyone, including me, though these cards never actually served any real purpose other than to make us feel serious and important. My title was "Director de Deportes" (sports director). For months, we all worked on a play to be performed by the community about the heroic struggles against the rich and powerful. When the church authorities learned about this, they took away the key to the chapel and forbade entry to the building. The show went on anyway, outside the chapel, though Raul defiantly broke inside to ring the bell to signal the start of the performance.

That April, when the semester started, my mother enrolled me in the local elementary school and began to teach courses on dialectical materialism at the university. I have no idea how she managed to get that job, but she had always been good at talking her way into things. To brush up on Marxist theory, she bought all three volumes of Marx's *Capital*. On the surface, my mother exuded confidence about her theoretical sophistication in Marxist theory. But in her diaries she confessed her worry that she had never carefully or fully read *Capital* before and was sort of winging her way through teaching it.

Meanwhile, I was anxious about fitting in when I arrived at school for the first day of classes in my new uniform—dark gray polyester pants, a white collared long-sleeve shirt, and the school's red, yellow, and white insignia patch protected by a clear plastic case pinned to my gray sweater. Luckily, the rules for footwear didn't prohibit me from wearing my beat-up boots, which was the only pair of shoes I owned other than sneakers and rubber sandals. In uniform, all the students looked the same, all of us poor, some desperately poor. But despite our outward similarities, I was haunted by differences: my mother and I were poor by choice, out of political principle. Yet even as I secretly longed for the creature comforts I could have had—a car, a TV, hot water, separate bedrooms, a private bathroom, a real kitchen—I thought that being poor helped us look a little less like the gringo outsiders that we were.

I was wrong. On that first day at school, despite the blending-in effect of my uniform, I was clearly marked as an outsider. All the other kids seemed to know one another already, and they pointed and laughed when they saw my hair. They threw rocks, banana peels, and insults at me. I went home that afternoon in tears. "Mommy, you have to cut my hair. Please, all the kids are making fun of me, calling me a girl."

Silence.

"My teacher even said I have to cut my hair before coming back to class."

That got her attention. "Well, okay," my mother said with a sigh. "But just a bit shorter, no crew cut." She took out her scissors, sat me down on the chair in the middle of the room, and cut my hair. "There, that should do it."

I rushed to the bathroom to take a look in the cracked mirror above the sink. I looked exactly the same. "Please, Mommy," I begged her, "just a little bit shorter, please?"

Raul chimed in, "Carola, Peter is a Peruvian now and you should let him look like a Peruvian."

Finally convinced, my mother took out the scissors again, sat me back down, and snipped away more aggressively. I didn't care how bad the quality of the haircut was going to be; I just needed my hair to be shorter.

It worked. A few kids still picked on me, but the teachers protected me, yanking them away by their ears if they bullied or poked fun at me too much.

After school, still in my uniform, I'd spend the rest of the afternoon and evening playing soccer with kids from school on the dirt street in front of the house. My mother had bought me a soccer ball made of real leather, right after we moved to Ocopilla. And that was what did the trick: nothing helps make new friends like a shiny new soccer ball.

Passing the Hat

RAUL WAS STRUGGLING in his chemistry classes, often studying late into the night, sitting at the desk between our two beds, lights on and music blaring while my mother and I tried to sleep. Raul liked to pace while reading aloud passages from his textbooks. Before the end of his first year, he'd failed too many of his classes and decided to drop out of the university. I think my mother and I were actually relieved when he flunked; school made him a nervous wreck and nobody was getting any sleep because of it. Raul's parents in Lima, however, were upset with him—the first of the family to go on to higher education—for dropping out. They blamed my mother for distracting him with talk about revolution. "Politics is for the rich. Only the rich can afford politics," his mother, Berta, liked to tell him. Raul's parents warned him that my mother was a "hippie CIA agent," though they stopped saying that after the relationship lasted for more than a few months, and they eventually warmed up to her.

Raul himself didn't seem upset by his failure; it freed up more of his time to do what he loved most: street theater. He was always performing, always looking for an audience, as if the world were one big stage. In Huancayo's downtown plaza, he entertained crowds for hours with his political comedies. At the end of each act, enough people would drop money into his hat to allow him to scrape by.

At Raul's insistence, my mother and I went as often as we could to watch his weekend performances. He attracted his biggest crowds on weekends, especially on Sundays, when people had time to stop and watch. Then his audience could swell from a dozen or so people to a hundred or more, especially if the weather was nice. Weekends were also the days when people felt most generous, willing to drop a coin or two, or maybe even a bill, into Raul's hat when he passed it around.

Raul had an ever-expanding repertoire of skits, some carefully planned out and choreographed, others improvisational. Sometimes he made changes as he went along, including incorporating people from the audience into his acts, which always drew applause. Many of his skits were pantomime, a white painted face his only costume. He sometimes mixed in dialogue and revolutionary political commentary to get his point across. He also read poetry and sold copies of his typed poems. It was fun watching Raul perform in public—he was at his best then, entertaining, confident, charismatic.

All of Raul's skits shared a theme: the poor and powerless getting back at the rich and powerful. He portrayed endless versions of this dynamic: peasants playing tricks on the landlord; Indians taking revenge on the Spanish; local workers ousting the foreign companies; guerrillas defeating the military and their *Yanqui* imperialist backers; a bank robber getting away with the cash and giving it to the poor; and squatters cleverly evading eviction by the government authorities. If my mother was watching, Raul tried to incorporate a feminist theme: an abused wife kicking out her drunkard husband, for example. In these David vs. Goliath stories, Goliath was always a blundering bully outsmarted by the little guy. The crowds roared with approval.

The police were less enthused, though, and often tried to break up Raul's performances because he didn't have a permit. More than once they arrested him for ignoring their warnings, and my mother and I had to bail him out. When they kept him overnight, we brought him warm blankets. He was also arrested for disorderly conduct in the park after getting into a fistfight with evangelicals. My mother was proud of Raul; she thought he was brave and heroic. And I suppose he was in a way. I just hoped he would never turn his fists on us.

One day, when the police showed up to stop Raul's performance in the plaza, people in the crowd started heckling them to go away; they wanted the show to go on and for the cops to leave Raul alone. The crowd tightened around Raul, making it harder for the police to get to him. Then the wall of people parted suddenly so Raul could escape. As he ran away, he turned and thumbed his nose at the police, yelling, "Look, my fellow humble citizens of Huancayo, here come the sellout servants of the rich doing their dirty work, but they can't catch me, not this time!" The crowd clapped loudly and cheered him on.

"How would you like to be part of my skits?" Raul asked me one day, a month or so after we had moved in with him. "We could develop some skits together, do them on weekends, be a team."

"Yes, yes, I'd like that." I was flattered Raul wanted to include me. It sounded like much more fun than watching him from the crowd.

My mother didn't object, unconcerned that the police might now come after me, too. Raul started to incorporate me into his skits, usually as the bad guy—the Rockefeller, the boss, the landlord, or some other hated gringo authority. Raul's character was the underdog who won in the end. We would practice in our room the night before each performance.

Several months after we started doing acts together, *El Correo*, Huancayo's daily newspaper, published a picture of Raul and me performing a skit in the park with a crowd around us, with the caption noting that the police "discouraged such unauthorized public activities." This made my mother beam with pride. She told me, "Maybe you'll grow up to be a revolutionary actor like Raul."

Our acts were successful enough that Raul decided we should take the show on the road for several weeks, traveling by bus to Huancavelica, Ayacucho, Cuzco, Puno, and Lima. Although I was apprehensive about traveling around the country alone with Raul, mostly I

Performing street theater in Huancayo with Raul and
a recruit from the audience, 1974

thought of it as a fun and adventurous road trip. With our earnings,
we paid for our bus tickets, food, and lodging. To save money on
hotels and maximize time for our performances during the day, we
always took overnight buses when possible. Along the way, we sent
telegrams to my mother, keeping her updated on our travels. One
from me dated July 8, 1974, read, "We travel Wednesday to Lima
direct from Puno. Mama I am fine. It's my birthday. I like Cuzco.
With love." What I didn't tell her about was the young woman whom
Raul met on the bus and cuddled with all night on the ride from
Huancavelica. As we were getting off the bus early the next morning,
Raul sheepishly told me, "Don't worry, that was nothing. No need to
say anything about it to your mother. Promise me, okay?"

I nodded. I was enjoying the traveling and performing, and didn't
want anything to spoil it. Anyway, I didn't want to upset my mother,
and I was always a little afraid of Raul.

I loved the travel, and the idea that our performances were bringing in enough to pay for the trip made me feel grown up and self-sufficient. Our time onstage, acting in front of all those crowds every day, from city to city, turned our little duo into the center of the world. My role as the villain was always good for a laugh, ridiculous as it was for a little kid to play a Rockefeller. Raul patted me on the back after each show, always pleased no matter the quality of the performance or the size of the crowd. I was an enthusiastic, uncomplaining sidekick, which Raul appreciated. We bonded daily as we sat together before each show to paint our faces white, sharing the jar of makeup, black pencil outliner, and tiny round handheld mirror. We checked and touched up each other's faces before starting our act, and shared the grimy towel to wipe off the oily mask after the show.

Raul again said to me that he wanted to be my father and wanted me to think of him as my father. But to me, a father meant protection, comfort, security—and Raul was none of those things. Raul was more like my buddy and traveling companion who happened to also be my mother's lover.

When Raul and I returned from our road trip a few weeks later, my mother greeted us warmly, gathering us both in her arms. She had bought me a gift for my ninth birthday: a set of little books with stories about the Chinese revolution. For Raul, whose birthday was the same month, she'd gotten a book about Lenin written by Trotsky, and signed it, "Until the final victory. I'm your woman, you're my man, we have only one heart. Carola." Raul bought me a pair of white jeans for my birthday, which instantly turned gray. Though my mother's birthday wasn't for several months, Raul had bought her a gift as well with some of our road-trip earnings: the collected works of Che Guevara. As he gave her a book on guerrilla tactics, Raul said affectionately, "My Carola, this will help prepare you to become a guerrilla."

Piojos

AS SOON AS I started school in Ocopilla in April 1974, the lice arrived. I tried to draw in my notebook while lice fell from my hair onto the page and crawled around in circles, as if they were trying to get my attention. I thought maybe they were falling off my head because it was so crowded there was not enough room for them all. I imagined bloody fistfights as the tiny monsters fought over the land, a white landscape of thousands of tiny eggs.

At first I was startled, but the falling lice became so routine, I barely noticed them. I would have been embarrassed, but many other kids at school had their own personal colonies of *piojos*.

My mother spent many a late-evening hour patiently combing the eggs out of my hair with a special fine-tooth comb, the affectionate grooming routine reminiscent of monkeys picking insects off each other. We tried everything, special soaps and shampoos, even resorted to kerosene, leaving an awful smell in my hair that lasted for days. But nothing worked.

My mother probably spent more time combing lice eggs out of my hair than she did cooking. Even if she had wanted to cook it would have been much too difficult. All we had was that single-burner hot plate and no fridge. So a meal at home usually meant crusty bread and jelly for breakfast, along with tea or coffee. After school, my mother and Raul were often at a political event. My mother paid a neighbor to feed me those nights. The meals were better than at home, but still pretty basic—typically a bowl of rice or noodle soup, a piece of bread, and a main course consisting of a mix of rice, potatoes, and meat.

Esteban, his wife, Julia, and their two daughters treated me like family. Esteban was especially nice to me when he was sober, but he always smelled like sweated alcohol. One night, Esteban announced that he had a cure for my lice problem. It had worked on his kids. Did I want to try it?

His two girls giggled but wouldn't say what it was. "It works," they promised.

After dinner, he took me out back to the muddy, fenced yard where the family kept their goats, chickens, and ducks.

"Lower your head," he instructed. "I need to douse your hair. Stay still; don't move." I did as he said, bending over as far as I could in the dark. A lukewarm shower of sticky salt water landed on my head, and my senses swarmed in the unmistakable smell. Nothing stinks quite like urine, and there is nothing quite like having a pot of pee dumped on your head. "Now, rub it in real good," he said. Tentatively, I reached up and massaged the urine into my lice-infested scalp. "Harder! Use both hands." So I wouldn't offend him, I rubbed the pee into my head with gusto.

I began to stand up, but he stopped me. "You need just a bit more," he said. There was no pee left in the chamber pot, so he unzipped his pants, pulled out his penis, and released a hot stream right on my head, taking care not to miss any spots. I was so drenched that even my ears were full. "There, that should do it."

Gagging, I desperately wanted to rinse my hair and wash off my salty face. But he stopped me again. "Now, let it set there for a little while," he said. "It has to soak in." And so I sat patiently, pee drying on my eyelids, waiting for the minutes to tick by.

It worked exactly as promised. It turned out that the lice living on my head were even more disgusted than I was. A few weeks later, though, they were back in full force—perhaps because the other kids at school still had lice—procreating and laying eggs more enthusiastically than ever. But I didn't ask Esteban for another "treatment."

Was Jesus a Revolutionary?

AS MUCH AS they loved each other, my mother and Raul could argue about pretty much anything, especially if it had to do with politics. Their political wrestling matches simultaneously infuriated and invigorated them. Some lasted for hours, at any time of the day, with brief rests in between.

"I hate Christ," Raul suddenly declared one day.

He didn't seem to be trying to pick a fight, but my mother could not resist responding. "It isn't necessary to hate Christ to struggle against the evils of Christianity."

And off they went, a verbal fistfight between atheists. Was Jesus a proletarian or not? Was he really against the rich and powerful? Was he really a pacifist? If you believed in Christ, could you still believe in Lenin? "No," said Raul. "Yes," said my mother. If you defended Christ, were you a reactionary? "No," insisted my mother. "Yes," insisted Raul. "So that means you think I'm a reactionary?" she asked Raul, incredulous. He huffed and didn't reply.

My mother told Raul it was nice that Jesus wanted his disciples to wash each other's feet.

"Teaching humility—always it's the poor who are supposed to be humble," Raul replied dismissively.

My mother shot back, "It isn't realistic to expect people to throw away all their lifelong religious beliefs in one jump. It's politically smarter to attack the Church and its doctrines than to attack Jesus and his life."

"I don't care about convincing old people; it's young Peruvians who need to learn to hate Christ and all that he symbolizes."

"Oh, Raul, don't be so dismissive. Have you actually even read the Bible?"

Instead of answering, Raul declared, "Just remember what Marx said, religion is the opiate of the masses."

"Yes, but it doesn't mean there isn't anything to be learned from the Bible." Perhaps my mother was feeling defensive about all those childhood years she had spent memorizing Bible verses at church.

One weekend afternoon, Raul took a bunch of familiar religious songs and substituted the names Marx, Lenin, and Mao for Jesus. He thought it was a creative way to try to convert Christians to the revolutionary cause. Pleased with himself, he proudly showed the doctored song sheets to my mother when she came home, confident she would be impressed by his brilliant idea. He was hoping to sing the songs as part of his acts and maybe even sell copies on the street.

But it completely backfired. My mother was not only unimpressed, she was mad. "You've turned Marxism into a religion!"

Raul was stunned. "Carola, it's just a tactic to politicize the masses."

"No! It merely perpetuates the cult of personality. Simply substituting Marx for Jesus is not progress toward the revolution, Raul."

Angry, Raul lit a match under the song sheets until they caught fire right in the middle of the room. My mother and I both jumped up.

"Raul, you're crazy," she screamed at him, stomping out the fire, ashes from the burned sheets floating up and spreading across the room. "You could have burned the whole place down."

My mother and Raul also quarreled, always without resolution, about what my mother called the "root causes of machismo" and the "origins of female oppression." Frustrated by my mother's persistent focus on "the woman question," Raul sometimes lashed out, telling her that as a North American, she was "*la hija del imperialismo*"— the daughter of imperialism. She would then counter, "Well, Raul, always remember that you are not the most oppressed person in the world because you're not a woman." He never worked out an effective response to that line.

One Saturday, several months after we moved to Ocopilla, their debate about female oppression lasted the entire day. They argued on the walk into town to take a hot shower, they argued while we were in the shower together, and they argued on the way back. It was as if I wasn't even there. That day, they got so mad at each other over their differing interpretations of female oppression that they decided to part ways on the walk home from our shower outing, Raul kicking at rocks in the road and storming off. When my mother saw that I had started to cry, she put her arm around my shoulders. "Oh, Peter, don't get upset, everything will be fine with Raul. And if it isn't, well, we'll still be fine."

After Raul returned home a few hours later the argument picked up where it had left off and continued into the night. As they tried to make up, my mother told Raul sincerely, "I understand that you're just trying to get revenge against the *Yanquis*." She then added, "Getting to know me is your way of getting to know white imperialist society and seeing the enemy up close." I'm not sure that really made either Raul or my mother feel better, but they did stop arguing, at least for that night. Maybe they simply got too sleepy to keep at it.

A particularly sensitive topic was the size of my mother's breasts. One night Raul made the mistake of noting how different my mother looked, undressed, from those large-breasted blond "American" women who posed nude on the calendars that hung on the wall of many of Peru's small street-corner restaurants and stores. Raul tried to reassure her: "My massaging your breasts will get your juices going and make your breasts grow."

He surely meant this kindly, perhaps even lovingly, but my mother was incensed. "You suffer from the cult of breast worship, just like my ex-husband did." She launched into a lecture about "the breast fixation of European and North American society, and of those societies affected by colonialism perpetrated by the West." Raul didn't apologize, but the next day he did integrate the "cult of breast worship" into one of his street theater skits as a critique of machismo, thinking it would please my mother, who was watching. Her diary entry that day indicates she was at least amused even if not entirely convinced about Raul's sincerity.

My mother and Raul even fought about flying saucers and the influence of extraterrestrials on history. Raul insisted that alien intervention and their introduction of advanced technologies was a good thing for human progress.

My mother criticized him for his naive faith in technological fixes, assuring him he'd grow to understand as he aged.

Raul blurted, "Carola, I have a confession. I'm actually from the planet Omvi and I'm more than three hundred years old."

My mother couldn't help but laugh. "Okay, let's see how aliens make love," and that was the end of that argument.

Except that it sparked another argument. My mother's period had just started, which she thought was no concern and should not get in the way of their lovemaking. But Raul pulled away and turned over. My mother took offense. "Menstruation should never inhibit a woman from being sexually fulfilled. What, men get to decide what time of the month to make love?" She then grabbed for the nearest towel to put underneath her—which happened to be my towel hanging from my bedpost. I reached up and yanked the towel back, startling her.

"No, that's *my* towel, use your own," I insisted, no longer pretending to be asleep. At this point I had been awake for hours, staring at the long winding cracks in the ceiling in our moonlit room while listening, as I often did, to my mother and Raul go on and on.

"Peter, you're not supposed to be awake." My mother tried to sound cross, but she laughed. "Just go back to sleep. Don't worry, I promise I'll wash your towel in the morning. Now give it to me." I covered my ears with my pillow and tried not to think about my towel, hoping I might finally be able to fall asleep.

My mother and Raul also fought about more mundane matters, especially money. Raul was always either broke or almost broke, despite his earnings from street theater. Any money that my mother gave him from her rapidly shrinking savings would instantly disappear; he could not resist splurging on eating out. My mother was paying for things more and more, like going to restaurants and movies, which she increasingly resented.

Raul took it hard when my mother told him he should be more self-sufficient and more careful with money.

"I got along fine before—without you, your money, your bourgeois habits," Raul told her loudly late one night as we were getting ready for bed. My mother had scolded him for spending so much on dinner that evening. Raul then angrily promised her, "Oh, don't worry, I will work hard, day and night, to repay the money I robbed from you as your gigolo."

"Just stop yelling, please," my mother said, putting her hand on Raul's shoulder to calm him down.

He shook her away. "I won't lower my voice for anyone!" he screamed, kicking the bed for emphasis. "And certainly not for a bourgeois woman who wants to be treated like a flower."

The next day my mother wrote in her diary about Raul: "For the first time I really have been feeling maybe he's prostituting himself to me."

Even when my mother and Raul could not reconcile their arguments in person, they left poems and love notes for each other, reaffirming their eternal devotion. They made an agreement to die together. She wrote in her diary: "We have a pact to either die together in the revolution or walk into the sea together when we've outlived our usefulness," and that "We are both certain of dying a violent death, and it could happen any time, but we have big dreams and plans for the future and keep pursuing them as we can." I'm not sure how I fit into my mother's confident prediction about dying violently, but reading those lines now I'm relieved I never had to find out.

Ataura

"**SHOULD I MARRY** Raul?" my mother asked me one day while writing in her diary.

"No, Mommy."

She closed the diary and looked over at me. "Why not?"

"Raul is mean."

Raul had been bossing me around and barking at me more and more. Now that he and my mother were getting more serious, he seemed to want me to know who was in charge. I had never really challenged his authority, but I had also never truly treated him as a father figure, which he probably resented. Within just a few months, Raul had gone from being a buddy to a bully. And it's not as if I could avoid him, given our living situation.

Tensions came to a head one afternoon when I was pestering my mother to buy me a new soccer ball; my old one had worn out quickly from overuse. Raul took off his leather belt and folded it in two. "I need to teach you a lesson, like my father taught me: you need to treat adults with more respect and do what you're told. Now that you're my son, I'm going to treat you like a Peruvian, not like a spoiled American. Now lean over."

I stood next to my bed, frozen in disbelief. I looked at my mother, but she simply stared out the window, refusing to interfere in Raul's plan to punish me. She had never spanked me, had never disciplined me in any way at all. But maybe because she wanted Raul to think of himself as my father, we had to accept his way of doing things. The betrayal bit deep—my mother had taken Raul's side against me.

"Raul is your *papi* now, you need to listen to him more and treat him with more respect," she said. I gritted my teeth in anger, saying nothing, just wanting to get the punishment over with.

Raul asked my mother not to stay in the room and watch, suggesting that she should go run some errands. To my astonishment, she didn't protest, just picked up her purse and headed out. Maybe that was what this was really about—for Raul to see if my mother would stop him, for him to test his power over her as much as his power over me. I'm sure my mother was happy not to have to witness what was about to happen, though she could probably still hear my cries out the window as she walked away down the street in front of our house.

Raul never disciplined me again—perhaps he thought he had made his point clear enough with that first lashing—but the sting of his belt stayed with me. I was sure my father never would have done that. No, if he had been there, he would have tried to protect me. And he would have given me a new soccer ball.

Raul wrote me a poem and gave it to me the next day. Maybe it was meant as an explanation, or an apology, or both, but it did nothing to make me feel better about what had happened.

> You are a man imprisoned in a body of a boy
> Your psyche is suffering from my violent neurosis
> Your fragile mind
> is dealing with the explosive contradictions of your
>   parents
> Sometimes you are crying an inferno of blood
> over our fragile relationship
> But you always have dreams
> of love and to be loved in your nine years of age
> My strength is only a mask
> Carola is the ideal companion
> And you are the final object

of the explosion of our contradictions
You are the clock of sand in our love
You are always in our dreams
And in our egocentric love
we ignore you
And you Peter child man
Always forgive us with love

Although I was more fearful of Raul after that whipping, what I didn't realize at the time was that my mother was worried, too. In her diary she admitted: "Raul is so heated that he could kill me at some point. At the very least he will make me suffer a lot. But there is so much positive between us, I can't run away."

My mother chose to marry him, instead, though she had no illusions that they would live happily ever after. She wrote a note to Raul right before the wedding: "The price of love is suffering. And until the Revolution comes, love is the most valuable thing in life. We're destined to suffer together."

Raul and my mother were married in the tiny village of Ataura, not far from Jauja. For a small fee, the local doctor signed off on the marriage health certificate that same day without even asking to examine them. This was where Raul's parents were married, and where Raul's birth was registered. Here, my mother and Raul had carved their names into the trunk of a tree right after they had met. We all piled into Raul's uncle Felipe's pickup, along with Raul's mother and brother, for the short drive to Ataura. My mother wore her regular light-colored cotton slacks but made sure to put on her favorite shirt for the occasion—a colorful, handmade Indian one she had bought at the market in Jauja—and it was too late to change out of it when Raul whispered in her ear, with a laugh, that his mother had complained to him earlier that she hated that shirt. Raul wore dark blue pants, his everyday boots, and what my mother called his "guerrilla shirt," tan and green with lots of little extra pockets. I put on my school uniform—the dressiest clothes I had—but removed the school insignia pin.

The small wedding ceremony took place on the second floor of the mayor's office in a well-preserved old building, elegantly decorated. Through the big shuttered windows, we could see the whole village, nestled into the hill and nearly hidden behind flourishing eucalyptus. Immediately in front of the building was the open plaza, empty except for a couple of dogs sleeping and an old lady selling *chicha*. On the walls of the mayor's office were portraits of town fathers, including one of Raul's great-grandfather. We sat in front of the mayor's table—covered by red cloth with ALCALDE written in large embroidered letters in yellow—while the mayor, a small, wrinkled balding man with a whispery voice, read the marriage laws and then asked individually, "Do you still want to get married?" They then signed the registry. It was over in just a minute or two, and then we broke out the champagne. I kissed my mother again and again and took my first gulp of alcohol, which to me tasted like a strong, unsweetened version of 7-Up. I was glad that she seemed so happy on this day, even as I dreaded her being married to Raul.

After the ceremony, we went to Mama Juana's house in Jauja. Mama Juana was Raul's grandmother, and, as was typical of traditional Jauja women of her generation, she wore dark, homespun-wool clothing, including a long dress and a tall white straw hat wrapped with a strip of black cloth. She cooked a huge dinner of roast guinea pig, corn and *avas* (a flat bean), sweet potatoes, and duck salad. Dozens of guinea pigs lived on the dirt floor in the kitchen, making little squealing noises and scampering about, eating vegetable peels and whatever other food scraps were discarded from above—fattening up before they themselves became a meal. Mama Juana had killed a few of the biggest for this special occasion.

A hard, superstitious old lady with tough skin and a crackly high-pitched voice, Mama Juana had more affection for her three shaggy dogs than for people. She did not like leaving her house, certain that the neighbors were casting evil spells on her. She spent much of her time puttering around, muttering to the chickens and guinea pigs, and tending her fires. Mama Juana was not happy at all about the marriage and refused to attend the wedding. Raul wasn't grown up enough to be married, she said, and she was worried that all he and my mother ever did was argue.

But Mama Juana's sharp tongue softened when we arrived. At dinner, she made a toast, wishing Raul and my mother well. She concluded with some words of advice for both of them: "Carola, please make sure to wash Raul's smelly feet every day, and Raul, please make sure to take good care of Carola when she becomes old and ill." My mother and Raul smiled politely and thanked her.

We stayed that night at Mama Juana's. After the day's excitement, I couldn't fall asleep. For a while I watched a large white rat crawling across the rafters above my head. Eventually, curious about the noise coming from Mama Juana's room, I tiptoed into the hallway and peered through the crack in her bedroom door. Seated on a pile of sheepskins, surrounded by her dogs, a bottle of *aguardiente*, several candles, and a pile of coca leaves, Mama Juana was singing to herself. During the last lines of her song her voice broke and she fell into weeping. I was mesmerized, convinced that she was a witch casting strange dark spells.

For all the passion and romance in Raul and my mother's relationship, in the end, getting married was just about the paperwork. My mother was running out of money, and to finalize the property settlement agreement with my father, she had to go back to the States. Otherwise, the plan was to stay in Peru indefinitely. If Raul wanted to go with her, they had no choice but to be married. Although I didn't realize at the time how serious my mother's money problems were, I did know she wanted to settle things with my father. And that probably meant I'd finally be able to see him again, too.

We were set to depart for Miami on December 10, exactly one year after arriving in Peru. But there was one complication. As described in a November 1974 diary entry, Raul's medical tests at the U.S. embassy turned into an unexpected and somewhat awkward hurdle.

> *Raul had a "semi-positive" reaction to syphilis tests in Lima (embassy doctor), and was there for days getting more tests. Finally was cleared but still isn't sure what he has (had) or why and we've had weird discussions about it all. One doctor told him it's possible he's "too active sexually" and his symptoms are related to "constant stimulation." He returned from Lima determined to control his sexual life more carefully, I reacted with fury, and in the end we fell into heavy loving like always. Peter wakes up in the morning and looks at us cuddling in each other's arms and remarks (out of boredom, jealousy?), "oh damn, every day it's the same!"*

As we prepared for our departure, my mother helped me get up to speed with my writing in English, even as she was trying to fight off a bad cold. She wrote hundreds of sentences in English for me, with lots of repetition and easy progression of ideas so I could figure things out easily. I would go over these, again and again, and then try to write sentences of my own in English, which was more difficult, so I used some of the same words from my mother's sentences to form new sentences. This was pretty boring since it did not involve much originality, but I kept at it.

To break the monotony, I penned my first poem, all in English, and proudly gave it to my mother right before we left Peru.

> *I am poor and rich*
> *And life is sometimes sad*

And sometimes marvelous
For me it's both
The bathroom is full of shit
My mother is sick
My teacher never comes
And to me they all call me gringo
All the older kids in the barrio beat me up
I'm nine years old
I'm first in my class
My shoe is torn
Life is sad, dammit
My mother is teaching me English
And that's good
Chau

After reading my poem, my mother smiled, folded it, and gave me a kiss on my forehead. "Thank you, Peter, I'll make sure to keep this." I would find it in her diary four decades later.

IV.

VISITING AMERICA

As you know, Professor Andreas has been active in the communist movement in South America for the past two years. Since the overthrow of the Allende regime in Chile last September, she has fled to Peru but her whereabouts there is unknown. . . . She has prevented me from having any contact with my son since she left Michigan shortly after losing her court case here nearly four years ago. . . . [U]ntil a solution to the visitation and custody rights for Peter, there shall be no settlement on any jointly owned property. After the Peter problem is resolved there will be no problem on property. I only hope that my son's mind and body is not being destroyed in the meantime.

—Carl Andreas, letter to his lawyer, July 1974

Christmas '74

MY FATHER LIKED to call the long custody battle "the Peter problem."

"The Peter problem," he wrote to his lawyer, "is the only thing standing in the way of settlement." My mother wanted money from the divorce and my father wanted me—he refused to budge on money until my mother gave in on custody. And so they had a stalemate for years until we came back from Peru at Christmastime in 1974.

Having no idea where my mother was, my father would fire off a letter to his lawyer, Lawrence Warren, who would then contact my mother's old Detroit lawyer, Walter Denison, who would then try to track her down in South America.

My mother's lawyer alerted her that "your husband has made several allegations about you being connected to revolutionary groups in South America and if you could give us some type of resume as to your activities, we would be appreciative, as it may be necessary for us to secure some affidavits on your behalf."

My father despised lawyers, especially their fees; he called them "parasites" and "bloodsuckers." He was eager to solve the "Peter problem" without going to court. "Lawyers are the only winners in court" was one of my father's favorite one-liners. Through Selma, my mother's aunt in Kansas, my father offered a financial settlement sometime in 1974—on condition that I would be returned to him—and that included holding back 20 percent as a sort of security deposit until my eighteenth birthday, "to assure that Peter would not be absconded once he was returned to Michigan."

My mother balked when she heard the offer. She told everyone that my father was "trying to buy Peter." In a way, I suppose he was. My mother desperately needed the money, so she decided to fly with Raul and me to the U.S. at the end of 1974. Her plan seemed straightforward enough: we would visit her father in Kansas for the Christmas holidays, I would see my father and Grandma Andreas for a few days accompanied by Joel, she would get the money from the property settlement, and then she and Raul and I would return together to Peru. But it did not work out that easily.

My father could not stop sobbing.

"Don't do that, Daddy, don't cry," I said, hugging him harder. I had eagerly anticipated this reunion, having thought about it for years, but had not anticipated all the tears. I had never seen my father cry before.

My father's new wife, Rosalind, explained that they were happy tears, and enveloped us both in her arms. She was some fourteen years younger than my father and had a blond beehive hairdo that made her look almost as tall as him. My father had met her a few years earlier at church during a visit to see Grandma. Rosalind, who had no children of her own, had recently divorced her minister husband after he revealed he was gay. Now, hugging my father and me together, she was not only my father's new wife but also my new stepmother, a role she seemed happy to embrace.

A few weeks earlier, my mother, Raul, and I had flown from Peru to Miami, the cheapest flight to the U.S., then traveled by bus to North Newton, Kansas, getting there in time for the Christmas holidays. I pestered my mother to let me stay with my father and Rosalind at Grandma Andreas' house. My mother and Raul were staying at Grandpa Rich's house nearby. North Newton could not have been more different from Peru: flat, clean, quiet, orderly, and sparsely populated by soft-spoken and neatly dressed pale-skinned people.

My mother only agreed to let me stay with my father because Joel would be coming from Berkeley for the holidays. I was thrilled; I had not seen Joel since my mother and I had left for South America more than two years earlier.

"Hey, Peter, look how big you are," Joel exclaimed with a grin, hugging me warmly. He still looked like the Berkeley hippie I remembered, with long hair and black bare feet. He cast aside his previous brotherly indifference and seemed as genuinely happy to see me as I was to see him.

As I sat next to my father at dinner, I noticed that his soft dark hair that I had remembered so vividly was now starting to turn gray, especially his coarse sideburns. I reached up to touch them and asked him why they were so much grayer than the rest of his hair. "Oh, that's just my gray matter," my father replied with a sly smile.

Grandma looked more frail and thin than I remembered her, but was as pleased as ever to play the gracious host. For dinner, she made ham, green beans, and her famous scalloped potatoes. She brought out a homemade cherry pie for dessert, which we all ate with a scoop of vanilla ice cream on top. I had missed Grandma's cooking and inhaled my meal faster than anyone else at the table.

After dinner was bath time. I hated baths, but this was a special occasion and I did not want to make a fuss. I was grimy and sweaty from days of traveling. Afterward, Rosalind dried and combed my hair. "Part it on the left," I instructed her. "Boys in Peru never part their hair on the right." I was asserting a new identity I was proud of even though Peru was thousands of miles away. I hoped she didn't notice all my lice eggs; if she did, she didn't say anything.

We were up early for Christmas. I was eager to open my gifts— this was my first real Christmas in years—but Grandma insisted we first all hold hands and sing "Joy to the World" and then read the Christmas story. I waited as patiently as a nine-year-old boy could, but the number and size and variety of the shiny bounty under the tree was calling to me. My mother was terrified that my father would try to "buy me off" with presents—and she was right. I was showered with them like never before, and could not have been more thrilled: a rubber ball, watercolors, Magic Markers, scissors, a radio with headphones, a backpack, cowboy boots, a silver Timex wristwatch, a blue corduroy shirt handmade by Rosalind, navy socks, and a pair of Levi's. As soon as I unwrapped the Levi's, I tore off my old gray school pants in front of everyone and pulled on the new jeans. I wore them all week, even to bed. I could not stop staring down at my wrist and admiring the shiny new watch—my first.

Joel received a couple of shirts and a pair of tan moccasins, along with special oil for the thick leather. As he still absolutely detested shoes, he hoped that perhaps moccasins would be the closest thing to not wearing them. He put them on for the trip back to Berkeley and then never wore them again.

From my nine-year-old perspective, the day was idyllic, everything Christmas should be. We played Chinese checkers, Monopoly, and my favorite of all, Risk—the game of world conquest. War, it seemed, was perfectly acceptable in a pacifist Mennonite home as long as it entailed plastic pieces on a cardboard map. Rosalind asked if I played games with my mother.

I replied, "Yeah, but she won't keep score, she doesn't believe in competition, so she won't play games where people 'win.'"

"Ah, I see," said Rosalind. "So should we not keep score?"

"No, I like to win." I grinned.

But the real-life battle was taking place just outside of my field of vision. To me, this Christmas trip meant a chance to see my father after all these years, but what it was really about was an attempt, finally, to resolve the property settlement and custody dispute between my father and mother without resorting to courts and lawyers.

With my father and Grandma Andreas
at Christmas, 1974

Joel was my mother's designated representative and intermediary. So while I was happily engrossed in playing Risk with my bearded, pipe-smoking uncle Paul, Joel and my father argued over the settlement terms across the hall. I pretended everything was normal. Uncle Paul flashed his knowing smile and tried to keep me focused on the game. Rosalind, aware that everyone could hear my father and brother, got up and instructed them to move to another room and close the door.

A couple of hours later, Joel and my father finally emerged, both looking drained. Joel called my mother, saying he was coming over with a proposal. Meanwhile, my play battle raged late into the evening until all my armies had been demolished. "Sorry 'bout that," Uncle Paul said with a wink, resting his left hand under his pipe. "I guess I'm not such a peace-loving Mennonite after all!"

Opening presents with Joel at
Christmas, 1974

We didn't get to bed until midnight. I was not used to sleeping in a room alone, so I climbed in bed with my father and Rosalind, my father in the middle. They were surprised but didn't seem to mind.

The next day, my father and Rosalind asked me more questions about my life in Peru. They were especially curious about Raul and about my schooling. I explained that Raul had been a chemistry student, but I could not remember the English word for chemistry so I gave them the Spanish word and they were able to figure it out. I was used to mixing Spanish and English words, talking to Raul in Spanish and to my mother in both languages. Rosalind asked me if I liked Raul. I shrugged my shoulders and moved my hands in a so-so gesture. I tried to tell them I had learned how to multiply and divide, but again I couldn't remember the English words, so I explained the process until they understood. My father must have been disappointed to see that my Spanish was better than my English, but he didn't say anything.

I had my own questions—about old neighbor friends in Michigan, about my Hot Wheels toy car collection in the plastic blue and yellow carrying case I had left behind four years earlier. My father assured me it was still in my old room in the house, ready for me to play with whenever I wanted to come to Michigan. "Everything is like you left it, Peter, waiting for you," my father told me in a soft, soothing voice. "And the Ping-Pong table is also still there, all set up and ready for you to use in the basement."

Joel came back with my mother's counteroffer, just in time for dinner. My father was outraged by her proposal. "I thought she wanted to settle," he said again and again, shaking his head in frustration. He pulled out his documents and asked Joel to go over them with him one more time. Joel said no, that he was worn out, but my father persisted until Grandma told him to put the papers away and eat.

My father didn't say a word during dinner. He didn't reply when I said, "You look sad."

The dinner conversation turned to football. Suddenly my father exploded, "As if football is the most important thing in the world to talk about," and then stormed away from the table.

The weekend arrived, and still there was no settlement. But I was excited—Saturday meant Saturday-morning cartoons, which I hadn't seen since I was seven. I asked my father and Rosalind to make sure to wake me up early. It took some effort on their part to rouse me, but once I remembered why they were shaking me, I headed straight to the TV and stayed glued to it all morning, even staying there to eat my grapefruit and scrambled eggs. I invited Rosalind to watch *The Lost World* with me. She tried but quickly lost interest.

Sunday was church day, but I refused to go. My Mennonite relatives were startled. My father tried to talk me into going for my grandma's sake, and Rosalind tried to cajole me, but I declared that "religion is bad for the world." I think I simply didn't feel like sitting through a church service, never realizing how heretical that statement was in North Newton, Kansas. "My mother and Raul say religion is the opiate of the masses," I continued, not entirely sure what that meant but determined to make my case against going to church.

Grandma looked pained but did her best to smile through my unintentional insults. It was as if life for her was something to be endured, as politely, cheerfully, and respectably as possible.

No one ended up going to church that day, not even Grandma, who *never* missed church. So instead we looked at some old photos Grandma pulled out from the closet—of me when I was a baby; of a proud-looking Grandpa Andreas (who died long before I was born) when he was a young father; and of her own father, my great-grandfather, who had been a Mennonite minister and lived until he was ninety-nine years old.

My father and Rosalind were driving back to Michigan the next day. I was not ready for the nonstop gifts, games, and attention to be over. And I was not ready to say good-bye to my father after only a handful of days. "You know what I want?" I said to Rosalind. "I want to go back with you for a visit. And then I want to live with my dad half the year and my mom half the year."

Rosalind nodded and told me to tell my father this, and I did.

"That's not realistic," he said, "Why don't you spend the school year with us and summers with your mother?"

I didn't reply, but kept thinking about what that might be like.

As a special treat, my father and Rosalind took me out to dinner at the Ramada Inn that evening. On the way to the restaurant and back, my father let me sit on his lap and steer the car with him, my hands over his on the wheel of his brown Pontiac LeMans. Delighted, I asked him if I could have a car when I was sixteen, and he said sure. "But will you still be alive when I'm sixteen?" I asked.

Rosalind laughed and walked me through the arithmetic. My father was forty-eight; in seven years he would be fifty-five—almost certainly alive. We then figured out how old my brothers Ronald and Joel would be by then, how old Rosalind would be, and how old my mother would be—forty-one plus seven equaled forty-eight.

Then Rosalind asked, "How old is Raul?"

"Twenty-two."

She and my father exchanged looks.

"Well, he'll be almost thirty," Rosalind replied.

The next morning I wanted to sleep in, but Grandma coaxed me out of bed with apple pancakes. She then packed lunches for my father and Rosalind to take with them on the long drive to Michigan.

"I'm going with you. I'll talk my mom into it," I announced with more confidence than I actually felt.

Joel came over from Grandpa Rich's and we all discussed my plan. Joel looked skeptical. When my mother called, Joel talked to her before handing me the phone, shaking his head as I grabbed the receiver. I pleaded with her, both in English and Spanish. I started to cry. I would not be going to Michigan. That was that. After hanging up the phone I flung myself into a chair in Grandma's living room, tears flowing down my cheeks. "I'm not going. She says it's too soon, that I have to wait to visit until you all figure out the property settlement thing." My mother may also have worried, not without reason, that my father would try to keep me in Michigan—and that I might end up wanting to stay. But she didn't say that.

"I know, Peter. It's okay, you can visit another time," Rosalind told me.

"Yep, no surprise," my father growled. "*That* woman, she always has to have things her way." He looked at me with a tired smile.

"Peter, we'll do everything we can so you can come be with us. Now come on over here." I ran over and sat on his lap.

"Peter, just remember three things," Rosalind said. "First, your daddy and I love you wherever you are. We love you whether you come with us or stay here. Second, you're a special, neat, fine boy. Three, we've had so much fun being with you." She gave me a long hug.

Later that morning, my father and Rosalind dropped me off with my bag and all my gifts across the street from Grandpa Rich's house. They waved and honked, and then they were gone. I had no idea when I would ever see them again and already missed them.

As I crossed the street, I clutched my new radio and thought about how fancy I looked in my new watch and jeans and boots. My mother wrapped me in her arms; I was all hers again. But in just those few days, I had been seduced by the American materialism she had spent years trying to shield me from, and gotten an enticing taste of what it might be like to live with my father and Rosalind.

The Wait

ALTHOUGH MY MOTHER now had me back, my new possessions and all, we couldn't simply return to Peru because she and my father had not reached an agreement on the money. To force a property settlement, my mother would have to go through the Michigan courts and that would include risking a custody battle over me. She decided to gamble; she desperately needed the money, and for some reason had confidence she wouldn't lose me. The court date—the showdown with my father—was set for August 11, many months away. It would be a long wait. We would remain in the U.S. until then.

After Christmas, we stayed on at Grandpa Rich's for several weeks. Immobilized from the neck down by multiple sclerosis and requiring a full-time caretaker at home after Grandma Rich died several years earlier, he was happy to have company. My mother winced whenever he introduced Raul to visitors as "the last Inca" and when Aunt Selma told Raul that "cleanliness is next to godliness," but Raul didn't mind or didn't understand these paternalisms; he and Grandpa got along just fine, perhaps because they didn't speak the same language. Raul would chatter away to him in Spanish. Flat on his back, Grandpa would listen intently and smile even though he had no idea what Raul was saying. There weren't many other people for Raul to talk to. He might as well pass the time talking at Grandpa.

We moved back to the old Berkeley commune early that winter. My father was outraged when he found out from Joel that I was living there with him, my mother, and Raul. He wrote Joel: "Does that mean that you have become a party to your mother's scheme to keep Peter and his father apart? You had said that Peter should be able to decide where he wanted to go and then after his mother prevented him from coming to Michigan you took him off to California. What right or obligation do you have to raise my son?" My father added at the end of the letter: "I also want to help out Ronald but am at a loss to know how. Both you boys want your independence but neither you nor society appear able to cope with it. Too bad that Peter is forced to follow in the same footsteps."

When Joel did not respond, my father again wrote to William McGuiness, the Alameda County judge who had given my mother a divorce and custody of the kids years earlier, pleading with him to do something about the situation. Though the judge sent no reply, my father continued to send letters, including one that read: "I am again writing to you as I need to know if you are investigating the living conditions under which my nine year old son, Peter, is being held. The last word I had was that Peter was being kept in a commune at 1516 Walnut Street, in Berkeley, the residence of his 18 year old brother Joel." The clerk's office finally sent a two-sentence reply, informing my father that "investigation of living conditions is not a matter serviced by the court as an ex parte action."

I started the term late at my old school in Berkeley, Whittier Elementary. I was placed in fourth grade, but I couldn't keep up and after a few days refused to go back. So I was then dropped to third grade, and handled it well enough to stay. The commune hadn't changed much, except that everyone, other than Joel, who had lived there before had moved on and been replaced. Ronald, now seventeen and more worldly after his solo adventures in South America, was living on his own somewhere else across town. We hardly saw him. He had been reinstated in high school and was close to finishing but had no interest in going on to college. In a rare letter to our father, he wrote:

> *School is going along in a boring way. Most of my classes*
> *are too easy for me and the students seem very young.*
> *A lot of what I read and study is literature created by*
> *the academic world. When I look at the university*
> *community I see through the trivial uselessness of its*
> *intellectualism. Among my friends in Berkeley are many*
> *college students. . . . I'm familiar with the life of college*
> *students and all the ridiculous bureaucratic bullshit and*
> *wasted time. For these reasons and others I have decided*
> *not to go to college.*

I remember Ronald coming by the commune a couple of times, wearing lots of leather, revving his motorcycle. I was envious. I wanted a motorcycle, too, and begged him to give me a ride. Ronald liked to show off his bike, so it didn't take much prodding.

"What kind of motorcycle is it?" I asked, gliding my hand across the chrome handlebars and squeezing the black rubbery grips.

"It's a Honda 350."

"Can you give me a ride? Please, please?"

"Hmmm." Ronald paused and then smiled. "Oh, all right. But only around the neighborhood. I've got to get going."

We took a spin up Shattuck Avenue past Live Oak Park and then wound around the curvy roads through the Berkeley Hills. It felt strange sitting behind my brother and holding on to him, my arms tightly around his waist—this was the closest I could ever remember being to him.

My mother, Raul, and I moved into a vacant upstairs room in the Walnut Street commune. It was about the size of our Ocopilla room back in Peru except now we had hot water, a real kitchen, and the run of the house. And I was happy to see that the old little black-and-white TV was still there sitting in the living room, which hardly anyone ever turned on, leaving it all to me for my Saturday-morning cartoons.

Almost everyone in the commune was gay at this point, and, as in the past, vegetarian. The members of the commune jokingly called it the commune of "fruits and nuts." Susan, a small, round-ish lesbian, was the friendliest and funniest, except when she was depressed and wouldn't get out of bed. Michael, a tall, curly-haired gay man, worked at a library and danced ballet. Marci was the loud-est, laughing and talking constantly, and seemed to have appointed herself head of the house. Jeff, a church organist, was the quietest. He had a young lover named Max—as well as a wife and child who lived nearby—and had taken over the basement of the house after Ronald moved out.

Each person in the commune had a set of chores and was re-sponsible for cooking one dinner a week. Raul intentionally scared people away from his first dinner by cooking a main dish made from cow stomach. On his next turn, figuring no one would show up, he bought a huge pork roast—his favorite food—and ate it almost entirely by himself, grinning the whole time. I, too, was tired of the bland vegetarian stir-fry we'd been eating nearly every night, so I enjoyed Raul's pork roast as much as he did.

"People in the house say you're not very respectful about food," I said to Raul between bites.

"Ah, to hell with 'em," he replied with a laugh and a dismissive wave. "They should learn to eat like real men, like us!"

Communal living did not dampen Raul's and my mother's enthu-siasm for arguing. It just made their arguments more public. They frequently yelled at each other in Spanish while everyone was eating dinner. Raul would stomp away from the table to sulk in our bedroom, where the arguing would later continue when we would go up to bed. Everyone else in the house just tried to ignore them, but that was harder for me.

One evening after dinner, my mother and I brought dessert up to the room for Raul as a peace offering. "Raul, look, we saved you a piece of pie," I said in my most cheerful voice, holding the little plate in both hands. But he refused to touch it or even look at it.

I begged my mother not to fight with him anymore: "Please, please, not tonight." She nodded, gave Raul a quick kiss on the back of his neck while he was reading, and went to sleep.

I thought that was the end of it, but Raul woke my mother up in the middle of the night, eager to argue about the book he had just finished reading. He accused her of not being a "true believer in the Third International," the communist organization founded in Russia in 1919 with the aim of uniting communists worldwide. He insisted that there was only one correct political line and interpretation of history.

My mother groggily replied, "Raul, the Third International was dissolved more than thirty years ago, replaced by the Communist Party—which is hardly worth defending at all costs."

This enraged Raul. He accused my mother of not being a "true communist," that he had the right to inform her about what he was reading, that she had no right to respond if she was not also reading the same book, and that he would have to guide her "political development." Pointing a fist at my mother, Raul boldly declared, "I will be the theoretician of the Peruvian revolution, for I feel the lifeblood of Peru's poor in me."

"Oh, really?" my mother asked. "And what will my role be?"

"You will have to immerse yourself with the masses in a distant place and do what you can to not hate me and not be affected by my tyranny."

Raul then started stomping around the room, screaming that my mother was driving him crazy and that she hated all men and was trying to get vengeance on men through him. At one point, he yelled out that he wanted to kill her. Both my mother and I were trembling. She motioned for me to join her in her bed, where we sat, side by side, holding each other closely with our backs pressed up hard against the wall. Raul was so agitated that he didn't seem to even notice that he was frightening us.

After declaring that he could not wait to get back to Peru to "organize the revolution," Raul finally started to calm down, motioned for me to go back to my own bed, and then climbed into bed next to my mother. He said to her, "You know, I'm a little bit crazy." And then he immediately fell sound asleep and started snoring.

Still wide awake, I whispered softly to my mother in the dark, "Mommy, please leave Raul."

She whispered back, "Raul will be better when we're in Peru again; he's just homesick and feeling alienated in America."

I was miserable the day after. I lay on the bed and sobbed about everything in general, declaring, "This is the worst day of my life." I'm sure it was partly the sleep deprivation, but the truth was that the situation was wearing on all of us. As my mother wrote in her diary, "These kind of nights are all too frequent and I am really at a loss to know what we should do about it."

"Please leave Raul, please," I again pleaded with my mother when we were alone one afternoon a few days later.

She didn't respond, though she had plenty to say about it in her diary: "Raul and I do seem to be constantly on the verge of splitting up, but we just can't do it. We are so romantic and so easily hurt and so stuck on each other I sometimes laugh aloud to myself when I think about it. Raul would kill me if he knew that." She also wrote, "Raul and I are so dramatic all the time, who knows, maybe we'll get bored of it all and finally settle into a more tranquil existence. But if boredom would overtake us, it would be even worse."

Raul was up early the day after the big fight. When we came down and joined him at the breakfast table, he was casually playing with a set of dice.

"Come on, play with me." He smiled at my mother like a child who had found a new toy. It was as if the previous night's blowout had never happened.

"No," my mother said, "you know how I feel about gambling."

Raul stiffened and became defensive, telling her, "You don't gamble because you've never had to."

My mother countered, "People who are responsible for feeding children should not gamble because they can't afford to." She added, "Women are the ones who lose out because men are the ones who gamble."

Raul shot back, "Women don't gamble because they don't know how." On and on they went. Eventually, I left the room, glad to be able to escape this time.

That April, my mother announced, "We're moving to Denver until the trial." She didn't explain why we were moving, or why Denver—though I knew she liked to be near mountains, and Colorado was also next to Kansas, where Grandpa Rich lived. My mother's diaries also give no real rationale for the move. Maybe she just got sick of living in groovy Berkeley again and thought the change might also be good for Raul. I had several months of school left, but I didn't protest the move. I was used to moving; we never stayed in one place for long. And we had not stayed in Berkeley long enough for me to really make new friends and get too attached.

The latest plan my mother and Raul had come up with was to buy a big van, drive it to Colorado, and then, after the Michigan trial, live in the van while driving it down through Latin America. At a used-car dealer, we found an old Chevy laundry van that looked exactly like a brown UPS truck. We spent days gluing beige shag carpeting to the inside walls of the van, trying to insulate it and convert it into a livable space. My mother and Raul proudly named the van "The Messenger of the People." She happily wrote to her father in Kansas about it in early May of 1975: "We've started working on converting the van into a home and it feels good to be really doing something together—Raul, Peter, and me."

But the van kept breaking down, at one point leaving us stranded by the side of the highway as we tried to cross the Rockies. Raul didn't know how to drive, didn't want to learn, and had no interest in car mechanics.

The van did get us to Denver, where my mother would eventually get rid of it at a substantial loss. Raul started taking English classes at the Colorado Migrant Council, though his real intent was to form a Marxist study group there. My mother was looking for a good cause, one that she could believe in, so she took a volunteer job, every day except Sunday, from 8:30 to 6:00 p.m., as a staff person for the UFW—the United Farm Workers union—which was in the midst of a boycott against grapes and Gallo wine. We lived in a small run-down apartment on West Fourth Avenue in a mostly Mexican neighborhood on the west side of Denver. To pay the rent, on Saturdays and three nights a week my mother put on a red skirt and a black ruffly blouse to wait tables at a local Mexican restaurant, La Posada, a mansion converted into a folkloric family-style restaurant. Raul worked part-time as a busboy at another nearby restaurant. We were close to broke.

Instead of enrolling me in school to finish the term, my mother took me everywhere on her UFW work that spring and early summer. Each of us proudly wore our little UFW pins, on which a black eagle spread its wings against a red background. My mother worked as a Spanish-English translator at UFW business meetings; organized showings of *Fighting for Our Lives,* a documentary film about the UFW campaign; helped put together press conferences to denounce police harassment; set up protests at jails where UFW staff were detained; and shuttled people around to keep picket lines going.

I spent many days with my mother picketing local liquor stores that sold Gallo wine, with typically twenty-five to fifty people at each picket. We called them "dirty" liquor stores that needed to be "cleaned up." I could belt out "¡El pueblo unido jamas será vencido!" (The people united shall never be defeated)—a line I remembered from our time in Chile—as loudly and with as much gusto as any adult. I was the only ten-year-old who was a regular at Bootlegger Liquor on West Alameda Avenue. For the Fourth of July, the UFW threw a big potluck party at Sloan Lake, dumping Gallo wine into the water as a sort of Boston Tea Party protest, and used the event to get new recruits to join the picket lines. When we picketed liquor stores, the police often showed up and made arrests for "blocking entrance."

My mother and Raul also sometimes collaborated in political activism. One time, the manager at Denver's Aztlan Theatre agreed to let Raul do a performance, in Spanish, in the break between the Spanish-language movies. Raul asked my mother to sing Violeta Parra's "Jose se fue para el Norte" (Jose has gone to the North) in the wings of the theater while Raul pantomimed the life of an immigrant worker in the United States. Then he talked to the audience about Chile and the need for worldwide revolution. At the end of his performance, my mother came out onstage and sang the anthem of the Chilean resistance movement with him. The song begins "De pie canta que vamos a triunfar" and ends with "El pueblo unido jamas será vencido" (Stand up to sing of victory to come . . . the people united will never be defeated). The whole performance was a sort of guerrilla theater because the manager of the place did not know Raul's act would be anything other than "entertainment." The audience clapped, and since the manager did not know Spanish, he clapped, too.

That summer, my mother and Raul also started a small Spanish-language newspaper. It was called *Chispa* (Spark), after the title of the newspaper Lenin published while in exile. They pitched it as "a newspaper for the Latinos of the West Side" and sold it for ten cents a copy outside the Spanish-language theaters in Denver.

While Raul and my mother kept busy with political activism around town by day, at home late at night they kept busy arguing with each other, as always, over politics. Lenin was one of the most persistent problems in their relationship. One summer day, Raul bought a large cloth portrait of Lenin and put it above the bed he shared with my mother. Just as I was falling asleep that night, I heard them yelling. The dispute was over the portrait's location.

Raul's cloth portrait of Lenin, with
a United Farm Workers badge
pinned to the lapel

Raul had made the mistake of not asking my mother's permission before hanging it. She exclaimed, "What, you're now making Lenin the patron saint of our bedroom? No way. You'll have to put it somewhere else."

"But, Carola, it's Lenin. Lenin! Above the bed is where he should be, looking down on us, watching over us, we should give him the proper respect he deserves."

After hours of arguing about it, neither one of them would give in. It was as if the fate of the revolution were at stake.

The next day, Raul moved out with Lenin and rented a room in a dilapidated house three blocks away, which he could barely afford on his busboy wages. The only thing he put on the wall in his new place was that Lenin portrait. Raul told us that he had convinced the landlord that it was actually a portrait of his father, whom Raul said was a "Quaker minister." Raul's real father had spent most of his life hauling junk to and from Lima's La Victoria flea market. I doubt the landlord would have cared if he'd known it was Lenin, but Raul enjoyed those sorts of jokes.

As a sign that he still loved and respected my mother, Raul pinned to Lenin's lapel a farmworkers' badge to recognize that my mother was working for the United Farm Workers union. Raul had long accused my mother of romanticizing the peasantry and not recognizing the role of the urban proletariat in leading the revolution—so this may have been a gesture of reconciliation he hoped my mother would notice and appreciate. Within a month or two, Raul was living with us again. The arguments continued. It had never been a real breakup, just a pause during which they visited each other constantly, but I had enjoyed the quiet break from full-time Raul.

While Raul was renting his own room, he'd read Nadezhda Krupskaya's biography of Lenin. Krupskaya, also a leading Bolshevik revolutionary, was Lenin's much-older wife. Raul was especially eager to reconcile with my mother once he decided that she was his Krupskaya. When he informed my mother of this revelation, another huge argument erupted. When the hostilities eventually subsided, as they always did, Raul told my mother, "Actually, Carola, you're Lenin. And me, well, I'm a mere Trotsky, vacillating and weak."

The Trial

THE TRIAL DATE was fast approaching. My mother and I traveled to Michigan by bus the first week of August while Raul stayed behind in Denver. Old friends of my mother's let us stay at their place in Detroit and let us borrow their car to drive back and forth to the courthouse. I had not been to Michigan for five years—half my life ago at that point. I was looking forward to seeing my father and Rosalind again, even while dreading the impending trial.

My father finally had my mother back in Michigan, on his home turf. This was his one chance to get me back. In the many documents he put together for the trial, he charged that my mother was a radical hippie, a church-hating atheist, an anti-American communist, and an anti-male and anti-marriage feminist who promoted polygamy and was determined to destroy the traditional family. He used a copy of my brother's polemical comic book about the Rockefellers as evidence of my mother's poisonous radical influence.

But winning custody was an uphill battle for any father; my mother was counting on the reluctance that courts usually showed when it came to taking a child away from the mother. My father was going to try to even the odds by depicting my mother as totally unfit, psychologically unstable, and downright dangerous, not only to her children but to American society and to Western civilization.

During the trial days I waited, tense yet bored, sitting on a long bench outside the courtroom, hoping for it to end. During court recesses, both my father and mother would emerge with forced smiles, trying to act as if they had not just spent hours engaged in the courtroom equivalent of trench warfare.

The trial was unexpectedly interrupted when Ronald was arrested back in Berkeley after a huge fight with his girlfriend, Beverly, a pretty redhead some ten years older than him. When the fight happened, she called the police. After the cops came and took him away, Ronald sat in the juvenile detention center for days until my father flew out to get him. During his days behind bars, the jail staff only fed Ronald hot dogs, and as a strict vegetarian, he only ate the buns. Ronald always projected such an air of dignified control that I imagine it must have really shaken him to be treated like a criminal, shoved into a police car, and made to wait in a cell without a decent meal, day after day, until my father finally arrived. No doubt the Michigan judge took notice that it was my father, not my mother, who made the trip to rescue Ronald. The trial resumed as soon as my father got back.

Right before the trial ended, the judge called me into his chambers, all by myself. He was a heavyset man with puffy cheeks, and his black robe made him look even bigger. The shelves were filled with thick, dark hardbound books, and the walls were decorated with framed diplomas. The room was hot and stuffy, and I was desperate to escape. I sat in an uncomfortable oak chair in front of the judge's enormous desk, dangling my feet nervously, staring at the floor. The judge leaned back in his brown leather chair, arms folded behind his head, and looked across the desk at me. All he asked me was one question: "Peter, who do you want to live with, your mother or your father?"

I wilted into the chair. Instead of replying, after a long pause I tried to deflect the question by asking a question back: "Can I live with both of them, equally, half of the year with each? That's what I'd like to do."

He shook his head. "No, young man, I'm afraid it doesn't work that way."

"But why?"

"Well, you should really be in only one school during the school year, not going back and forth all the time between different schools in different places, and certainly not between Michigan and Peru. That's just not good for you, or for any kid."

After a long silence, I said, "Well, then, I guess I should just stay with my mother." My reasoning was simple: my mother needed me more than my father did. I had a hard time imagining my mother without me, or me without her for that matter. And I knew my father would be okay without me, and me without him, because we were already doing okay. And he had Rosalind.

The judge stood up, extended his fat, sweaty hand, and said, "Thank you, Peter, we're done."

And then I went back to my bench in the hall and waited, watching the courtroom door.

An hour or so later, Rosalind came through the door with a huge smile on her face. She rushed over to me, crouched down, and put her hands on my shoulders. "Peter, you're coming home with us, to live with us!" She gave me a hug. I hugged her back but felt numb inside. What had just happened?

My father then appeared, beaming. "Peter! It's finally over." He hugged me stiffly.

I was relieved the trial had ended, but startled by the outcome. We were supposed to be heading back to Peru now; we had only come to the U.S. for an extended visit and for the property settlement agreement. But that whole plan was now derailed.

Minutes later, my mother, wide-eyed, stumbled from the courtroom. She made a beeline for me, pulling me off to the side.

"What did you tell the judge?" she asked. Her voice shook with accusation. Her eyes filled with tears.

"I told him I should live with you. Really, I did."

Maybe the judge would have chosen my father regardless of what I'd said or how I'd said it, but, either way, the decision had been made, the trial was over. And my mother's worst nightmare had come true. She had the property settlement she had come back to Michigan for, but she'd lost me in the process.

Looking back, it's not surprising that the judge trusted my father to provide a more stable home for me. The real surprise is how confident my mother had been that she would win. Even her diary entries leading up to the trial reveal no worries at all. A few days into the trial she wrote a letter to her father saying she remained confident in the outcome even though "Carl is taking every opportunity to make me seem like a wandering, irresponsible degenerate."

My mother took the loss as a devastating failure—not just a personal one, but a political one, too. At the stroke of a judge's pen, her dream of raising a revolutionary boy, free of the vices of mainstream America, was dashed. The Establishment had prevailed. And, worse, she had been an accomplice; by fighting for the settlement, she'd succumbed to the temptation of, of all things, money.

We all walked outside to the parking lot. It was a hot August afternoon and my mother, shoulders hunched, took my hand. We were both shocked that I was about to go home with my father and Rosalind forever. I looked up at my mother's face. Her skin was pale and her lips were trembling. I'd never seen her look so defeated. She met my eyes and tried to smile. "Don't worry," she said, bumping her arm into mine. "I'll figure something out."

"Don't worry about me," I told her, suddenly painfully aware that this was much harder on her. "I'll be fine. Just take care of yourself, okay? Please?" I wrapped my arms around her waist.

After wiping away her tears, my mother put her hand on my head, tousled my hair, kissed my forehead, and then gave me a long hug. "I'll get you back, I'll come get you, I promise." Her words were confident, but her tone and body language screamed defeat.

I didn't realize how hard on herself my mother had been over losing me in the custody battle. Her first diary entry after the trial read:

This page should be all black and all bloody. I have hurt myself badly and don't really want to write it down. The system has come down on me and I was too dumb to not let it hap-

pen. I was like a cow walking into the slaughterhouse, know-
ing and not knowing, attracted by some stupid thing like food
or shelter or sex. I went to Michigan and I lost custody of Pe-
ter. And Peter is there now with Carl and I don't know what
to do. I am tired of talking about how it all happened. I am
amazed at how difficult it is to focus my anger, to recuperate
my forces, to concentrate on anything else but Peter.

For my father, the "Peter problem" was finally settled, or so he
thought. I had never seen him happier. Now he would have his
youngest son back and we would live together in the nice suburban
Michigan home he had originally built for the family. My old room
was all set up, waiting for me to move back in, as if I had never left.
The green-and-white quilt that Grandma Andreas had made for me
when I was a toddler still covered the bed, with neatly embroidered
squares featuring pictures of ducks, giraffes, and other animals. My
little rocking chair was still there, too, right next to the bed, though
I could no longer fit in it. A small maple desk hugged the wall, ready
for me to do my homework on. Everything looked perfectly comfortable, but it would take time for me to actually adjust. I was suddenly
stepping back into a life I had not occupied since I was five years old.
In a few weeks I would go back to Meadowbrook Elementary School,
the same school my mother had taken me from in late 1970 for our
clandestine move to Berkeley.

To celebrate the start of our new life together, my father took
me to Farrell's Ice Cream Parlour the day after the trial was over. It
was just the two of us. We both loved ice cream, so this was a real
treat. The waitress showed us to a booth and handed us menus as
we sat down. I studied the shiny plastic-laminated menu carefully,
salivating over all the pictures of sundaes and banana splits. I was
overwhelmed by so many choices and looked across the table at my
father for some guidance.

"Order anything you like," he said with a smile.

"Really?" I wasn't convinced he meant it. My father hardly ever ate out, preferring to save money. That included ice cream, since he always had a well-stocked freezer.

"Sure, go ahead," he replied in an encouraging voice. "Special treat."

I studied the menu for another few minutes before noticing what I wanted. When the waitress came around and asked for our orders, I pointed to the featured dessert at the top of the page—by far the most expensive item on the entire menu. My father let out a muffled gasp. "Ah," the waitress said with a knowing smile, "that's the Pig's Trough. You sure you can handle that all by yourself?" I quickly nodded.

"Maybe we should share that, Peter," my father chimed in. I shook my head.

"Well, okay then, the Pig's Trough it is," the waitress said, giving me a quick wink and then scribbling it down on her notepad. She looked over at my father. "And what can I get for you?"

"Oh, just a small sundae. I might need to help my boy finish."

When the Pig's Trough arrived I stared at it admiringly for a few seconds before diving in. It was a beautiful creation: a double banana split with six scoops of ice cream topped with whipped cream, sprinkled nuts, and a cherry in the middle. I didn't even leave my father a bite, just to prove I could eat it all by myself.

The waitress was mighty impressed. As a reward, she gave me a pin that read I MADE A PIG OF MYSELF AT FARRELL'S. I grinned. Calling someone a pig was a political insult in my old life with my mother, but now it didn't bother me. I was proud of my accomplishment.

Within days of my moving in with my father and Rosalind, my mother wrote to me, in Spanish, so my father and Rosalind couldn't read it:

I will be back in Michigan next week to demand a
retrial to reclaim you. The trial will not be right away,

and I will bring friends and make a public case of it
because the first trial was very unjust. So you should
know I am doing all I can. With enough organization,
we—the poor people of the world who are in the
struggle—still have some power. Many are thinking of
you, Peter, and are going to help.

I could not bear the thought of yet *another* long trial, but I couldn't say that to my mother. In truth, her plan to legally appeal the custody decision was mostly, according to her diary, "a cover for more concrete plans to take Peter out of Michigan about Christmastime—it's not a capital or extraditable offense." But she wasn't going to bring me into my own kidnapping plan until she was ready.

What my mother also didn't tell me is that many people were actually trying to convince her that she should see losing me as a blessing in disguise. She wrote in her diary: "Old friends in Detroit think it's convenient for me to put my kid in cold storage while I make the Revolution. . . . Some people, including Dad and Mary Lou [her sister] . . . think maybe Peter will be better off with Carl and I should feel unburdened." She angrily wrote to Grandpa Rich: "I am really hurt by your attitude in this matter—as if delivering my child to the enemies of the revolution would 'free me up' somehow to make revolution. That's not the kind of revolution I'm into." My mother rejected any thought that there was a tension between prioritizing her role as a mother and prioritizing the revolution. For her, the two were the same thing; we were in it together. Those who thought otherwise just didn't get it.

When my father asked me about my mother's letter, I replied casually, "She misses me. That's all."

"Why does she write to you in Spanish?" he asked.

"Oh, she just doesn't want me to forget the language."

"Ah, I see." My father looked at me for a long time, saying nothing. How could I admit to him how divided my loyalties still were?

My mother's petition for a retrial was denied, perhaps as expected. Still, she tried to stay optimistic in her next letter:

> *I spent the whole night talking and making love with*
> *Raul. We're determined to get you back. Peter, you know*
> *it made me very happy to remember your words: "Don't*
> *worry!" It hurts me greatly you are not with us but I*
> *know everything will turn out well in the end. I love you,*
> *and I have confidence in you, my dear son.*

She worried, though, about my increasing comfort at my father's house, which I didn't hide from her very well. After one phone call to see how I was doing, she commented in her diary: "I talked to Peter earlier and felt kind of numb afterward knowing he is genuinely attached to Carl and Rosalind."

Back in Denver, my mother was not used to being alone with Raul without me and spent much time brooding over my loss. But at the same time, Raul was becoming more important to her than ever. In her diary, she reminded herself to "trust Raul. He trusted me when I went to Michigan and came back without Peter. He didn't put me down. He didn't tell me what I 'should have done.' He didn't tell me what I 'should do.' He felt with me the full grotesqueness of the situation."

Privately, as time went on, her confidence began to crumble:

> *I wonder what I have to give to Peter, on what basis I am*
> *hoping to "reclaim" him. I don't want him to be alienated,*
> *gullible, competitive, but I wouldn't want him to be bitter and*
> *frustrated like me, either. Raul might have more to offer him*
> *than I do, but if Raul and I are in conflict all the time, Peter*
> *will get the short end of it and may yearn for the safer, pre-*

dictable life he's having now. I FEEL PETER'S REJECTION
TERRIBLY AND AM NOT SURE I CAN RECOVER ENOUGH
FROM THAT TO SUSTAIN OTHER HURTS.

Still, she put on a good face for me. When I wrote to my mother that September, telling her that I had started school and was liking it, she replied, "I am happy to know you are doing well in school. Later, when you are back with us and we return to Peru, you will not have so much time for studies, so it's very good that you do it now."

Raul added a short scribbled note at the end of her letter: "Hello son, you know I miss you a lot. I have confidence in you and I expect that when you watch TV—the idiot box—you critique what you see. And you should always think about the poor and the workers. Today I fought with four men using Karate. I had many wounds—thirty cuts!—but I beat them." He signed it, "The communist with a Kung Fu punch, your papi, Raul." It felt strange to get this from Raul, who still thought of himself as my father even though I was now living with my real father. I didn't reply.

As the weeks and then months passed, my mother's weekly letters got heavier and heavier. She worried that I might be getting too used to my comfortable suburban life and would be reluctant to give it up, that I was being bought off by my father and gradually turning my back on her and Raul.

She was right to worry. I *was* enjoying my new life, much more than I let on. I'd gotten used to the predictability of life in the modern and spacious suburban home at the top of a wooded hill. I liked having my father around, knowing when he'd be pulling into the driveway after work every day and hearing that comforting sound of the garage door opening, seeing him in his corduroy suit walking in smiling and asking me, "Well, how's Peter today?" Then we would sit down together for a quiet, argument-free dinner every night and enjoy a bowl of Friendly's ice cream after, maybe followed by a game of cards or Ping-Pong. I'd been making plenty of new friends and doing well in school. I was reading lots of books (*Paddington: The Original Story of the Bear from Peru*, was my favorite, even though, as I had learned from living in Peru, there were no bears there); and with my English much better by now I had earned an A on a spelling test for the first time. My teacher even said I was going to be skipped to the fifth grade to catch up to my age group after the Christmas break. I had a small part as a toy clown in the play *The Velveteen Rabbit*. I was surviving the weekly sermons at church by sitting next to my father and discreetly playing tic-tac-toe with him—fortunately for me, he believed more in *going* to church than in actively participating in it.

I did feel guilty about how easily I was adjusting, even ashamed. This was not how a good revolutionary boy was supposed to be—so quickly seduced by the comforts of suburban America. It was nice to own more than a few pairs of socks and not have to wash our clothes by hand. I had gone soft and I knew it. I kept asking myself, *Am I a sellout? Am I betraying my mother? What would she think?* Fearing the answers, I told my mother as little about my new life as I possibly could, and with my letters and phone calls to her getting shorter and shorter and less and less frequent, she became increasingly suspicious.

> *Dear Peter,*
> *The judge and the lawyers are still playing around*
> *with me about the settlement money. I'm furious, and this*
> *makes it even more difficult accepting your incarceration*
> *by people who treat me so unjustly. I have written you*
> *many letters that I do not send because I imagine you*
> *will not want to hear about my preoccupations. You want*
> *to be free to enjoy your new life as the king of the universe*
> *and I don't know how to remind you that you are a child*
> *of the people. You do not see the people from where you*

*are and you start to view the people as a threat to your
privileged life. The rich waste their time accumulating
and buying, and guard against the poor. They may help
the poor sometimes, but they will never want the poor
to kick the rich out and take power. The thing that
preoccupies me about you, Peter, is that you will fear the
poor when the poor rebel (just like the rich always have),
rather than rejoice when the poor rebel. You are so far
away that you never see the rebellion. You are so far away
from the realities of the world, Peter. You perhaps carry
with you memories of what you once knew of the world,
but that will fade if you stay there. And Peter, I very
much hope you don't feel that your "real home" is with
the rich. I know that they try day and night to make you
feel that way, showing you photos of your previous life
there, and making you think that because your father
entered my body one day to make you grow there that this
somehow gives him rights over your life.*

*Carl is trying to get ahold of your passport. If the
judge agrees to this and doesn't allow me to receive the
money if I don't hand over the passport, we will have
serious problems, Peter. Don't talk about this with them,
Peter. It's very delicate. I just want to tell you this so you
don't trust them too much. Rosalind wants to give me
rights and promises but she doesn't have the power, and
Carl is very slippery and manipulative, as always. You
always love those who are around you, Peter, if they treat
you well. But you must also think about what you are
losing, if you stay there for years, how that will affect
your mind, your attitudes, your personality. I continue
to believe you are a sane boy, Peter. That's why you easily
adjust to new experiences, but you now need to think
very seriously whether you want to totally adopt the life*

*of luxury and security. Raul and I are a little crazy, for
sure. We do not care at all about respectability. You have
to think about why we have chosen to be this way. You
can be stronger and more conscious from having spent
a few months there, or you can sell out to the experience
without caring. It was a risk to leave you there. You are
young to be risking your life, but you have lived much
and you are not so innocent. I may visit you within
weeks—don't announce that! You are in prison there
without knowing it.*

 I love you,
 your mama.

My mother wanted me to feel like I was in some sort of prison,
but that's not how it felt to me. She wanted me to feel like I would be
a sellout if I stayed with my father, and I feared she was right. I didn't
know how to respond to her letter, so I didn't write back.

A few weeks later, in early November, my mother came to Michigan to reveal her kidnapping scheme to me and to try to convince
me to leave the country with her. Her plan was to pick me up at
school during recess, drive across the border into Canada, and then
travel to the Mexican border by air the next day to meet up with Raul
and start our journey south to Peru. She kept phoning me over the
weekend from her friend's house in Detroit, hoping I was ready to
go. But I wasn't ready, and wasn't sure I ever would be. I tried to stall
her, saying, "Can't we wait until school is over, I'm getting better at
reading and writing English; I'm finally learning cursive," and "I'm
in this play, everyone is counting on me."

My mother's frustration boiled over through the phone. "But,
Peter, don't you want to live with me?" Yes, I do, I reassured her.
"Well, then, let's go now, okay?" But it wasn't okay, at least not right
then. As much as I told my mother that I wanted to be with her, it
was hard to hide the fact that I was nervous about escaping to Peru

and facing the possibility of once again being separated from my father for years.

My mother could tell I was reluctant to help her carry out my kidnapping. "Two short intense secretive conversations with Peter have produced nothing more than trauma for him," she wrote in her diary. "It looks as if we're in for a long separation." She added, "I'll have another chance after school today, hopefully, to make contact with Peter and if this doesn't succeed in effecting a getaway (i.e. if he has overcome his reluctance, which is doubtful), I will leave for Denver tomorrow morning."

That night, as my father, Rosalind, and I finished dinner and then sat on the couch watching TV in the living room, none of us suspected that my mother was spying on us, camouflaged by the trees behind the house, observing our every movement. She never told me about it, so I was startled to find out from her diary that she had spent the evening "watching the scene in the 2970 Heidelberg house through the back windows."

My mother returned to Denver without me, the kidnapping plan on hold. But she would be back a few weeks later to try again. In the meantime, she sent me a poem:

A child travels between worlds
His heart in one
His body in another
He listens to the music of the people
He plays, reads, and studies
Doubts what his teachers say
Doubts what his friends say
Doubts what the grownups who take care of him say
*   (they smile too much)*
He does not think much about his future
He is not scared of God
He is a communist, and always will be

> *He guards his secret*
> *He is a wise and calm child*
> *Aware that history is on his side*

I threw away the poem after reading it, ripping it up into little pieces so that my father and Rosalind wouldn't find it. But decades later I discovered a copy of it, folded in half, tucked away in one of my mother's diaries.

V.

RETURN TO PERU

Called Peter a couple of days ago and he says he'll be waiting for me on Wednesday, but was mixed up on what day is Wednesday. He's just barely old enough to pull this off—maybe!

—Carol Andreas, Detroit, December 1975

RETURN TO PERU

Kidnapped

THE WARRANT FOR my mother's arrest was issued by the sheriff's department a few hours after my teachers at Meadowbrook Elementary School reported me missing from the playground. The official charge was "enticing away child under 14 years of age." An all-points bulletin with our descriptions was sent out by the police to authorities at airports, train stations, and bus stations. But it was too late. We had already crossed the border. I know exactly what I was wearing that day because it was recorded in the sheriff's incident report: "Peter was last dressed in brown cowboy boots, blue jeans, a beige turtleneck shirt, gray sweater with a white stripe on the midriff, and a green ski coat with a fur-trimmed hood." These were my only clothes until we reached Peru a few weeks later. My father contacted the FBI and the State Department, but they told him that no extradition would be granted from Peru.

I had finally agreed, however reluctantly, to collude in my own kidnapping, which took place at noon on Wednesday, December 10, 1975. Early that morning in my father's house outside of Detroit, I ate my Frosted Flakes at the breakfast table as if it were any other day. Holding back tears, I said good-bye to my father and Rosalind as casually as possible. "See you later," I called back as I headed toward the door to catch the school bus.

"Have a good day at school," my father hollered after me, taking a sip from his coffee cup and momentarily lifting his head from reading the *Detroit Free Press*. He was the picture of a 1975 working dad— dark corduroy slacks, Harris Tweed sport jacket, brown sweater-vest, and a fat, striped tie—and was about to start his forty-five-minute commute into the city.

"Maybe we can play canasta again after dinner tonight," Rosalind added as she took a last bite of her breakfast.

"Sure," I said, trying to sound calm. I glanced back at the two of them sitting there at the table. I paused and took a deep breath. The faint clean smell of my father's aftershave and the aroma of freshly brewed coffee filled the air.

I shut the front door behind me and was gone.

I had been extra careful this time with my mother's kidnapping plan. As my father and Rosalind sat nearby in the living room, my mother and I had gone over it on the phone in Spanish. I'd screwed it up the first time, a couple of weeks earlier before school one day, when I had asked my father for my allowance in advance.

My father was puzzled. "You know you always get your allowance at the beginning of the week. What's the rush?"

I fidgeted and stared at the floor.

"Peter? Is there something wrong?"

I hesitated and then said, "It's just that, well, I'll need it."

"But why?" My father was growing suspicious.

"I'm leaving for South America with my mother," I blurted out, not having prepared a lie.

"What? When?"

"Today. This afternoon, I'm meeting her at school, during recess." The confession brought an immediate sense of relief, but this quickly gave way to feeling intense guilt for having botched my mother's plan.

After a long silence my father said, "Peter, you'd better stay home today."

My father and Rosalind kept a close eye on me that weekend as I helped sweep leaves off the deck.

"What if my mother got me?" I asked Rosalind as she made dinner.

"Well, we'd try to find you."

"But what if she took me out of the country?"

There was a long pause. "Always remember that our love goes with you wherever you are."

"My dad isn't happy if I don't live with him, but my mom isn't happy if I don't live with her." I sighed.

"Just remember, Peter, you're not responsible for your parents' happiness."

I nodded, unconvinced. I'd been getting the opposite message my whole life.

As much as I loved my mother, it was hard to imagine giving up the security and stability of my new suburban life and returning to the never-ending political squabbles between her and Raul. But if I declared a decision to stay, I'd be letting her down and abandoning everything we'd fought for together. I didn't want her to give up on me and I didn't want her to think of me as a sellout. My mother's faith in me was worth sacrificing everything else.

Right after that first failed escape, my mother wrote me a letter:

> To Peter,
>
> They say you would be missing something if you were with me.
>
> Yes! Missing alienation.
>
> Missing the privileges of having a nice home, family, riches.
>
> Missing respect for the terrible laws that bring injustice to the poor.
>
> Missing racism that makes one think white skin is superior to colored skin.
>
> Missing sexism that makes one think women should serve the vanity of men.
>
> Missing the pacifism that makes one think the poor should be patient with the rich, waiting for the poor to solve the problems created by the rich themselves.

They say it is right that you now know the
patriarchal family, that it is right that you now know the
authoritarian perspective, the piety of the church, that
you should experience a life inhibited and restricted by
cleanliness, elegance, the English language, the bourgeois
language.

Bullshit, Peter!

The truth is that we are suffering from the repression
of male pigs that still control this society. We are suffering
from the disappearance of a free spirit, and the rampant
consumerism that confuses a child—who is bought off by
smiles and gifts and personal attention.

We are suffering from the domination by the rich
who always punish those who are fighting to change the
system.

We are suffering from your betrayal, my child, because
you are very young and you do not yet understand the
value of what you have lived.

My mother never sent me the letter. She put it away in her diary
once she was sure I wouldn't choose my father over her. Reading it
now takes me immediately back to the impossible choice I'd faced.
I wanted to be with both of my parents, but it was clear that could
never happen. It was one thing to disappoint my father and Rosalind, quite another thing to lose my mother's love. I knew my mother
would blame me if I stayed with my father in Michigan, whereas I
knew my father and Rosalind would blame my mother if I went with
her back to Peru. If I told my mother I wanted to stay in Michigan,
she would see my decision as the ultimate personal and political
failure. She would never forgive me, or herself.

And so, that chilly December day, I kept my promise to my
mother. When I sneaked out of the schoolyard during the lunch
recess, she was waiting for me outside the playground in a red VW

Beetle, the engine running. She had disguised herself in oversized dark glasses and a thick black wig. I would not have recognized her if she had not waved to me from the driver's seat. I walked quickly toward the car and got in, and we sped off. Despite the cold, my mother's forehead was sweaty, and she looked pale against the heavy winter coat she'd wrapped around her slender frame. The faint odor of sweat was familiar, comforting. She had never worn deodorant, preferring her own human smell to flowery chemicals.

"Everything go okay?" My mother squeezed my hand as we turned the corner. "No one suspects anything this time?"

I shook my head and squeezed her hand back. I didn't say anything, fearing my words would betray my ambivalence.

We drove in silence. As we approached the Detroit-Windsor Tunnel, which runs under the Detroit River and links the United States to Canada, tears started rolling down my cheeks.

My mother pulled over to the side of the road. "Do you want to go back? We're almost at the border." She was trying hard to seem calm, but I heard the wobble in her voice.

"No," I replied, wiping away my tears with my coat sleeve. I wanted to be in the car with my mother right then—but I also wanted to still be running around the playground back at school. I did not look at my mother, fearing she would see the indecision in my eyes. She did not press me. She maybe realized she'd get a different answer if she asked again.

I changed the subject, teasing, "You look really goofy with that big puffy wig and those ugly glasses." I had never seen my mother in glasses, and the wig made her head seem huge.

She laughed and started the car again. "Yeah, you're right. I'll take this thing off as soon as we've crossed into Canada."

We made it to Toronto by evening, and checked into a downtown hotel.

"Now you should call your father," my mother said as we sat on the edge of the bed together, staring at the black phone on the nearby nightstand. "Tell him you're with me and you're fine, that you're not coming back, and that he shouldn't look for you. No need for a lot of details."

I glanced around at our hotel room. My mother reached for the receiver. "Here, I'll dial for you," she said impatiently. She seemed more eager than I was to get the phone call out of the way. Anticipating the sound of my father's sad voice filled me with dread. She handed the phone to me as soon as it started to ring on the other end. The receiver felt heavy in my small hand as it reconnected me with the life I had just left behind.

My father answered. "Hello?" I knew exactly where he was standing in the house—not far from the kitchen table where I had said good-bye to him for the last time that morning.

"This is Peter, I'm with my mother. Please don't try to find me, I promise I'll write you from South America." My mother nodded and smiled as I spoke. I tried to sound confident.

"Peter, we've been so worried about you all day." My father sounded relieved to hear my voice, but then began to plead with me. "Please, just come home. Can't we sit down and talk about this together?" He kept repeating, "Let's all sit down and talk about this and work it out, okay?"

I didn't reply, fearing I might start crying if I did.

Rosalind got on the line. "Peter, is your mother there? Let me talk to her." I handed the phone over, glad to be rid of it and feeling sick with guilt.

"I don't care if the police are looking for us, we're out of jurisdiction," my mother snapped. "Good-bye." And she hung up.

That was the last time I would speak to my father or Rosalind for more than three years.

My mother turned to me. "Peter, I know that was hard, but it was the right thing to do. I know part of you liked living with them, but you really didn't belong there." I choked back tears as my mother, satisfied that we'd done our duty, picked up the phone again and quickly dialed Raul at his El Paso, Texas, hotel room.

"Peter's with me now," she announced triumphantly when Raul answered the phone. "Yes, yes, everything went as planned. You'll be there when we arrive tomorrow, right? I assume you mailed the boxes to Lima before you left Denver. It's a good thing you got out of there yesterday, the cops are probably knocking at the door as we speak. You have all the money with you, right? Okay, then we'll see you tomorrow!"

Early the next day, my mother and I flew to El Paso, our gateway to Latin America. Raul was waiting for us at the airport, waving his arms over his head as we stepped off the plane. He blended right into this gritty southwest border city where Spanish seemed to be as common as English.

Raul greeted us with his signature backslapping hugs. "We're all together again!"

I hugged Raul back stiffly.

My mother gave him a kiss and squeezed both of his hands. "We made it."

"Well, what are we waiting for? Let's get across the border then," Raul declared, as if he were now in charge, and then proceeded to lead the way, not even looking back to make sure we were following. He was clearly eager to head south as soon as possible. He had waited for this day the whole year the three of us had been in the States. He'd never gotten comfortable there, just hanging around with little to do, knowing hardly any English, while my mother battled my father over my custody and squabbled over their shared property.

From Denver, where he and my mother had been living while I was in Michigan, Raul had taken the bus down to El Paso with my mother's savings, all in cash, including the nearly $40,000 that had just been released from the property settlement agreement with my father. My mother had sown pockets inside our pants to hide the money and keep it safe. Stuffed with cash, the three of us walked across the border bridge from El Paso into Juarez. I was flattered by my mother's trust in me, but the bulky pile of crisp $100 bills in my pants, poking out around my waist, made me self-conscious.

Could the Mexican border guards standing lazily to the side as we went through the metal gate and walked across the bridge tell I was moving awkwardly? Fortunately, unlike entry to the U.S., there was no inspection of any sort going into Mexico.

Entering Juarez, a bustling, grimy Mexican border city that dwarfed El Paso across the Rio Grande, was like entering another world. The toxic smell of exhaust fumes, the sight of shantytowns crowding the hills, and the constant noise of the traffic congestion overwhelmed my senses. Only the weather was a welcome change, a relief from the transition to early winter back in Michigan. We checked into a small hotel near the main bus station, and ate *tacos al carbon* from one of the many vendors lining the streets. Then we celebrated our escape across the border by going to a movie. Raul insisted we see *Jaws*, which was fine by me—my father certainly would not have let me go to such a violent movie at age ten—but the gory scenes gave me nightmares for days and left me with a permanent shark phobia. Still, the movie was a useful distraction from thinking too much about my father and Rosalind and the comfortable life I had left behind.

The next morning, the three of us huddled in the back of a packed bus for the two-day ride to Mexico City. The driver kept everyone awake with nonstop mariachi and *corrido* songs blaring from the radio, his crucifix dangling from the windshield bopping and swinging to the beat.

In our hotel room in downtown Mexico City, we washed off several days of sweat and dirt, grabbed a quick bite to eat on the street, and headed to the local theater. This time my mother chose the movie, *El Fin del Mundo—The End of the World*—a Japanese film about the hazards of industrialization that were destroying the planet, and its apocalyptic message terrified me even more than *Jaws* had.

I kept my mother awake with questions late into the night. "Are we really going to die from pollution?" I asked as the three of us tried to fit together in the hotel room's one double bed. Exhaust fumes and the noise of traffic seeped in from the busy street below. Raul was already snoring, apparently not perturbed by either the noise or the fate of the planet.

"Industrial capitalism is killing this planet, but we still have time to save it," my mother murmured. "One more reason we need a real revolution, and not only in one country—it has to be worldwide. Otherwise we're all doomed." She rolled over, toward Raul, with her back facing me. "Now go to sleep," she mumbled. "The revolution won't come overnight, but don't worry, the planet won't die overnight, either."

I insisted we sleep with the lights on, as if that would keep the pollution at bay.

From Mexico City, we kept moving south by bus, to the Guatemalan border, a remote jungle crossing that bore no resemblance to the hustle and bustle of the El Paso–Juarez border. We had to walk across the border to switch buses. I paused for a minute at the border demarcation sign that read MEXICO and GUATEMALA, and hopped back and forth—one foot in Mexico and the other in Guatemala. "Look at me," I yelled to my mother and Raul, who were walking well ahead of me. "I'm in two countries at the same time!" They turned and laughed, and I hurried to catch up to them. The next bus would take us to the capital, Guatemala City. I was starting to have fun again being on the road with my mother—we had always been good traveling companions—even if I was less than happy that Raul was with us. At least they seemed to be getting along.

The following day I sent my father and Rosalind a brightly colored postcard from Guatemala City with a picture of majestic Maya ruins. I made sure my short scribbled message on the card was light and upbeat, as if I were on a fun, extended vacation abroad. At the end of the card I wrote in caps, "HAVE A GOOD NEW YEAR, LOVE PETER."

We made it to Lima by Christmas, some two weeks after we fled Michigan. I was back in Peru, but in my mind I was still straddling two worlds. I imagined the little red-and-white-checkered birdhouse ornament I had made just a month earlier in fourth-grade art class hanging on the Christmas tree in my father's living room. The brightly decorated tree would have many carefully wrapped presents underneath it, spread neatly on the tightly woven gray wool carpet, but none would bear my name. My wool stocking, if it hung above the fireplace, would be empty and our color TV would be tuned to my father's ABC evening news.

We spent that Christmas dancing and lighting fireworks with Raul's family—his mother, Berta; his sister, Victoria; and his three brothers, Lucho, Carlos, and Juan—at their small home on the outer edge of Villa El Salvador, a sprawling shantytown of several hundred thousand inhabitants on the southern outskirts of Lima. My mother and I were warmly welcomed. Their home had no Christmas decorations or tree with presents underneath, but this did not dampen the family's festive mood, lubricated by beer and *aguardiente*.

A few years earlier, Villa El Salvador had been nothing more than an empty desert when squatters from Lima's overcrowded slums organized a nighttime takeover in bold defiance of the government. When the police came to try to evict them and tear down their makeshift shacks, the squatters refused to move. Wishing to avoid a potentially bloody confrontation, the government eventually relented, and the trickle of new squatters turned into a flood as thousands of people rushed to stake out plots of land. Though the sandy, harsh terrain was not exactly welcoming, squatters were attracted to the prospect of open land not far from the capital.

Villa El Salvador had no electricity or running water. Tanker trucks came by once a week to fill up the two rusting fifty-gallon metal barrels in front of Berta's straw-mat shack. The toilet was a hole in the sand in a screened-off area, with old newspapers for toilet paper and a can of lime powder to dissolve the shit. With no streetlights to illuminate the sand streets and keep the muggers at bay, it was dangerous to go out at night. We all slept together on straw-filled mattresses and woke up with our legs covered in itchy fleabites. I intensely missed my flea-free bed, Saturday-morning cartoons, and Frosted Flakes, but I resisted saying that to my mother. And this time, unlike our first arrival in South America more than three years earlier, I knew what to expect and adapted without complaint.

Comas

A MONTH OR so after our escape from the U.S. and return to Peru, my mother began to question her relationship with Raul. "Should I leave him?" she asked me.

I don't know what answer she thought she'd get, but to me there was no question. "Yes, please, Mom. Do it," I urged. But I knew it was unlikely.

That evening at dinner, she was picking at her food, heaving deep sighs. Raul was out of town, so it was just the two of us.

"What's wrong?" I asked her.

She gave me a sad smile. "Well," she said. "I've been thinking a lot about suicide."

I put my fork down. I couldn't swallow the food in my mouth.

"Hypothetically, of course," she said. "I've been thinking about all the different ways I could do it—pills, razors."

I couldn't even look at her.

She continued. "Suicide is a human right. Besides, the people left behind usually manage fine. Look at Violeta Parra." Parra was a famous Chilean singer who had killed herself in 1967. "*Gracias a La Vida*" ("Thank You, Life"), one of her best-known songs, was one of my mother's favorites.

I stared helplessly at my plate. I had long been terrified by the possibility of my mother suddenly dying. I'd imagined a violent, gruesome death. I'd imagined her tortured by the police. When she left on errands, I sometimes smothered her with good-bye kisses, telling her that they would help keep her alive.

"And if I die anyway?" she once asked.

"Well, then, the kisses will make sure you're reincarnated."

It had never occurred to me that my mother's death might actually be self-inflicted. I grew quietly angry. How could she even think, let alone say, these things? How could she contemplate leaving me alone to fend for myself, after all that effort to get me back from my father? After I had abandoned a secure life for her? After she had forced me to choose between her and my father, even if it meant agreeing to my own kidnapping? My fury began to bubble, but I said nothing. I continued to stare a hole through my untouched food. My mother was so self-absorbed in her woes that she seemed completely unaware that her talk of suicide was upsetting me.

My mother sighed again. "Okay," she said, "I have to tell you something."

I glanced up at her. "What?"

"I found something."

"What do you mean?"

"I found an old letter to Raul from some woman named Julia."

"Who's Julia?"

"Some classmate of his from those English classes he was taking in Denver." Her voice cracked. "It's a love letter."

She pushed her chair away from the table, knelt on the floor next to the bed, and stuck her hand beneath the mattress. She pulled out the crumpled letter. "See?" She waved the letter in my face. "I found it in one of his books. It's several months old, written when we were in Denver. This woman says she's pregnant."

With that, she turned from me, got into bed, faced the wall, and cried. I looked at her for a long time, wondering if I should go to her. But I didn't. I was still too angry at her for even mentioning the unthinkable possibility of suicide. I did not feel like comforting her; I felt like shaking and slapping her. Looking back at that moment, I still feel that same anger today: a mother should never tell her ten-year-old child that she's thinking about killing herself. And my mother was well aware of how terrified I already was of the possibility of her suddenly dying. A diary entry around that same time read, "Peter was very affectionate saying goodbye today. He's always afraid I'm going to die, even when we just separate for a few hours or a few days."

When my mother confronted Raul about the love letter days later, he somehow convinced her that Julia was not actually pregnant, that the wording in the letter meant she was worried she *could* get pregnant *if* they were to have sex—and that's why she didn't want to have an affair with him. My mother bought the story. Perhaps the alternative was simply too hard for her to take.

We were in the middle of moving to Comas, a grimy slum extending up the bare rocky hills from the highway north of Lima. There was not a blade of grass or a tree in sight. Nowhere on earth, I thought, could be more different looking than the lush, wooded neighborhood with sprawling homes and two-car garages I had left behind in Michigan. The drab terrain matched the drably dressed inhabitants, as well as the perennially gray skies. The highway at the base of the hills was jammed with traffic, people, and storefronts.

Our home in Comas, like all the others in the area, was a one-story utilitarian brick and cinderblock house. A large patch of bare dirt served as an enclosed backyard; everything we tried to plant in it—grass, vines, flowers, vegetables—died instantly. Not even weeds could grow. It made my mother depressed.

Raul told her to cheer up. "Someday it will look just like Berkeley, with flowers and trees." This made my mother laugh, but it didn't make her feel any better about Comas. As she described it in her diary, "Comas is the ugliest place in the world—pure dust and cement and trash and garbage."

Still, Comas was a real step up from Villa El Salvador. In Comas, we at least had electricity, even if it was erratic. And we had plumbing, although the water only came on for an hour or so a day—usually early in the morning, but it was never predictable. The sewers were constantly bursting, and sewage could run down the long road to the highway for days at a time. We boiled water to make it safe for drinking. We had no phone, but there was a public pay phone seven blocks away. There were few streetlights, so walking home or going out at night still brought with it the fear of being mugged.

The house in Comas belonged to Raul's family—which meant it was rent-free, the main reason we were there. The whole family had lived in the house years earlier, until Berta finally got tired of her husband's drinking and of the steep mile-long walk up the hill from the bus stop. So she and the kids moved to the sand dunes on the outer edge of Villa El Salvador.

Raul's father and sister still lived in the small front part of the Comas house, but the rest had fallen into disrepair. It took us days to make it livable. The place was full of dust, grime, trash, and bugs. Ten years' worth of garbage and junk had been building up in the backyard. The kerosene stove needed to be fixed, and it was a challenge for us to learn how to use it.

After we cleaned the place up to make it more habitable, two of Raul's younger brothers, Lucho and Carlos, moved in with us. My brother Joel and his girlfriend, Gabrielle, freshly arrived from the U.S., also decided to take a room. They had spent three months taking buses and hitchhiking through Mexico and Central America, all the way down to Lima from Berkeley. I had been eager to reconnect with Joel and hear all about their long trip south to join us. With no road from Panama to Colombia, they had hitched a ride on a boat carrying contraband goods, and were dropped off somewhere along the Colombian coast—essentially smuggled into Colombia, along with the contraband, since they had no entry stamp in their passports. They were robbed twice en route, including once in Bogotá when some kids grabbed Joel's glasses right off of his face and then sold them back to him for a few pesos the next day.

Joel's stories reminded me of when Ronald had showed up at our home in Santiago in early 1973 and told us all about his adventures traveling through the remotest parts of southern Chile. But unlike Ronald, Joel seemed genuinely enthused about seeing us and planned to stick around. My mother and I were more than happy to have him and Gabrielle move in, making us feel more like a family. Having Joel there also made me feel less stuck between my mother and Raul. Joel and Gabrielle even took me traveling with them on a three-week trip through Peru and Bolivia. It took no pleading on my part for my mother to agree to let them take me along. To save money we hitchhiked, mostly catching rides on the backs of trucks, lying flat on our stomachs on top of the open-air cargo and holding on tight while winding up and down narrow mountain passes, day and night. We got all the way to La Paz, visited Lake Titicaca on the Bolivian border, and also made it to Cuzco and Machu Picchu. It was the only time I had ever traveled with Joel.

When we returned, Joel and Gabrielle earned money teaching English part-time. Joel also worked with a local publisher to have his *Incredible Rocky* comic book translated into Spanish. Gabrielle, meanwhile, got caught up in a New Age mystical cult, growing increasingly absorbed in self-discovery and spirituality. A few months later, when she ran off with one of the cult members, Joel didn't seem all that upset about it.

The house in Comas was large enough that I even had my own room, though it doubled as the living room during the day. Raul's father and sister kept to themselves in the front rooms and we rarely saw them. Raul's mother, Berta, dropped by now and then, and sometimes chastised my mother for not washing and ironing Raul's clothes. My mother gritted her teeth and listened to her politely rather than argue. Nothing she said would have changed Berta's mind anyway, and she didn't want to fight with Raul about his mother.

That April, I started school six blocks away, halfway down the

My mother and Raul with Raul's mother,
Berta, 1976

hill between the house and the highway. I was ten years old, enrolled in the fourth grade. Classes were from 1:00 to 6:00 p.m., but the teacher would often let us out an hour early. No one took school all that seriously, and I was happy to have the extra playtime. The most important thing was to always arrive at school on time—the penalty for getting there late was having to clean up all the piss and shit that missed getting into the holes in the ground in the bathroom.

The biggest challenge was not my schoolwork, since there was little of it, but keeping my dark blue uniform clean. On weekends, I washed my school pants over and over again by hand because I only had one pair and no washing machine. My mother said it was important that I wash my pants myself, "like all men should." The neighbors let me borrow an iron to press them.

Before and after school, I played for hours with the neighborhood kids—usually soccer, or spinning tops, or marbles on the dirt street right in front of the house. Unlike at Meadowbrook Elementary, there was no school playground, but the streets and alleys of the neighborhood provided a playground of sorts, where one could always start or join a game. Like in Ocopilla, it didn't take long to get in on the street fun, especially if one had a decent soccer ball to share. We had no television, but I went to the house of a family up the block to watch TV on their little black-and-white set—mostly reruns, with Spanish subtitles, of American shows like *Bonanza* and *The Beverly Hillbillies*. My mother did eventually get a radio, which we quickly regretted because Raul would get up early in the morning and blare it, singing along loudly, while everyone else was trying to sleep.

Just like at the Berkeley commune, chores were carefully divvied up. At each meal, the quality of our food depended on who was cooking and was always complicated by our having no refrigerator or oven. But we all took turns going to the nearby street market every morning where we could buy most everything we needed. Whoever went to the market got to drink a *surtido*—a blender concoction of mixed tropical fruits, sometimes with vegetables and herbs. A *surtido especial* contained raw eggs, milk, and various fruits mixed in a blender. As a special treat on Sundays we often made ceviche—raw fish marinated with lemon, onion, and red pepper, served on lettuce with a whole sweet potato. We'd also sometimes boil two or three red-purple ears of corn for several hours, let the water cool, then add sugar and lemon to it. This made the popular drink *chicha*. We hardly ever had desserts other than fruit, but from time to time we bought sweets from street vendors—ice cream bars and *chupetas* (fruit-flavored ice); or we'd buy a box of *manjar blanco*, a sweet, creamy paste made by boiling sugar and milk for many hours, and fight over it until it was gone.

The trickiest and most important chore was filling the water containers every morning. The person responsible had to make sure to wake up early, open the faucets, place the water containers underneath, then wait patiently for the water to come on; it could be anytime between five and seven in the morning. Oversleeping meant the whole house would go without water. And falling back to sleep with the faucets open while waiting for the water could be disastrous. One morning when I was on faucet duty I nodded off with the faucets on, and while everyone else was still sound asleep the entire house flooded. By the time everyone woke up and figured out what had happened, the water on the concrete floor was already at least an inch deep.

One day a week was designated as a "free day," meaning no one had assigned house chores and duties, but what this meant in practice was that nothing actually got done. This especially frustrated my mother. She wrote in her diary: "No one bothered to sweep or fill the water containers or do dishes yesterday since we had agreed it would be each one for himself or herself for one day, and Peter never ate anything after breakfast and was complaining of being hungry at midnight when there was nothing in the house to eat."

The house in Comas was a sickly place. It seemed like someone was always coughing, sneezing, throwing up, or running to the bathroom, and my mother seemed to have it worst of all. She mostly had colds and stomach problems, but once, during a bad bout of hepatitis, her skin turned yellow for weeks. I took special care of her during those weeks, bringing her *surtidos* from the market, and she gave me a new set of drawing markers in appreciation. At least for those weeks, I was intensely aware that diseases rather than dictators were the biggest threat to my mother's life. It was at moments like these that I felt most needed by her—that while my father and Rosalind *wanted* me to live with them, my mother truly *needed* me to live with her.

Like everywhere else we had lived, one thing never changed in Comas: my mother and Raul argued and argued, and then argued some more. The only real change was that the fights kept escalating, the next one building on the one before it. A typical entry in my mother's diary from that time: "We talked and loved and fought literally all night long." Or: "Raul says I'm an ultra-feminist and no one will have me (but he still will, he says, only his conditions and concessions vary from moment to moment)."

At least my mother and Raul had their own room now, so the rest of us had some insulation from their yelling. But Raul's younger brothers contributed to the tension. Carlos, twice as round and half as smart as Raul, sparked a fight one afternoon when he blurted out, "A man needs to beat his wife if he wants her to really love him." My mother shot Carlos a look to let him know he had just declared war on women. I'm not sure if Carlos really believed what he said or if he was just trying to provoke her. But even Raul, seeing that look on my mother's face, jumped in to take her side.

"You idiot," Raul yelled at Carlos, slapping him dismissively on the head. "It's no wonder girls don't want to go out with you." Carlos laughed it off and walked away.

But that was a rare moment; most of the time Raul and my mother were on opposite sides of the shouting. And unlike in the past, it started to get physical, though I didn't realize how bad it had gotten until I read through her diary entries from this time:

> We fight violently. He threatens me with death by bullet (first time). I attack him physically to show him I'm not afraid, and he responds with violence. I tell him I will never accept bringing a gun into the house because even though I promise to love him forever I don't want to risk an impulsive moment in which he uses the gun to demonstrate his fury.

One Saturday when my mother and I came home together from the market we found Raul sobbing in bed, surrounded by the thousands of dollars in cash we had brought with us to Peru from my mother's property settlement agreement with my father. Raul and my mother had hidden the money in the house and were drawing from it sparingly to live on. After a particularly explosive argument with my mother, Raul had decided to take off with all the money while no one was home. But at the last minute, he changed his mind and broke down crying. My mother sat there for a moment on the bed in stunned silence. "What's going on, Raul? What are you doing with all the money?"

"I couldn't do it, I couldn't do it," Raul sobbed. "I was going to leave. But I couldn't do it. See, I love you too much to do that. Now I know I can never leave you."

Raul and my mother kissed and made up by the end of the day, put the money back in its hiding place—a hole in the wall hidden by their bed—and decided that the solution to the imbalance in their relationship was to find manual jobs, because Raul's problems were "typical of lumpen proletariat" and hers were typical of "petty bourgeois intellectuals." My mother told Raul, "Remember, according to Mao, it takes many years to grow out of bad habits."

But at the same time that Raul and my mother were reaffirming their love to each other, she was expressing more and more doubts about their marriage in her diary, sometimes concluding that it was only a matter of time before it ended: "It makes me feel weak to think about moving again, uprooting Peter again"; "I don't feel personal defeat, but I do feel that I've been on a romantic binge that was doomed from the outset."

My mother never did get a manual job in Comas, nor did Raul for that matter, but our block elected her its representative for the neighborhood Comité de Lucha organized by the Partido Comunista del Peru, already known informally as Sendero Luminoso (Shining Path), which would transform into an armed insurgency years later. My mother was proud to be chosen; it made her feel like she had truly become not only an accepted member of the community but a political leader. Raul couldn't believe they had selected my mother, a foreigner, as their representative, and teased her about it, and this of course only added to the tension in the relationship.

As things worsened between Raul and my mother, I became more open about urging her to leave him. I associated living in Peru with all of my frustrations with Raul, and began to complain about it. I tried to tell her that I wasn't rejecting the choice to leave Michigan, but my denials were halfhearted, and she knew it. My complaints hurt my mother to the core. As she confessed to her diary:

> One of the worst days of my life. . . . I talked with Peter about the future and he was bitter about my decision [to stay in Peru]. He says he wants to study in a sane school in the U.S., have real friends, is tired of Peru and sick and tired of Raul. He doesn't think Raul can change. He's exasperated by my vacillation. I replied calmly, but today he found me crying and tried to comfort me, telling me I should do what I wish. I asked him if he regretted his decision [to leave Michigan and come to Peru] and he said no. He bought me a chocolate to take care of my depression. Perhaps the day was not totally bad, thanks to Peter's comfort and support in the end.

It's clear from my mother's diaries that she was sinking deeper and deeper into a depression in Comas, something I didn't fully grasp at the time. She hated the place and her fights with Raul and couldn't shake the suicidal thoughts, though at least she kept them from me. Instead, she turned to Joel. "I talked with Joel today about my suicidal tendencies," my mother wrote in her diary, "and he convinced me that I shouldn't see suicide as something romantic or heroic—quite the opposite. He's a saner person than I."

Animal House

IN ADDITION TO its usual human inhabitants, the house in Comas was filled with all sorts of creatures, large and small, cuddly and creepy, welcome and unwelcome. It was debatable who really ran that house, the humans or the animals, including the thousands of flies, ants, fleas, ticks, spiders, and the winged cockroaches I had first encountered in Guayaquil. There was little point in resisting: we kept killing and the bugs kept coming.

I'm not sure why, but the ticks were only interested in Dingo, the mutt we'd adopted as a puppy when we first moved to Comas. He'd quickly grown into a skinny adolescent in only a couple of months. There was no such thing as "dog food" at the local outdoor market, so we fed him leftovers and sweet potatoes boiled together in a large pot. But no matter how much food he consumed, he was always skinny and hungry, probably due to the fact that, as we later discovered, he had worms. We originally attributed his nightly yelping to fleas, but an even bigger nemesis were the many ticks on his body, mostly congregating under the big flaps of his ears.

Every evening, someone settled on the steps in the courtyard to pick plump ticks out of Dingo's ears. The rock we crushed them with soon turned red with blood. Joel's girlfriend, Gabrielle, was particularly skilled at it, and happily spent most evenings helping dislodge the ugly bloodsuckers. When she left, Dingo was devastated. After that, getting him tick-free was a lost cause as long as he was free to roam around Comas with the other dogs in the neighborhood.

No one ever took Dingo for a walk, leash or no leash. In Comas, most dogs ran around on their own, returning home only to sleep and hopefully get some scraps of food. Despite the ticks, Dingo was spoiled by our neighborhood's standards.

Dingo did manage to coexist with the unnamed kitten that Carlos brought home one night. With her soft, smoky-gray fur, she was perfectly camouflaged in Comas. She took a special liking to my mother and often curled up in her lap while she sat at the table writing in her diary or reading about the life of Lenin.

Perhaps if the kitty had been bigger and more menacing, she would have been of some use in keeping the mouse population under control. But that, too, was a lost cause. As soon as we turned the lights off at night, the mice took over, leaving tiny black pellets as evidence of their nightly rampages. We could hear them squeaking and scurrying about, but we didn't realize quite how many there were until one day, while cleaning, my mother and Raul lifted their bed frame up and an extended family of mice scattered frantically in every direction. The makeshift bed frame was really just a wooden crate filled, absurdly, with paper—the perfect material and place for a very large mouse nest.

When we first arrived in Comas, the neighbors gave me two little gray-and-white bunnies as pets. They were adorable, with the silkiest fur, and spent all day either nibbling alfalfa and carrots we brought from the local market or cuddling with each other. We dug a wide, deep hole in the backyard to put them in and covered it with wire mesh. But the rabbits soon dug tunnels and sneaked out, hopping around until one of us caught them, at which point, they happily returned to their hole-in-the-ground home. It was as if their half-hearted escape efforts were just temporary fun.

I often took the rabbits out to play. It turned out their favorite playmate was Dingo himself. And he seemed to understand to be gentle with them: he would bark at them, charge at them, chase them around, and even touch them with his teeth, but he would never bite. As soon as he lost interest, they would hop toward him, and the whole game would begin again. It was great entertainment for everyone.

One day, one of the rabbits disappeared. We never figured out what happened, but poor Dingo was never fully above suspicion. In the end, though, the worst threat to the life of my remaining pet bunny turned out to be my own brother. Joel had been a vegetarian since his early teens, but when he arrived in Peru, he discovered how difficult it was to live meat-free in South America. People kept offering him plates of meat, so he decided to embrace his dormant inner carnivore, so much so that within his first few weeks in Peru he had eaten guinea pig, lamb's head, cow's heart, and tripe.

Joel liked to say that if you make the decision to eat animals, you should also be willing to kill the animal yourself. One day, to prove his point, he pulled my squirming pet rabbit out of the hole by the ears. We were about to give the rabbit back to the neighbors, since he seemed lonely without his mate, and I had not been diligent about feeding him and cleaning out his pen. But Joel had other plans. As he saw it, the neighbors were going to make a meal out of the rabbit, so we might as well have him for dinner ourselves.

"Hold the legs firmly," Joel instructed me. "Make sure he can't move." He grabbed a big knife and sawed at the throat as the terrified rabbit twisted and strained.

How could I have agreed not only to let Joel kill my bunny but to help him do it? I was too eager to impress my older brother. I felt I had to show him that I could handle it like a big boy. But the truth was I couldn't handle it, and was immediately nauseated. I just hoped my brother didn't notice.

Worst of all, after slitting his throat, Joel had no clue what to do with the rabbit. He managed to skin it, but then forgot to gut it, so intestines and feces ended up in the stew. I didn't eat any, and I don't think Joel or anyone else did, either. After that, I had a hard time believing my brother had ever actually been a vegetarian—and I've never eaten rabbit.

A Dangerous Place

COMAS WASN'T SAFE, especially in the black of night. With too few streetlights, the long trek up the hill from the highway bus stop to our house became treacherous. One night, Raul was walking home late and was mugged just a block from the house.

He was livid. "I'm going to get those sons of bitches," he declared as he bandaged up his bloodied hand. "Those fuckers don't realize who they've messed with. I'll show them."

He rushed back out the front door, taking a kitchen carving knife and his brother Lucho with him to hunt down his attackers. Raul and his brother were looking for vengeance, but when they found the muggers, one pulled out a .38 revolver and shot Lucho in the leg. The police ended up arresting everyone involved—Raul, Lucho, the shooter and his accomplices—and they all spent the night together in a cell.

My mother was disgusted. "Look at the mess your male macho behavior has gotten you into this time," she yelled at Raul as she bailed him out of jail.

"You have no sympathy! Lucho was shot. We could have been killed!"

"Well, you never asked me about it before stupidly rushing to avenge a crime."

Raul then got upset at my mother for not allowing him to have a gun. "If we'd had a gun we could have defended ourselves."

"No, if you'd had a gun you would more likely have used it on me," she countered.

That shut him up. In the midst of a particularly intense late-night argument a few months earlier, Raul had said that if he had a gun he'd put a bullet through my mother's head. She never forgot that threat, and never let him forget it, either.

Then things got messier. The assailants ended up pressing charges of their own against Raul and Lucho, claiming that they were actually the ones who had been attacked that night on the street. Everyone started bribing the police to take their side. When Raul asked her to contribute money to the bribe bidding war, my mother refused. "You got us into this awful mess with your macho crap, and now you want me to help you buy your way out of it? No way."

Meanwhile, Lucho, who was on crutches and medication and was supposed to be spending his time resting up and healing, snuck out of the house one afternoon. Raul yelled at my mother for not watching over him. "Do you realize he may never walk again if he's not careful?"

"Well, I'm not his mother," she shot back.

Lucho did recover from his bullet wound, but he ended up being killed in Lurigancho prison years later when he and hundreds of his fellow Sendero Luminoso guerrilla inmates were gunned down by guards during a prison uprising.

In the end, the biggest danger in Comas was not the muggers but the cops. General Morales Bermúdez, who had taken power after a bloodless military coup against the nationalist military regime of Juan Velasco the previous summer, imposed harsh new measures to try to keep the economy from continuing its downward spiral. He drastically devalued the currency, and gas prices doubled overnight. This sparked street protests and demonstrations in Comas and across the country. The police cracked down, and tanks and soldiers were deployed to our neighborhood. The government imposed a state of emergency.

At one street demonstration at the local outdoor market, some eight blocks away from our house, Raul and Joel were handing out leaflets protesting high prices and calling for a general work stoppage. The police rushed in to break up the demonstration and went after Raul and my brother. Raul escaped his pursuers by running into the crowd and blending in by removing his glasses and outer shirt.

But Joel, a sandy-haired gringo, stuck out in the crowd. One policeman started running after him. Joel took off as fast as he could, but the policeman kept up. By the time my brother neared the house, his pursuer was less than a block behind him. I happened to be standing at the front door. Not wanting to reveal where we lived, Joel ran right by our house, didn't even glance at me, and kept going. It was surreal to watch my brother sprinting past, pretending he didn't know me, with an angry cop in hot pursuit. It happened so fast I didn't have time to call out to him, luckily. Around the corner, Joel ducked into a small local store, where the owners sheltered him. They shut the door as if the place were closed, and the policeman ran right by.

That close call worried us all. It wasn't clear what would have happened to my brother and Raul if they had been caught, but certainly they would have been arrested, maybe beaten. There were few civil liberties protections during the state of emergency. After the escape, police helicopters buzzed over the neighborhood for hours; the whirring propellers sounded like they were right above our house. That evening, a policeman told a local shopkeeper that "the gringos are troublemakers" and that the police knew from aerial photos where we lived. "We're going to get the gringos tonight," he boasted. As soon as word got back to us, my mother, Raul, my brother, and I quickly packed our bags and moved a few blocks up the street to stay the night with some neighbors. Early the next day, we left Comas entirely and headed to the highlands. We were on the move yet again, but this time I was relieved. I would not miss Comas at all, and neither would my mother.

Huertas

AS GLAD AS we were to get out of Comas, the house in Huertas—a small peasant community on the outskirts of Jauja—wasn't much of an improvement, but it was free. It was where Raul's grandparents had lived when they were young. No one had lived in the house for many years until my mother, Raul, Joel, and I showed up. Comas, for all its filth and drabness, had in some ways been luxurious compared to our new home. In Comas, at least we had plumbing and a real toilet, with running water for an hour or so a day, not to mention electricity.

Huertas was more like camping. We used candles and a kerosene lamp at night. We cooked over open flames in the crude fireplace and boiled our water to disinfect it. I slept on the dirt floor in my navy-blue polyester sleeping bag with red-flannel lining until we built a loft space with a eucalyptus ladder right above where my mother and Raul slept. We also made simple furniture out of eucalyptus, using green, freshly cut trees because it was impossible to put nails in the dry wood. The hut had no windows until my mother managed, with great effort, to chip a hole in the hard adobe wall to let some daylight in. Mama Juana gave us two guinea pigs as a housewarming present. Dingo also fled with us to Huertas, and although he was not as besieged by ticks, he was constantly hungry. The hope was that we would grow our own food in two fields nearby, but that would take time. Somehow my mother and Raul thought we could fit in, even though we were the only people in the community who didn't get up at dawn and go to bed at sunset.

The worst thing about living in Huertas was the toilet—or, more accurately, the shithole. We had neither an outhouse nor an out-of-the-way place to build one behind our single-room adobe hut. So we simply dug a hole in the ground in the front yard, if you could call it a yard; it was more of a grassy pasture surrounded by crumbling mud walls. The shithole wasn't even discreetly off to the side. No, it was on display, without anything surrounding it for protection, dug only fifteen or so feet from the front door for convenient late-night use. If the wind was blowing in a certain direction, you got a strong whiff of the stench.

Worse, it was in my way. This was the same grassy area on which I kicked my soccer ball around. Somehow I always managed to save the ball from falling into the hole, but one day while I was practicing dribbling with Joel, I moved backward a few feet before realizing where I was and then it was too late. My left leg sank all the way down to my knee. I pulled it out as fast as I could, but not fast enough. Piss and shit flooded my boot.

Watching us from the doorway, Raul burst out laughing. "Oh, I'll bet you'll never do that again. You should have seen the look on your face!" He kept laughing as he ran to get a bucket of water to help me wash off my boot and foot.

The primitive living conditions took some getting used to, but at least Huertas was bright and sunny. My mother's mood picked up immediately. She didn't seem to mind that we had no plumbing or electricity and no market nearby. All the adobe houses were on little dirt roads lined with eucalyptus trees. The surrounding hills were dry but spectacularly beautiful—yellow, ocher, and speckled with dark green trees. The sky was a brilliant blue, the air cool and fresh. Women were outfitted in bright traditional wool skirts and tall white straw hats with a dark cloth band around the top. Sheep and llamas walked down the lanes and colorful trucks and buses bumped down the narrow roads.

Joel stayed with us in Huertas for a month or so before heading back to the States. He helped us rebuild the red-tile and straw roof of the adobe hut, carrying supplies from town on one of the two rickety old bicycles we all shared. While my mother used our tiny supply of wood to build a fire and cook oatmeal for breakfast, Joel and Raul would sometimes play chess. Eventually, I convinced Joel to teach me the rules. When he decided it was finally time to hitchhike back to Berkeley—it would take him three months to get there, mostly by catching rides with truck drivers—he coaxed me to come wait with him by the side of the road with the promise of a final chess match.

I eagerly followed him out to the road, then crouched and set up all the pieces as fast as I could. But I wasn't fast enough. A rust-spotted car slowed to a stop and the driver leaned his head out the window and offered Joel a ride.

Joel looked at me and shrugged as he slung his backpack over his shoulder. He could tell I was upset. "Sorry about the chess game. Next time." He bent down to give me a quick hug and jogged around to the passenger-side door.

Speechless, I watched the car drive away, the exhaust pipe puffing tiny clouds, until my brother disappeared. I had no idea when I'd see him again. My throat ached. Rejected, I looked down at the chessboard. I was still holding the king, hovering it over its square where I'd been about to set it. I placed it carefully next to the queen. Then I drew my arm back and angrily swept the chess pieces off the board, leaving them in the dirt by the side of the road.

I cried all the way home, for several miles. I found my mother sitting at the kitchen table, jotting something down in her diary. She looked up when she heard me sniffling.

"Joel didn't even start the chess game. I'll never see my brother again." I had gotten used to my brother living with us, having another family member around, and now suddenly felt left alone again with my mother and Raul.

"Of course you'll see him again," she said, setting her pen down on her notebook. "But you can't expect him to stay here living with his mother. He's a grown man now. And you know how hitchhiking works. You take the first ride you get."

I nodded, knowing she was right, but it didn't make me feel any better. Joel later sent me a note from Caracas: "I should have played one complete game of chess with you before I even started hitchhiking just to be fair, but when the car stopped, well, I just couldn't refuse the ride. I owe you a game of chess and we'll play it next time I see you."

The only thing that Raul and my mother hung on the wall in our Huertas home was the large black-and-white cloth portrait of Vladimir Lenin wearing a dark suit and tie—the same one they'd fought so fiercely about before. It seemed rather out of place in our rustic surroundings, where, frankly, not much in the way of revolution was occurring. My mother and Raul were arguing about Lenin and everything else, perhaps exactly because they could not figure out what to do with themselves in Huertas. They handed out political leaflets and at night scribbled revolutionary slogans on the walls of the police station in nearby Jauja—posing as nighttime lovers when anyone passed by—but that was hardly satisfying. While my mother dreamed of working the land and organizing local farmworkers, Raul's interest in the countryside was halfhearted. He was really a city boy. Doing manual labor in the fields was not his thing. With no audience to perform in front of, he was lost. So it wasn't surprising that whenever there was a communal workday—when everyone in the community was supposed to work together on a common project every few weeks—Raul always found a way to be at this or that political meeting or event in town, leaving my mother and me on our own to help dig ditches and haul water with the rest of our neighbors.

In the past, my mother and Raul's heated late-night political debates ended in equally heated lovemaking, but now that was happening less and less. One late night my mother got upset that Raul was masturbating in bed, and this fight turned into a screaming match that woke me up.

"I'm sure Lenin masturbated," Raul barked.

"I'm sure he didn't do it in front of his wife," my mother screamed back in tears, pounding on Raul's chest with her fists. "You're just another male pig."

And then, to my immense surprise, she finally left him. Our Huertas experiment in extreme rustic rural living came to a sudden end after Raul accused my mother of being "politically backward" because she put feminism first and solidarity with the working class second. He accused her of being merely a "petty bourgeois feminist" who had no place in his revolution. My mother responded bitterly that she was actually doing nothing for the feminist cause, that she was even putting up with his exploitation of her, as evidenced by the fact that she was doing most of the cooking and other work around the house. Raul snapped, "If I'm exploiting you, why don't you leave me?"

So she did. A few days later, while Raul was out of town, my mother told me to pack my bag.

"Aren't we waiting for Raul to come back?"

"He's not coming with us this time," she replied, biting her lip as if she couldn't believe she'd let the words escape.

"Where are we going?" I asked, trying to contain my excitement.

"Back to the States, probably Denver. We'll never really be able to leave Raul unless we leave Peru." She then added, "The school term in the U.S. begins at the end of the month. You can even start classes on time for a change. Wouldn't you like that?"

That's all I needed to hear. I crammed my clothes into my old duffel bag as fast as I could; there was just enough room for three or four shirts, a couple of sweaters and pairs of pants, and some underwear and socks. My mother and I always traveled light—we still used the same duffel bags we had brought with us when we first came to South America almost four years earlier—which was especially handy now that we were making a quick exit. We took a taxi to Huancayo and boarded the overnight train to Lima.

My mother cried quietly as the train swerved back and forth through the high mountain passes. I held her hand and put my head on her shoulder. "Mommy, please promise me it's for real this time. Promise me."

She kissed my head and nodded. In her diary, she noted that "as soon as we left, Peter helped me stay firm, made me promise not to change my mind again—told me it had to happen someday."

When we arrived in Lima we checked into the Hotel Europa, a cheap but clean and airy hotel near the train station where we'd stayed several times before. We bought the least expensive one-way plane tickets to Miami, which left a few days later. I was eager to start our new Raul-free life back in the United States.

But when we returned to our hotel that evening, Raul was there, waiting for us in the small lobby. It hadn't been hard to guess where we'd be. My mother and I stopped cold in our tracks and I grasped her hand. Raul looked up at us with tears in his eyes. He stood, but neither he nor my mother took any steps to close the gap.

"Okay," she said to him from a distance. "You can come into our room. Since you're here. But you're not getting into bed with me."

That night, while I squeezed my eyes shut and tried to sleep, Raul spent hours begging my mother to change her mind.

"Please," he kept saying. "I can't live without you. I'll kill myself."

"Raul," my mother said. "We both know this isn't working."

"I'll devote the rest of my life to making things right," he said. "I'll even come back to the U.S. with you if you want."

"No," my mother kept saying. Her mind was made up. I couldn't believe it.

I was amazed and relieved in the morning when she kissed Raul good-bye. "I love you," she cried into his shoulder, "but I can't live with you."

Raul and I never spoke to each other that whole long night, but at the end he gave me an awkward hug, telling me, "It's now up to you to take care of your mother."

We left Peru for good.

VI.

MILE-HIGH HIDEOUT

The truth is that I am not a North American woman or Latin American nor European nor Asian. I'm a woman of the world trapped in Denver. Waiting. Waiting. Waiting. Waiting for the economic crisis. Waiting for total repression. Waiting for the definitive encounter. Waiting for the revolution in Peru. Waiting for Peter to become an adult. Waiting for the birth of the Revolutionary Organization of the Women of the World.

—Carol Andreas, Denver, 1980

South Bannock Street

NOW THAT WE were back in the States, hiding from my father, my mother legally changed her name to Andrea Gabriel—combining her old last name, Andreas, with Gabrielle (she liked my brother's ex-girlfriend's name), and shortening both. Maybe the police would still come knocking at our door, we thought, but my mother would at least make it a little harder to find us by changing her name.

It took us a few days to travel by bus from Miami to Denver, where my mother still had some friends and where Ronald was now living, though we would rarely see him even after we were in the same city. It was now late August 1976. I had just turned eleven the month before. My mother was determined to start a new life, on our own this time, away from Raul and hidden from my father. We would end up spending seven years in Denver, longer than anywhere else I'd ever lived. I wanted to visit my father and Rosalind, but less than a year after the kidnapping, I knew that was impossible. So I resisted the urge to contact them.

Whenever I broached the question of seeing my father, my mother would say, "I really don't know, Peter. It might be a while. You need to be old enough so that your father doesn't try to get you again. And if he knows we're back and where we live he might still legally go after me for taking you out of the country like that. We're already taking enough of a risk that he could track us down."

"Maybe in another year?"

My mother shrugged.

"Two? More?"

"Let's just wait and see. But we have enough other things to worry about right now."

We rented a first-floor apartment in a large, run-down brick house on South Bannock Street on Denver's west side. The house was originally built for a single family but had been carved up into six one-room apartments. It badly needed a paint job, especially the front porch, where the wood was almost bare. The yard was overgrown, neglected by everyone except the neighborhood dogs.

Our apartment was one long room on the first floor. It had once been an adjoining living room and dining room, but we never used the sliding pocket doors. The kitchen, along the wall at the back of the room, was marked by a beat-up table with two metal chairs. My mother threw a colorful tablecloth over the table. "Good as new," she declared.

Below the front window, an old faded-green velour couch doubled as my bed. The fabric was worn down in places and entirely worn off on the armrests. Beside that couch stood my mother's bed, the foot nearly touching the front entrance. Against the wall opposite her bed, my mother's Olivetti sat on a small oak desk, her growing collection of books stacked in piles on the floor. This included the forty-five volumes of Lenin she had bought right after we moved to Denver. She was going through them all, making dozens of pages of notes, in order to write what she called "the feminist critique." I didn't really know what that meant; to me they were mostly notable for taking up too much of our floor space. I hoped she was a fast reader.

The bathroom, shared with the other apartment on the first floor, was squeezed under the staircase across the narrow hallway. We could barely stand up straight in the shower stall or sit on the toilet without bumping our knees against the sink. The floor consisted of layers of peeling greenish linoleum. The four tiny apartments upstairs, mostly occupied by single, elderly men, all shared one bathroom and a kitchenette.

The house sat on the corner of the block, with the yard open to the sidewalk and street. Our landlord, Mr. Anderson, a friendly, plump man in his sixties with thick silver hair tucked neatly under his baseball cap, offered to take $25 off the rent as long as we kept the yard poop-free, mowed the grass, pulled the weeds, cleaned the shared bathrooms, and swept the hallway and front porch every so often. It was also my job to collect the rent checks once a month from the others in the house. So our rent was $50 instead of $75 per month, utilities included.

Flaws aside, at least our new home was cheap and furnished. And it felt downright cushy compared to anywhere we had lived in Peru. Even though we shared a tiny bathroom like we had in Ocopilla, it was only with one small family. There was hot water, which ran all day long. Without Raul there, we had peace and quiet around the clock. The neighborhood was a bit run-down, but it seemed safe enough; certainly nothing like Comas or Villa El Salvador. So I no longer worried that my mother might die at any moment. She was still hoping to be part of a revolution, but Denver seemed manageable compared to Chile or Peru.

Yet my mother wasn't really as happy as I was to be back in the States. She missed Raul, sometimes crying into her pillow at night. I tried to take his place, explaining how we'd take care of each other, just the two of us. She would pat me sweetly on the head. But I couldn't stop her from dreaming about him—or fighting with him in her sleep—and I didn't realize they were still writing long, detailed letters to each other through our first months in Denver.

Soon after we moved into our Bannock Street apartment, we adopted a puppy from the local shelter. Her given name was Tinkerbell, which we immediately changed to Incabell, and then just Inca. She was either a husky–German shepherd mix or a Norwegian elkhound, but it didn't matter to me; Inca was the most beautiful dog I had ever seen. Like Dingo and the other dogs we'd had, Inca was low maintenance; we simply let her out the front door to roam the neighborhood and do her business. But unlike Dingo, who was presumably still with Raul back in Huertas, Inca was happily tick-free and healthy. Unlike the local market in Comas, Denver grocery stores stocked plenty of dry dog food.

My mother also decided to get us a little green parakeet we named Maya, who lived in a tall wooden cage we hung from the kitchen ceiling. Then we adopted Lucifer, a stray black cat. Inca and Lucifer got along just fine, and so did Inca and Maya. But Lucifer and Maya were not such a good match. The problem was that my mother liked to leave the birdcage door open so that Maya could fly around the room. She said the poor bird needed some freedom and it was cruel to leave her caged up all the time like a prisoner. Maya seemed to enjoy her freedom, but so did Lucifer, who one day leapt up and swatted Maya down. It was a fatal blow. When I found the little bird on her side on the floor, breathing heavily, I knew immediately what had happened and yelled at Lucifer, who seemed very proud of himself. There was nothing I could do but watch poor Maya breathe her last breath. We never really forgave Lucifer for killing our bird, and perhaps that's why when he got out one day he never came back. Eventually we got another parakeet, which we named R2-D2, and my mother continued to leave the cage door open. One day, R2-D2 flew out the window, never to return.

A few months after we came to Denver, my mother managed to squeeze an old, scratched-up upright piano into the room, along the wall by her desk. She had gotten it for a good price from neighbors. More than anything else, that piano helped me understand that, at long last, we would no longer be living out of our duffel bags.

I didn't even know my mother could play the piano. But she had taken lessons while growing up in Kansas. She mostly played tradi-tional songs from her childhood, even religious hymns, despite her declared atheism. But my mother's favorite was the folk song "*De Colores*," the unofficial anthem of the farmworkers movement. She seemed happiest when she was sitting at that piano, tapping the keys and singing to the world at the top of her lungs. However far off the revolution might be, she wasn't letting herself give up. And soon enough she'd find plenty of local political causes to adopt.

My mother also picked up a record player at a garage sale and bought a dozen or so used LPs, including some by her favorite Chilean singers, Violeta Parra and Victor Jara, as well as Nina Simone and Keith Jarrett. We played these albums over and over again, especially on weekends. My mother also made waffles on weekends. She was a purist when it came to waffle toppings: just real maple syrup and butter, not the fake stuff, and nothing else. No matter how sleepy I was, I always got up with her. She hardly ever slept in, so if I wanted waffles, I had to eat them at the crack of dawn. Afterward, I went straight back to bed.

The only thing we splurged on was a car, our first since the failed Chevy laundry-van experiment. My mother bought an old Datsun station wagon with a new lemon-yellow paint job so sloppy that it even covered the black rubber trim and bumper. The yellowy foam popped through the tears in the black plastic front-seat cushions, but it drove fine. The car meant that on occasional weekends we could drive up to the mountains with Inca. After years of getting around by overcrowded public transportation in South America, it felt luxurious to have such freedom to travel, to simply jump in the car and be able to go wherever we wanted.

Like most other places my mother and I had lived, the Denver apartment had a mouse problem. Usually, I was responsible for washing the dishes, except when my mother offered to do them in exchange for me setting and emptying the mousetraps. My mother sympathized with the mice, even admired them, comparing them to guerrilla insurgents, but she couldn't handle how the critters were always chewing up her newspaper clippings. So she decided they had to die, as long as she had nothing to do with it. I didn't mind disposing of the bodies, since it took less time than washing dishes.

Our neighbor on the first floor, Diane, was a round and short single mother on welfare. She lived with her two young kids, Jesse and Olivia. Whenever my mother invited Diane over for tea, I would play with Jesse, who was a year or two younger than me. Years later he would end up in prison. There was a lot of turnover in the upstairs one-room apartments. One elderly tenant, who was so frail and quiet that we often forgot he was even there, died suddenly one night, apparently from a heart attack. His was the first dead body I'd ever seen. When the ambulance wheeled him out, the landlord paid us to clean out the room. The place had a distinct musty and stale old-person smell. The old man had hardly had any belongings, only a suitcase of clothes and a pair of tan Frye cowboy boots sitting by the side of the bed, begging to be worn. After a moment's hesitation, in which I imagined him taking them off right before dying, I claimed them. It did feel creepy wearing a dead man's boots, but they fit perfectly and were the nicest pair I'd ever had. They were certainly a huge upgrade over the old beat-up boots I had brought with me from Peru. I wore them daily until I finally outgrew them.

About six months after we moved to Denver, the smallest upstairs room, right above the front porch and bordered on three sides by windows, opened up. When it didn't get rented again right away, my mother decided it was finally time for me to have my own room and for her to have some privacy. It would cost an extra $25 in rent per month. I was ecstatic.

Not much more than a single bed would fit in there, and it would be hard to keep that room warm in the winter due to all the leaky windows, but it was like having my own apartment. There was enough space for a nine-inch black-and-white TV that we bought at a garage sale. My mother had finally given in to me having a TV, especially since it wouldn't be in the living room. I had long outgrown *Speed Racer*, but *Battlestar Galactica*, with Starbuck and Apollo fighting the evil Cylons, was even better. And it was on that tiny TV that I, like many other kids in Denver, became a diehard Broncos fan during the 1977 season when they made it to the Super Bowl for the first time. Slowly but surely, I was becoming an American kid again, rediscovering my love of television and replacing my previous love of *fútbol* with American football. And just as I had successfully pestered my mother to get me a soccer ball in Peru, now I convinced her to buy me a Wilson football made of real leather.

My mother got an odd assortment of part-time jobs, none of which seemed to last very long. She worked at a cardboard box factory for a few months and then at a hummingbird-feeder factory. At one point she worked as a maid at the Denver Hilton and as a janitor at Denver General Hospital. She also waited tables, first at Mary Lou's Café on Broadway, where she would slip me an extra large piece of cherry pie, and later at the 1st Avenue Café. She also spent a couple of months driving vehicles at a car auction but got fired for stalling them too many times. She was never a very good driver, especially of manual-shift cars. Though these jobs helped pay the bills, none of them had anything to do with my mother's radical politics, beyond keeping her connected to the working class.

What she wanted, more than anything, was to return to teaching. Finally, a year or so after we moved to Denver, she found part-time adjunct positions at the University of Colorado at Denver, Colorado Women's College, and Red Rocks Community College. Compensation was terrible, but the work was satisfying. For my mother, teaching was an opportunity for political advocacy. As she always had, she saw students as dupes of the system, and her job was to inspire them to challenge it by exposing capitalism and imperialism as the root cause of so many of the injustices of the world. Common as such a fate was for adjuncts, my mother was convinced that each time her contract failed to be renewed it meant that the FBI was sabotaging her because she was a threat, or at the very least that some rich corporate types on the board were trying to get her fired. She suspected that FBI informants were in her classes and that the FBI was behind her being blacklisted from the tenure-track academic jobs she applied for. The FBI had kept a file on my mother when she was an antiwar activist back in Detroit in the late sixties—a copy of which she obtained through a Freedom of Information Act request—and ever since then she assumed that the FBI was monitoring her.

My mother was unconventional all the way down to her grading system: she never gave exams and never included a grade with her written comments on papers. At the end of a semester full of discussion and oral presentations, each student wrote up a self-evaluation, discussed it with her, and gave themselves whatever grade they wanted. My mother called it an "honor system," insisting that most students didn't give themselves a higher grade than they deserved. I think she really believed this—she wanted her students to feel empowered, to not have to compete with one another for grades, and

My mother speaking at a Denver feminist
rally in the late 1970s

to not have to relate to her as their grader—but it was also a convenient way to avoid doing all that grading. Students either adored or despised my mother, depending on whether they liked her radical politics and style of teaching, but none of them ever complained about her grading system.

The hub of radical political activism in Denver for my mother was RIP (Radical Information Project) Bookstore on East Seventeenth Avenue where she volunteered. I doubt many books were actually sold there. The place proudly called itself "anti-profit" instead of "nonprofit," and I joked to my mother that they should really call it "anti-money" since they never seemed to have any customers. It was mostly a hangout for local activists who wanted to show political documentaries, hold discussion groups, and organize petitions, fund-raisers, marches, and demonstrations ranging from protests at the Rocky Flats nuclear plant to monthly rallies in front of the state capitol.

In exchange for the nights I sat through anti-imperialist documentaries at RIP, my mother would take me to see second-run Hollywood movies at the old Mayan Theatre on Broadway. Then she was the one struggling to stay awake, unless she had chosen the movie. Her favorite was *Harold and Maude*, perhaps because she identified so closely with Maude, the oddball old lady who has a wild affair at the end of her life with an equally oddball teenager. For my twelfth birthday, I was able to convince my mother to take me to a weekend matinee showing of *Star Wars* on the huge curved screen at the Cooper Theatre, but she fell asleep within a few minutes. Han Solo and Luke Skywalker bravely leading the rebellion against the Empire was apparently not anti-imperialist enough to hold her attention, or maybe it was just that it took place "in a galaxy far, far away" rather than closer to home, where she thought the real revolution needed to happen.

Lesbians Will Lead the Revolution

DESPITE HER CLEAR attraction to men, politically my mother desperately wished she were a lesbian. She had concluded that the lesbian movement, which she saw as the radical vanguard of the feminist movement, would lead the way to a revolution not dominated by men. Almost all of her Denver friends were feminist activists of various types, and most of them were lesbians. They liked to hang out at Woman-to-Woman Bookstore on East Colfax Avenue; my mother taught night seminars on Marxism in the basement to the dozen or so women who showed up. Many lesbian activists admired my mother: she was older, more worldly, spoke Spanish, had a PhD, had been involved in the early feminist movement in Detroit in the sixties, and seemed so self-assured in her political beliefs and commitments.

She gained admirers in the lesbian community after writing an article for the *Big Mama Rag*—a locally produced radical feminist newspaper with national distribution—titled "The Case of the Crumbling Pedestal: No More Domination in Lenin's Name," in which she criticized revolutionaries for deifying Lenin and neglecting the "woman question." The article opened with the line "For the past eight years, I have been doing battle with Vladimir Ilych Lenin and I am finally ready to come out of my heterosexual closet and seek support from other women in facing up to the enigma that Lenin has been in my life." She then went on to recount her long and bitter fights with Raul over Lenin "that I imagine left an indelible political mark on my 9-year-old son, who witnessed it all."

Being a lesbian, my mother had decided, was politically the right thing for a good feminist to be. As she explained it to me, "Lesbians are the purest feminists—they don't have all the hang-ups about pleasing men and attracting men." But she just couldn't bring herself to do it.

"Mom, you're definitely not a lesbian," I said, rolling my eyes at her one night when we got home from bowling with a bunch of her lesbian friends.

"I know, I know," she replied with a sigh, taking her coat off.

For my part, I wondered if some of my mother's lesbian friends weren't secretly in love with her. Kim tried the hardest to talk my mother into giving lesbianism a try, although Kim herself later decided that she also preferred men.

One lesbian couple that befriended us soon after we arrived from Peru, Clair Kaplan and Deb Taylor, became my mother's closest friends in Denver. They always brought over their dog, Jenny, to play with Inca. I'd never seen two dogs more ecstatic to see each other, and I thought to myself that if love existed between dogs then they must certainly be lesbian dogs in love.

In solidarity with women's rights issues, several of the male activists in my mother's orbit formed a Men Against Sexism group, which often met at the house the men shared on Adams Street in Denver's old Capitol Hill neighborhood. The Adams Street house was a popular gathering place for "consciousness raising" meetings that doubled as potluck dinners, to which my mother would often bring me along. I was startled one evening when some of the men in the house announced that they had decided to get vasectomies—which I confused with castration—to show their solidarity with women's liberation and help free women from the chains of child care. Only one of the men actually went through with it, and some suspected that he was just trying to avoid his girlfriend's pressures to have a baby. He had also refused to be a sperm donor to a lesbian couple who wanted a child, telling them that they were not sufficiently committed to radical politics to be worthy of his sperm.

The person I made the deepest connection with at the Adams Street house was one of the organizers of the Men Against Sexism group, a kind and charismatic man named David Gilbert. Unlike some of my mother's other friends, he was not constantly giving political lectures, though one time he did give me a gentle but stern warning about the evils of pornography and how it perpetuated male exploitation of women. "It objectifies women," he explained. "Don't succumb to it like I once did," he warned me with an earnest look, perhaps thinking that I needed to hear that since I was nearing puberty. At that point, I'd never seen anything resembling porn other than the popular pinup calendars of bare-breasted blond women decorating the walls of many restaurants I'd been to in South America.

As a protest against the pornography industry, he and others spray-painted the porn shops on East Colfax Avenue in the middle of the night. On weekends he organized house outings to the mountains for gun-shooting practice in the woods, setting up wooden targets that were made to look like white cops. His day job was moving furniture, but he was secretly a member of the Weather Underground, the armed revolutionary faction of Students for a Democratic Society. A few years later, he ended up going to prison for life for his role in a botched robbery of a Brinks truck that left two policemen and a security guard dead. My mother thought it was terribly unjust that he had to spend the rest of his life in a prison cell but greatly admired that he had sacrificed so much for the cause. All I wanted was for my mother to keep herself out of jail.

Separate from her own personal inclinations, my mother was convinced that lesbians would be essential to the revolution. This was so important to her that it kept her from joining a traditional Marxist-Leninist political party. She sent a strongly worded "Dear Comrades" letter to the Chicago headquarters of the Marxist-Leninist Organizing Committee, criticizing them for not accepting lesbians and gays in the organization and for not acknowledging their critical role in

the political struggle and coming revolution. "I suspect that a proletarian victory of any kind will not happen until these forces are in the
lead," she wrote. "White men from present Marxist-Leninist groups
who can accept the validity of their taking a secondary place in such
an organizational force will be a valuable cadre." She then offered to
personally talk with the vice chairperson of the organization's central
committee about her criticisms and concerns.

The response letter from the "Political Bureau" of the party,
which of course followed the party line, bluntly informed my mother
that "We do not agree with your assessment of white men in the revolutionary struggle." Moreover, "We do not promote homosexuality
among the working class," and "homosexuals are not allowed into
the organization." Nevertheless, "We do not think that this question
is one that should keep comrades outside of the party who are not
practicing homosexuals." And, finally, "We do not think that this
is a matter that requires your speaking to our vice chair." The letter
ended with the words "With revolutionary greetings, Political Bureau, MLOC." This response, predictably, made my mother furious,
and she became even more disillusioned about formally affiliating
with a Marxist-Leninist group.

But my mother's biggest fights over this issue were not with
political party leaders, whom she soon gave up on as hopelessly
backward and homophobic, but with Joel. He was now living in
the Berkeley area again, even though he was no longer comfortable
hanging out with his old hippie friends, who he didn't think were
true revolutionaries. He wrote to us: "When I first got here I got real
depressed. What am I doing in this fake high-class hippie town? I
still feel that way. I'm sick to death of hippyism. It's stinking rotten
decadent." Now in his early twenties and a devout Marxist-Leninist,
Joel worked the night shift on the assembly line at the Fremont GM
automobile factory to pay the rent but mainly to try to get new recruits for the Marxist-Leninist organization he was involved with. As
in her fights with Raul, both my mother and Joel seemed to think

the success of the revolution, which they assumed was just around the corner, depended on who won their endless ideological debates.

My mother and Joel were always trying to convince the other of their own "correct political line." They argued on the phone, they argued by letter, and even Joel's once- or twice-a-year visits were often consumed by their disagreements over feminism and revolutionary strategy. They each had their own distinct critiques of Mao, Stalin, Lenin, and other revolutionary leaders. Joel had replaced Raul as the political debater in my mother's life. My mother's feelings were hurt when Joel didn't want to read the dozens of pages of handwritten notes she took from reading the full forty-five volumes of Lenin, and Joel got offended when my mother poked fun at him for putting so much faith in Enver Hoxha's revolutionary Albania as a model for the rest of the world. "They don't even allow long beards in Albania," she said, laughing dismissively. "Karl Marx had a beard!"

Their single-minded obsession with debating each other began to frustrate me more and more, but my mother took it all in stride. In a P.S. to Joel at the end of one of her letters, she wrote, "I'm so inattentive to Peter these days that he holds me down on the bed to get me to listen to his small talk, says he is going to cut the cord on the phone. He's in good humor about it, though."

The debates between my mother and Joel were perhaps extra intense because they had once been such close political allies; after all, not only had my brother taken my mother's side in the divorce and the custody battle, but in 1977, not long after returning from Peru, they'd collaborated in putting together a booklet denouncing China's new political leadership following Mao's death, and made hundreds of copies to distribute. They called it "a study for the use of Marxist-Leninist comrades," titled *The Capitalist Roaders Are Still on the Capitalist Road: The Two-Line Struggle and the Revisionist Seizure of Power in China*. My mother and Joel had already been leery of Mao's rapprochement with the United States, and after his death they were sure that China was veering dangerously off course—toward global capitalism and away from the more radical self-sufficient communist path originally blazed by Mao—and they wanted to sound the alarm. Rather than putting their names on their booklet, they listed the more authoritative sounding "China Study Group" as the author. They were actually the only members of the group, with our Denver apartment listed as the official address. My mother managed to distribute hundreds of copies at home and abroad, but hundreds more ended up in our closets, gathering dust for years.

One day, after another one of my mother's long arguments on the phone with Joel, I sat on the floor at her feet and asked her the question that I thought would most likely keep her attention. "Who is most radical," I asked, "you or Joel?"

"Well," she paused, trying to figure out the simplest way to answer. "Each of us thinks we are more 'pure Marxist'—Joel because he sees that revolutions were made in Russia and China by a party under centralized control and that's what he wants here, and me because I see that where revolutions were made under centralized control, women and minorities, who were the most exploited, didn't come into power."

Seeing the puzzled look on my face, my mother went on. "Your brother has organized political forces behind him. I'm more radical because I'm the one swimming against the tide—but not against the tide of history!"

"Oh, okay, you're each more radical in your own way," I said, regretting my choice of subject.

"Here, I'll let your brother speak for himself." My mother opened her desk drawer and handed me a letter from Joel in which he laid out their differences, emphasizing how wrong my mother was to focus on the "bourgeois lesbian movement."

Dear Andrea,
    It is deeply disturbing but undeniable that our differences are major. I consciously identify with the

Marxist-Leninist movement and ideology that has been
developed by Marx, Engels, the Paris Commune, the
October Revolution, Lenin, Stalin, the Chinese and
Albanian revolutions, Mao Tse-tung, and Enver Hoxha,
as a movement and ideology which is and will lead the
world proletariat and the whole world to communism.

   I believe you have an incorrect outlook that you have
carried from bourgeois aspects of the women's movement
that has been strengthened by your sinking roots in the
lesbian community in Denver. You have conciliated,
more and more, to friends in the lesbian movement who
take a cultural separatist and fundamentally bourgeois
outlook, look at all Marxist-Leninist groups in this
country and around the world as consolidated male
chauvinist groups, oppose looking at capitalism as the
primary enemy and put the woman question above the
class question and aim the main blow at patriarchy,
and now apparently are looking towards a woman's
communist party or a woman-initiated communist party.

"Your brother's problem," my mother said with a sigh, "is he
always thinks he's figured it all out." She laughed. "I succeeded in
turning my oldest son into a communist, but I totally failed to turn
him into a feminist." And then she added with a smile, "It will sure
be interesting to see how you'll turn out, Peter. Who knows, maybe
not a communist or a feminist! I just hope you won't become a total
conformist like your father." That was my mother's real fear. She said
this to me without even a hint of bitterness or resentment toward my
father. At this point, with the divorce long behind her, it was more
like she felt sorry for him somehow, as if he, too, had been duped
by the system. One of my mother's life missions was to make sure I
avoided a similar fate.

Don't Vote!

TUESDAY, NOVEMBER 2, 1976, was Election Day, including at Denver's Lincoln Elementary School. The excitement had been building for weeks as students prepared their campaign speeches, buttons, banners, signs, and posters. Teachers, administrators, and students of all grades would gather for a special assembly in the school auditorium that afternoon. It was Jimmy Carter vs. Gerald Ford.

My mother had enrolled me in fifth grade at Lincoln as soon as we arrived from Peru, in time for the fall term. I was so eager to be accepted as an American, to fit in, that I swore off speaking Spanish and didn't tell anyone we had just moved from Peru. But I had other strikes against me: I was too old for fifth grade—at eleven, I should have been in sixth—and worse, during the first week of school, my classmates noticed all the white specks in my hair, the lice eggs that I had brought with me from Peru.

It turned out that lice treatments actually work if none of the other students have lice. Once I used the special shampoo, I was finally lice-free. But the sound of the students snickering as they pointed fingers at me those first few days in school rang in my ears for months afterward.

When I told my mother that everyone at school was busily preparing for Election Day and that there would be a special event to celebrate it, she squinted at me across the dinner table. "The elections are a sham," she said, picking up her fork.

My enthusiasm suddenly deflated.

"All they do is perpetuate ruling-class domination. They trick people into thinking they can work within the system. But the system must be smashed, and that means we need a real revolution."

I picked at my broccoli.

"Participating in American elections is about reform rather than revolution," she said.

I could tell by the way she said it that *reform* was a bad word. Anyway, if reform was opposed to revolution, it had to be terrible.

She reminded me of the U.S.-supported coup in Chile, after Allende had tried revolution through elections. And she explained how Democrats and Republicans are both parties for the rich, though the Democrats make more of an effort to pretend otherwise. I told my mother I didn't know much about Carter or Ford, other than that one was a Democrat and the other was a Republican.

"Don't worry about that," my mother said. "There's no real difference between them."

"So you're saying the elections are for dupes and sellouts?"

"Yes, exactly!" She leaned back in her chair. "Now you understand."

My mother always said that there were three types of people in the world: dupes of the system, sellouts to the system, and those who fight the system by converting the dupes and denouncing the sellouts.

At first, my mother wanted to keep me at home on Election Day as a sort of boycott or protest. I was all for playing hooky. But then she came up with another idea.

When the big day came, I was brimming with confidence, delighted that, unlike my teachers, my classmates, and their parents, I had escaped the dangers of "false consciousness." Being "in the know" politically made me feel special, and also made me feel sorry for those who didn't recognize the evils of the system and the need to bring it down.

The school hallways were decorated in red, white, and blue. After lunch, everyone gathered in the auditorium. Students brought banners and signs from home that their parents had helped them make, with large bold lettering: VOTE FOR CARTER!, VOTE FOR FORD!, CARTER-MONDALE '76! None of us could actually vote, of course. But no matter: we were being groomed to be future voters.

I proudly unfurled my cardboard banner, which my mother and I had made the night before, and held it high above my head. The banner had only two words painted in bright red capital letters: DON'T VOTE!

Jaws dropped. Heads turned. My teachers looked either terribly disappointed or mildly amused. Some of my classmates simply looked puzzled.

Perhaps I should have expected that reaction, but I didn't care. For one moment, after more than two months of doing my very best to fit in and be accepted as a normal American kid, I tossed that all aside. As my whole school stared, I simply grinned and held my head up high and wished my mother could have seen me. She would have been so proud of her radical little boy.

Playing Hooky

I LIKED SCHOOL, but I didn't always feel like going. Whenever I told my mother I wanted to stay home, she never asked why; when the school called to inquire about my whereabouts, my mother gave me a wink as she explained to the receptionist, "Peter isn't feeling well today." Sometimes she simply said, "Peter has decided to sleep in, which is fine with me." Occasionally, I would even walk right out of school during the mid-day recess if I felt like it, knowing that when the school called home my mother would vouch for me. To an eleven-year-old, this made her the best mom in the world.

She didn't believe in strict rules at home, either, or even loose rules, for that matter. As had been true in South America, she had total faith in me, perhaps knowing that the last thing in the world I wanted to do was betray her trust. I never had a curfew or a bedtime. I never got into trouble anyway, which I suppose gave her extra confidence about her no-rules rule. My mother's attitude was that she could count on me to be responsible, use good judgment, and do the right thing. Then again, she didn't give me a lot of tips about what exactly that meant. She never said a word to me about sex education or staying away from drugs or alcohol.

My mother didn't see herself as an authority figure in my life; she saw me as her accomplice and best friend. In fact, she seemed to get a little thrill from being complicit in my defiance of authority. Of course, she wanted me to learn the basics of reading, writing, and arithmetic, but, as she always told me, she thought mainstream education socialized kids to be obedient conformists. She never looked at my report cards or even asked about my grades—she refused to grade her own students, after all. So I never tried to impress my mother with my schoolwork and never took it personally that she showed no interest in the fact that I was doing well in my classes.

My mother's worst fears about students being turned into sellouts were realized when the Denver Public School System launched the Adopt-A-School program, in which giant corporations like Coors, Exxon, and Chevron provided services such as career counseling and tutoring. Desperate for new funds and resources, my teachers supported the program, but my mother was appalled that corporate America was invading the classroom. She condemned the involvement of special interests in an article in the Denver weekly, *Westword*, titled "Adopt-A-School, Co-opt A Student? Denver Public Schools Teach Children the ABC's of Big Business." She followed that piece up with another in Denver's *Rocky Mountain News*, titled "Big Business Feeding Propaganda to School Kids."

Shortly after these articles were published, my English teacher, Ms. Johnson, stopped me as I was leaving class one day. She peered at me through her large round glasses. "Your mother just doesn't appreciate a helping hand," she said, reaching up to push her glasses closer to her face. "What's her problem?"

I didn't know how to reply and didn't feel like arguing with my teacher anyway. So I just put on a smile and shrugged my shoulders.

My favorite time to skip classes was when it snowed. The more snow, the better. After asking my mother to call in sick for me on days with some snowfall, I would go door-to-door through the neighborhood, offering to shovel steps and walkways and driveways for a buck or two. At the end of the day, I'd blow all my money on pinball machines. Sometimes I would coax a friend or two to go shoveling with me, although it wasn't as easy for them to skip school. But I knew I could always count on Robert Vega, who lived a few blocks away, to play hooky with me; he hated school, was barely passing, and missed classes all the time. He probably thought I was also getting in trouble by playing hooky when it snowed, not realizing my mother was in on it, and I never told him. A few years later, Robert Vega would be the one to almost get me in trouble.

My mother herself was sometimes the reason I skipped school. If we got home late from one of her evening political events we would both be tired the next morning. She would wake up, make breakfast, and call in sick for me. Then we would both go back to bed.

I usually made sure not to skip more than one day in a row, not wanting my teachers to be suspicious. But one time my mother took me out of class for an entire week. It was November 1977, right in the middle of the fall term. We spent that week in court.

My mother had been arrested the day before my twelfth birthday. She was picketing at the main gate of the Adolph Coors Brewery Company in Golden, Colorado. More than a thousand brewery workers had been on strike since April, protesting racial discrimination and forced polygraph testing of employees, among other things, and my mother was eager to organize it. The Coors strike brought together an eclectic coalition of labor, environmental, gay-lesbian, and social justice activists. Members of the Coors family were outspoken backers of right-wing causes, which made Coors the company that everyone on the left loved to hate, my mother most of all (secretly, years earlier, she and Raul had fantasized about kidnapping Joseph Coors and forcing him to "listen day and night to a recording of helicopter, police car noises, and other highly selective tortures"). My brother Joel even joined the cause long-distance by drawing an anti-Coors comic book, which was handed out at rallies and other strike events.

In a speech at a brewery workers' rally in front of the state capitol building, my mother told the cheering crowd:

Cover of my brother Joel's comic book in
support of the Coors strike

It's not just our ANGER at Joe Coors and his lie de-
tector tests and forced physicals and harassment of
workers and of minority people in the community
that's keeping us together. It's our HOPE that working
people can take their lives in their own hands—that
they can, in building up their own power as workers,
take power away from those who only use it against
the people. Anger is enough to make people go out
on strike, but without hope, and the organization and
discipline that hope inspires, we can't win the strike, or
the larger battles that we all face as working people. The
coalition that community people have formed is dedi-
cated to keeping alive that hope and helping build that

organization and discipline. The courage of the strikers in voting to stay out on strike even when money has run out inspires us to a greater sense of unity. Many of us in the coalition are living with meager resources, too, and working on the faith that the sacrifices we make now will help create a better life in the future for ourselves, for our children, and for all our sisters and brothers who are living in fear of losing their jobs or who are tired of being made to work intolerably long hours and under intolerable conditions just to keep some rich man's pockets lined with gold.

Que viva la lucha!

Hasta la victoria siempre!

For six months, my mother made the strike her full-time passion as a coordinator of the Coors Boycott and Strike Support Coalition. In early July, she and four members of the coalition were arrested and charged with "harassment, resistance, and trespassing." The cops claimed they had crossed ten to fifteen feet inside the Coors property line and refused to leave, although my mother insisted that the whole thing was fabricated, that the local police were in cahoots with Coors to harass and disrupt the protesters. The trial date was set for November.

I couldn't wait. Not only would I get to skip school for days but I would get to see my mother take on the evil empire of the Coors Brewing Company. It never occurred to me that if she was found guilty, my mother could end up going to jail; for her part, she didn't seem worried, either. She was energized by the coming fight.

When we arrived that first morning of the trial, a picket line of protesters stood yelling slogans and waving BOYCOTT COORS! signs in front of the Jefferson County Courthouse. They cheered my mother on as she walked up the steps, with me proudly by her side. I felt like a celebrity; some local press was there. Inside, the courtroom was packed. I sat up front with my mother's activist friends. There was a lot of camaraderie in that room. Unlike the last time I had been at a courthouse—during my parents' custody battle—this felt more like a party. I thought to myself, *What would my father say if he could see me now?* He worked as a contract negotiator for a big union, so presumably he would have been supportive of the Coors strike, but he certainly wouldn't have approved of my skipping school. And he would have distrusted, on principle, anything my mother was involved in.

Contrary to my expectations, though, the trial dragged on tediously, through the jury selection and cross-examination. I doodled in my notebook, daydreamed, and even nodded off, except when the proceedings focused on my mother. In addition to the trespassing charge, the prosecution accused her of screaming, "Stick it up your fucking ass!" to the police and the security guards. As soon as they made this allegation, everyone who knew my mother burst out laughing. My mother could yell in a picket line as loudly as anyone, but she never swore. No one, including me, had ever heard her use

With my mother at the Coors strike trial in Golden, Colorado, November 1977

the F word. Maybe she said "bullshit" on occasion, but even that was pushing it. There was no way this was true.

To kill time during the courtroom breaks and intermissions, I strutted up to the front, stood behind the podium, and pretended I was a trial lawyer. "Your Honor, I would like to call Andrea Gabriel to the witness stand. Ms. Gabriel, is it true that you are an anti-capitalist, God-hating, homo-loving communist agitator?"

"Well, yes, I am, and proud of it," I said, switching to a defiant falsetto. All those hanging out in the room during the break, including my mother, laughed and cheered me on.

I switched to the defense: "Your Honor, I would now like to call Mr. Joseph Coors, president of the Coors Brewing Company, to the witness stand. Mr. Coors, is it true that you are a fat capitalist pig who hates homosexuals, communists, and labor unions?"

"Well, yes, I am, and proud of it."

Everyone laughed and cheered me on even louder, though the stuffy prosecuting attorneys returning from the break didn't seem to find it all that amusing.

Impersonating a court lawyer during the
recess at my mother's Coors strike trial in
Golden, Colorado, November 1977

In the end, none of the charges could stick. At the conclusion of the weeklong trial, all of the defendants were acquitted and the case was dismissed. The defendants held their fists up high for the celebration group photo.

My mother felt triumphant. As soon as she got home, she typed up her own statement to the media, with "PRESS RELEASE!!!" in bold caps at the top, declaring that the effort by Coors to intimidate strikers and their supporters had backfired, and that, regardless of the ultimate outcome of the strike, the workers were part of a "growing movement against the totalitarian practices in the industry, and they will be seasoned in the struggle for working class solidarity." I never saw that any news outlets picked up on that press release, but I do know that the next day I finally, reluctantly, went back to school.

Gun Crazy

BOYCOTTING EVIL CORPORATIONS like Coors was one thing, but my mother firmly believed that it would ultimately take armed struggle to destroy capitalism. That's why she not only tolerated but encouraged my brief love affair with guns. I first learned to handle a real gun with real bullets in the basement of Al's Pool Hall on Broadway, a half mile or so from home. I was in the sixth grade. I often stopped at Al's on the weekends or on my way home from school to shoot a few rounds of pool or play pinball until I ran out of money. I then replenished my supply by helping myself to the loose coins at the bottom of my mother's purse.

Many of the teenagers from the neighborhood—kids a few years older than me—hung out at Al's, killing time, quarter by quarter. Al, the sixty-something, chain-smoking owner, sat silently in the back and watched customers come and go. His friend Clyde was a regular. A short pudgy man with a potbelly and greasy, graying hair, he bore a notable resemblance to Manuel Noriega and treated kids to free games of pool.

As a friend of Al's, Clyde had a special privilege: access to the makeshift shooting range set up in the basement. The kids who hung out with Clyde not only got free pool games but also shooting lessons. After we played pool and did target practice with his .22-caliber rifles, Clyde would sometimes give us rides home in his black Cadillac Fleetwood with shiny black leather seats and sharkfin taillights. It was bigger and fancier than any car I had ever been in, a classy Batmobile. Once in a while, Clyde also took us in his big black cruiser to go bowling, see a movie, or play miniature golf.

I liked Clyde's attention and all the free fun things to do that came with it. He spoke at length about reincarnation, what our auras looked like, finding past lives through hypnosis, extrasensory perception, the writings of Edgar Cayce, and extraterrestrial visitors. "The aliens are everywhere around us, impersonating humans," Clyde warned us during one ride to the movies, adding, "I was abducted by aliens once, but only briefly." Clyde also claimed that he was a member of "The Clan," a vast, secretive old extended-family network that ruthlessly protected its members and stretched across the western United States and into Mexico. He said he could see the future and knew that he was going to die in the year 2025. Part of me believed him, but part of me also thought he was nuts.

My mother knew about Clyde, but she never really asked anything about him, what he did for a living, where he was from, whether he had a family. I suppose she thought that I needed a father figure, which was certainly true. She saw that I liked to do things that cost money even though I didn't have any of my own. The one time my mother met Clyde, she hit him up for a donation for one of her political causes. I was embarrassed by my mother's forwardness, but Clyde didn't seem to mind. He gave her twenty bucks. He wanted my mother to like him, and my mother wanted him to support her cause.

One day at the shooting range, Clyde brought out a .22-caliber Ruger, a carbon black pistol that resembled a WWII-era German Luger. He told me I could use it for target practice whenever I liked. It was sleek and shiny and beautiful. It had a nice heft to it, heavy but not too heavy. Nothing like the flimsy plastic toy pistols I had played with before. I could not wait to use it.

Clyde even let me take it home. Problem was, I hadn't yet told my mother about my new love of guns. "There's a shooting range for target practice in the basement of Al's pool hall," I said to her casually over breakfast. "Clyde has been teaching some of us how to shoot." I held my breath, waiting for her reaction.

She was scanning that morning's *Rocky Mountain News*, scissors in hand, ready to clip any article of political interest. "That's nice," she said. "Just be careful."

I could barely hide my relief and excitement. I tried not to think about how my pacifist father would have reacted. He hated guns, and would have been horrified that I was anywhere near them.

Later, I showed my mother the Ruger pistol, displaying it for her on our kitchen table. It turned out that my mother was actually supportive of my gun obsession. "Ah, I see," she said as I rattled off the key specs. "You know, learning to use a gun will prove handy for when the revolution comes." This was the same person who less than a decade earlier had led a campaign to abolish war toys. In between, the pacifist Mennonite had become a Marxist revolutionary.

My mother didn't even seem to mind that I kept the gun in my bedroom upstairs. As always, she trusted me. On weekends, she sometimes drove me to the mountains so I could shoot at bottles and cans in the woods. She never wanted to shoot, hold, or even touch the gun herself—maybe it was the last bit of Mennonite left in her. And for as much as I loved it myself, I was glad she was uninterested. Otherwise, I thought, she might be tempted to run off and join some guerrilla group somewhere and get herself killed.

Joel, who was living in the Bay Area, heard about my interest in guns and sent me a used copy of the *Shooters Bible* for my birthday. Like my mother, he wanted to give me useful skills for the coming violent overthrow of the ruling class. I pored over the hundreds of pages of pictures and the detailed descriptions of guns of all shapes and sizes, from revolvers to rifles to shotguns. Barrel length, caliber, weight, features—all the specs were there. It was like pornography for a prepubescent boy. I kept it by my bedside.

In the winter of 1978, halfway through sixth grade, I woke up late at night to the sounds of a drunk man shouting and pounding on a door downstairs. It was our neighbor Diane's ex-husband. Diane was screaming through the door that she would call the police if he didn't go away. He persisted, and started threatening to kill Diane if she didn't open the door.

This was not a good moment for a twelve-year-old boy to have a loaded gun in his bedroom. I suppose I wanted to play the hero. I grabbed the Ruger, tiptoed from my bedroom in my underwear, and slowly made my way down the stairs to the first floor. I stopped halfway, sat on a step, and leaned against the wall, my heart pounding. I thought, *Okay, I'll just yell out to him that I have a gun and that he should leave.* I told myself that would be enough to get him out; I would never have to use the gun or even point it at him.

Meanwhile, Diane kept crying and her ex kept pounding, yelling, "You fuckin' bitch, I'll kill you if you don't open this fuckin' door right now, let me in."

I kept wondering if he would really kill her, and what would happen if he broke down the door. Despite my mother's long-standing hatred of the police, I kept hoping they would come and stop him. I crept down a few more steps, then stopped again, trying to steady the gun in my trembling hands. It felt heavy and unwieldy. The police were nowhere to be seen. But suddenly, just as I was getting up the nerve to confront him, silence descended. A car door slammed, tires squealed, and he was gone.

Overcome with relief, I sat frozen for a few minutes before quietly crawling back upstairs to my room, hoping no one had seen or heard me. There was no sign of my mother, and I wondered if she had somehow managed to sleep through the whole thing or perhaps wasn't even at home. But I was so wound up that I could not fall back to sleep. I sat in bed with that black .22 Ruger still in my hand, waving it around, fantasizing that I had bravely come to Diane's rescue. I took the small bullets out of the clip and rolled them around in my sweaty palm, thinking the empty pistol was now safe to play with. Tossing the gun from hand to hand, I even briefly put the gun to my head, put my finger on the trigger, and almost pulled it.

It suddenly occurred to me that there might still be a bullet in the magazine. I checked and, sure enough, there it was.

I never told my mother what had happened that night, but the next day I gave Clyde his gun back, stopped hanging out at the pool hall and the firing range in the basement, and never touched a firearm again.

VII.

TEEN YEARS

I want "the revolution" but I want a secure home and community, too. Future is scary. Poor innocent Peter, dreaming of going to elite college, and having trouble keeping on top of class assignments, and no time to learn ordinary skills like building and mechanics.

—Carol Andreas, 1980

Stealing from the Rich

MY MOTHER WAS arrested on my thirteenth birthday, a year and a day after her previous arrest. She was trying to find a present for me at Cinderella City Mall in Englewood, a Denver suburb. We arrived at the entrance of JC Penney's. "You wait here," she instructed. "I'll be right back with your birthday gift."

So I waited, and then waited some more, staring into the store windows and admiring the expensive-looking Seiko and Bulova watches and other items on display. After a half hour or so I went in to look for my mother. There she was, in the boys' department, near the jeans section, being detained at the counter and then, as I watched, escorted out by mall security guards.

This was not the first time that my mother had shoplifted, but it was the first time she had been caught.

My mother hated the mall, a concentrated form of everything she despised about America's materialist consumer culture. On the rare occasion that she did step inside a mall, she considered it a matter of principle to strike a blow, however tiny, at corporate America. She usually helped herself to small items, typically clothing, which she would slip underneath her coat or into her purse. As she explained it to me, it was only fair to take back from the capitalists who shamelessly robbed and exploited the poor. This was a convenient philosophy, given that otherwise we could rarely afford new clothes. Shoplifting gave us an alternative to the Salvation Army or other thrift stores.

Except for the stressful anticipation of the court date, I barely questioned my mother's shoplifting, though I would have been mortified if my friends had known. Neither explanation—that we were so poor that my mother had to steal, or that she was so mad at corporate America that she had to steal—would have helped my social status in junior high. But luckily, though I happily accepted her stolen gifts, I was never tempted to follow in my mother's footsteps.

Years earlier, when we lived in Berkeley before moving to South America, I had gone on a candy-stealing spree with my friend Garrett. We came home with an impressive stash of chocolate bars and several packs of bubble gum. It felt as if Halloween had arrived early that year. But as I was sorting through the illicit candy hoard spread out all over my bed, my mother walked in on me. I immediately confessed, and she gave me such a harsh scolding that I never shoplifted again. On her orders, I threw all the candy in the trash, though I did manage to sneak a few bars out of the garbage bin late that night.

Tempting as it was, I didn't remind her of her double standard when she explained to me the virtues of her politically correct shoplifting, perhaps because I was a beneficiary of her crimes. Did she see stealing candy as less legitimate than stealing clothing, or had her attitude toward shoplifting simply loosened and evolved from those Berkeley days? One thing I knew was that my mother would have been unhappy if I was the one who had been arrested for shoplifting.

My mother's arrest was in early July, but she wouldn't have to appear in court until October. Unlike with the Coors battle, we were both dreading that date, counting down the days until she would have to face the consequences. But when the day finally arrived, the shoplifting gods had mercy on my mother: we were the only ones who showed up, so the charges were automatically dropped.

After that, I'd imagined my mother's shoplifting days were over. But then Christmas came, and we headed to Sears on the weekend. Once again, I found myself waiting outside, staring absently at the fancy watches in the display window. Finally she came out with a long dark green wool scarf tucked away deep in her purse. Every day that winter I wore that scarf as a warm reminder of what my mother was willing to risk for me.

The Bout

BEING CALLED A "*Yanqui* gringo" and teased for my long hair had been a warm-up to more than a few fistfights in South America. I learned to stand up for myself, taking punches and throwing some back. Maybe I'd absorbed some of that Peruvian machismo. I thought my fist-fighting days were behind me when my mother and I moved back to the States, but Joey Gallegos changed that. Joey was a skinny little Chicano kid with a big mouth who seemed to constantly be getting into fights. Maybe it was just my turn when, midway through seventh grade at Baker Junior High, I bumped into him by accident in the hallway. The only two things that Joey and I had in common were the big fat Goody combs sticking out of our back jeans pockets (a necessity for 1978's perfectly feathered hair) and our crush on Jessica Duran.

"Fuckin' honky," Joey yelled at me as we passed each other in the hall.

I turned and countered, "Hey, fuck you, too."

That was enough to set Joey off. He spun around and strutted toward me. Joey and I went through the ritual of circling each other and shoving and throwing insults, but as a crowd began to form, Mr. Campbell, the gym teacher, arrived to break it up.

Mr. Campbell didn't give us the expected lecture about not fighting and threatening to send us to the principal's office. Instead, he simply instructed us to meet him at the gym right after school. When we got there, he was waiting for us with a smile. He handed us each a pair of boxing gloves, and seemed to enjoy the surprised looks on our faces. "Put these on," he said. "You want to fight? All right then, here's your chance. Beat each other's brains out, but you have to play by my rules. No kicking. No hitting below the waist. One continuous round until one of you drops or gives up. Got it?" And then he added, "Oh, and I already called your parents to get their permission and tell them you'd be home a little late today."

I wondered how my mother could have possibly approved. Didn't she distrust authority figures in schools? And wasn't boxing an example of the "macho male culture" she always complained about? But maybe, like when she'd approved of my short-lived gun obsession, my mother thought this would be a good experience to harden me up for the coming revolution. Either way, I knew my father would have disapproved. He didn't like sports, and I imagined he would dislike a violent sport like boxing most of all.

Mr. Campbell led us to the middle of the empty gym. He sat on a folding chair and leaned back to watch the entertainment. Joey and I stood there awkwardly, not sure exactly what to do. "Here, let me help you with those," Mr. Campbell said amiably, reaching out to tie the laces on our gloves. The padded gloves seemed comfy, but I knew from watching boxers on TV that they could do serious damage.

I looked at Joey. I was a lot taller, and had longer arms, but he was quicker. I wondered if he had ever done any real boxing before. Probably not, I thought. Hopefully not. "Go on, what are you waiting for?" Mr. Campbell egged us on.

Joey and I began to circle each other, figuring we ought to do something, just as we had in the busy hallway. This time, there were no insults exchanged, or friends to cheer us on or to intervene if things got too out of hand. There was only silence, and Mr. Campbell watching gleefully from his chair. "Come on," he said impatiently, "I want to see some good boxing."

And so we boxed, lunging at each other clumsily, arms flailing, trying to put on a show for our audience of one. We stopped at one point and looked at each other. Joey's jet-black hair was wet with sweat. I looked at his equally black eyes, trying to read his mind. Was he frightened? Tired? I couldn't tell. But this whole boxing thing was not much fun, and as we grew tired, we threw fewer and fewer punches. I didn't care so much about beating Joey, but I definitely didn't want to be the first to give up. *What would Jessica Duran think?*

Finally, Mr. Campbell intervened when neither of us would fold. He stepped between us and said, "That's enough, boys. Let's get those gloves off and shake hands."

Fifteen minutes had passed, maybe longer. Maybe Mr. Campbell was in a hurry to get home, maybe he thought he had taught us enough of a lesson, maybe he simply got bored. I was relieved that it was over. No one had "won" the match, and there were no knockdowns or knockouts, but neither of us minded. That was the last time I got into a fistfight. Joey and I kept a respectful distance in the hallways, and from then on we always gave each other a knowing smile.

When I got home that afternoon, my mother was clipping articles as usual. She looked over at me and saw my fat lip.

"Mmm. Someone from school called earlier, said something about boxing. You all right?" She didn't ask if I had won or lost. I didn't expect her to.

"Yeah, I'm fine, just a swollen lip and a sore jaw, no big deal."

"Did you use any of the karate moves Raul taught you?" This was the first time my mother had brought up his name in a while.

"No, Mom, it's boxing, not karate—no kicking allowed."

"Ah, that's probably good," she said, and reached up to clip a new article.

Surfacing

I'M NOT SURE when I started to call my father "Carl," the way my brothers did, but it must have been around the first time I contacted him after almost three years in hiding. Now barely a teenager, I was eager to be treated like a grown-up and to demonstrate my independence. I was determined that there would never be another tug-of-war battle over the "Peter problem." I was living with my mother, Denver was my home, I would stay there, and that was that.

But even so, I wanted to see my father. It just didn't feel right to continue living in hiding and be so completely cut off. In early December, my mother finally, reluctantly agreed that I could contact my father and Rosalind, just in time for Christmas.

We came up with a plan: for a few days over the holidays, I would visit my father and Rosalind in Michigan, with Joel flying in from California, and we would keep secret where I lived. Joel and I would connect through Chicago to Detroit so that they would not figure out my point of origin.

I sent my father and Rosalind a short letter via Joel, the first contact since we had returned to the United States.

> *Dear Carl and Rosalind,*
> *I am planning on coming to visit you for Christmas with Joel!! I will be arriving on the same flight as Joel. I haven't seen you in three years so I thought it would be a good enough time to now! I would like a letter from you though that says that you will not try to keep me there*

or try to get me back in any way whatsoever. I want to
make it clear to you that I don't want you to know where
I live. I am very happy that I am going to see you at
Christmas!
    Love,
    Peter Andreas

    PS: You can send your response to Joel

Reading that letter again now, I realize how badly those lines must have hurt. They may have assumed that my mother composed it for me, but I wrote it by myself.

All I cared about at the time was being able to reconnect with my father and Rosalind without risk, and to finally enjoy a real Christmas again. After moving to Denver from Peru, we even avoided visiting Grandpa Rich in nearby Kansas, though he knew we were back in the country. North Newton was too small a town, and word would have spread rapidly. So we stayed put, hiding out in Denver, with no Christmas tree with presents underneath, no feast, no family gathering. Nothing at all. My mother treated it like any other day, except most things were closed and there was no school. She always got me something for Christmas, but it was frequently shoplifted, never wrapped, and she often gave it to me early. My mother, if asked about her religion, liked to tell people she was a pagan and worshipped the Andean earth goddess Pachamama; to her, Christmas was an unfortunate name for the winter solstice and had been taken over by consumer capitalism.

As it turned out, my father actually knew we were back in the country; he just wasn't entirely sure where we lived. He had caught a glimpse of my mother on an August 7, 1978, ABC evening news story on the antinuclear protests outside the Diablo Canyon nuclear plant in California. He immediately contacted the sheriff of San Luis Obispo County, informing him that there had been a warrant for my mother's arrest. It was indeed my mother he saw on the news that evening yelling and carrying a protest sign, but she just happened to be visiting friends in California that week.

My father also had other clues that we were no longer out of the country. Grandma Andreas had sent me a $10 check, via Joel, for my thirteenth birthday that July. When Grandma received the copy of her deposited check back—stamped deposited at First National Bank in Denver, and signed "Andrea Gabriel"—she immediately notified my father. But he had no idea who Andrea Gabriel was. With my brother Joel as intermediary, I sent a thank-you note to Grandma for the birthday check and tried to give her the impression that we were still somewhere in rural Peru by writing, "Our corn is growing ears now." We weren't even living near any cornfields.

Despite his earlier persistence, though, my father didn't balk at my insistence that they not try to get me back. Maybe he understood that I was too old now to be his little boy, no matter what right he had legally. Back when I was ten, my father could have won me over—and had started to do just that—but by now that battle had been lost. My father and Rosalind wrote to Joel that they would welcome a visit from us, and that they had no intention of trying to keep me there.

And so my brother and I met at Chicago's O'Hare airport to catch a connecting flight together to Detroit. My flight from Denver arrived first, so I waited for Joel's plane to come in from San Francisco. I was glad I'd have my brother with me for this first visit to Michigan, and so was my mother. He'd make sure there would be no talk of me staying there and no trash-talking about my mother.

"Hey, Peter," Joel greeted me with a wave and a smile when he got off the plane. Joel had cleaned up—he now wore shoes, and no longer wore colorful tie-dyed shirts—but his sandy-brown hair was still nearly down to his shoulders, and his political views were more radical than ever. As we waited for our Eastern Airlines flight to Detroit, Joel asked me, "So, Peter, are you sure you're ready for this?"

"Yeah," I said. "It'll be okay. Just glad you'll be there."

When we stepped off the plane, I saw my father and Rosalind waving at us from the gate. My father had clearly aged; though he still had a full head of hair, it was grayer than before. Rosalind looked exactly the same. We walked up to them. "Well, hello, Peter," my father said, sticking out his right hand awkwardly, then leaning forward to give me a stiff one-armed hug with his left arm. My father was never much into hugs or public displays of affection, though I could tell by his watery eyes that he was happy to see me. And I was certainly happy to see him.

"Hello there, you two!" Rosalind chimed in cheerfully. "We're so glad you *both* could make it."

"How was your flight? Make your connection all right?" my father asked without asking where we had connected from. "Good that the weather cooperated." This was a big moment best handled by small talk.

"Yeah, everything went fine," Joel said, giving both my father and Rosalind a hug.

When we got to the house, all the trappings of Christmas were on display—the little red-and-white-checkered birdhouse tree ornament I had made weeks before my mother kidnapped me dangled from the colorfully decorated tree in the living room, with shiny, perfectly wrapped presents underneath. There was my old red-and-white wool Christmas stocking, with my name embroidered on it, hanging from the fireplace. It was, in so many ways, just as I'd imagined all those years ago, on the run in Peru.

At the dinner table that first night there, my father asked me safe, polite questions. "So, Peter, how is school? What grade are you in now?" He made sure not to ask where school was exactly, or even in what country.

"I'm in seventh grade. It's okay."

Rosalind joined the conversation. "Do you have a favorite subject?"

"Social studies."

"Hmmm." My father mumbled, "Just don't become one of those crazy sociologists."

Rosalind gave him a sharp look and reached over to squeeze his hand.

My father then continued. "Do you also take more practical classes, like woodworking? I remember enjoying that when I was in seventh grade."

After a long pause, Rosalind asked, "So what else are you interested in, in school?"

Before I could answer, my father jumped back in. "How about photography?"

"Nah, I don't have a camera, anyway."

My father sighed. "Well, I suppose you're still a little too young for that." He then leaned back in his chair, putting his hands together behind his head. "I remember, during my sophomore year at Bethel, I was the president of the camera club. Maybe you'll get interested in that sort of thing when you're in college."

I nodded. That was the first time anyone had ever mentioned college to me. My father noticed my hesitation.

"You are planning on going to college, aren't you? We've still been putting money into an educational trust fund for you. Not that your mother is going to help at all with that." Rosalind shot my father another stern look.

Despite the awkwardness, spending time with my father and Rosalind after three years in hiding made me feel normal, even if temporarily.

As always, my father did the dishes—it was the one kitchen task he was fastidious about—so my brother and I took turns standing next to him and drying. He disapproved of using the dishwasher, claiming it to be lazy and wasteful, and therefore insisted on washing everything by hand.

Afterward, my father showed me my old room. "See, it's just like you left it, Peter," he said to me as he opened the door. It was true. It looked exactly the same as I remembered. There was my Hot Wheels car collection in the blue and yellow plastic carrying case, though I was now too old to play with them. Grandma's beautiful handmade quilt still covered the bed. The maple desk that I had used to do my homework on was still there, too, against the wall across from my bed.

Everyone stayed on their best behavior during our few days there, eager to get along. There were no arguments except for a brief intense exchange, in hushed voices, between my father and brother off to the side, which I assumed was about my mother. Rosalind had no doubt carefully coached my father not to make disparaging comments about my mother, which must have been hard for him. To my relief, there was no talk of going to church. Instead, we stayed home on Sunday and played Risk for hours and hours, just as we had during Christmas in Kansas years before.

For a moment during that Christmas visit I fantasized about what it might have been like if I'd stayed living there with my father and Rosalind back in the fall of '75, in that big, comfortable suburban house with its huge windows overlooking the trees. And then I wondered what it might be like if I stayed there now. But then I thought about my mother; our beautiful dog, Inca; my teachers and classmates at school; the streets of Denver. Since coming back from Peru, the city had finally begun to feel like home. We'd only been there for a little more than two years, but that was longer than I had lived anywhere else since leaving Michigan at the age of five. I'd also turned into more of a city kid and had a hard time imagining living in the suburban sprawl where one had to drive to get anywhere.

While my father and Rosalind waited with Joel and me at the Detroit airport to catch our return flight a few days after Christmas, Rosalind leaned over and gently whispered into my ear, "Peter, we know you and your mother are living in Denver. It's okay. We've accepted that. You don't have to worry. We just want to see you. Maybe you can come for a longer visit next time, maybe next summer?"

I liked that idea a lot, and nodded. I was taken aback that they knew where we lived, but I was also grateful I no longer had to worry about hiding and keeping our location secret. I began to hope that I might finally achieve my version of normal. We all hugged good-bye.

As I said my good-byes and squeezed my father's soft hand, I felt both sadness and a rush of relief. For the first time that I could remember, I held some control over my own life. I was now no longer simply a rope pulled by my mother and father. My mother had yanked the rope out of my father's hands almost three years earlier, but now the tug-of-war was over. I wanted to live in Denver with my mother, and could, on my own, insist on keeping it that way, but I also longed for a real connection to my father and Rosalind, which was now possible again. As Joel and I boarded the plane to Chicago, we turned around to wave another good-bye.

The Science Report

I WAS A year behind my junior high classmates based on my age, and always assumed I would never catch up. But that was before Mr. Qualteri's science class and my discovery of drugs.

Mr. Qualteri never smiled; he was the most solemn teacher I ever had, but I suppose there was nothing lighthearted about dissecting a frog. Behind his back, the kids in the class made fun of Mr. Qualteri's permanently somber persona, daring one another to find a prank that would make him laugh, or even smile. The fantasy I harbored was snatching his thick, dark toupee, but Mr. Qualteri would certainly not find anything funny about that.

For the spring term, Mr. Qualteri assigned us two "science reports," for which the requirement was simply to pick a topic and go to the library to research it. There were no other instructions, nothing about what kind of sources to use, how many to use, how to cite them, or even whether to cite them.

At the small public library on the other side of Broadway, a mile or so from home, I told the librarian I needed to write a science report. "It just has to do with science," I said. "Anything scientific."

"Well, all right," she said. She went to a nearby reference shelf and pulled out a thick hardbound book, titled something like *The Science Encyclopedia*. I could barely lift it. She showed me the other books like it on the same shelf, with titles such as *Encyclopedia of the Human Body* and the *Encyclopedia of Science and Technology*.

I flipped slowly through the pages. I could not believe my good fortune. Writing that science report would be easy, I suddenly realized. It was only a matter of choosing something, anything, and copying down the information.

Maybe it was the fancy pictures—molar, incisor, bicuspid—that grabbed my attention, but whatever the reason, I pulled out my notebook and recorded word for word the entire entry for human teeth. In seventh grade, I'd never heard the word *plagiarism*. I even copied the pictures of all the different types of teeth and put them on the cover of the science report I handed in the next day in class. Mr. Qualteri was pleased; he gave me an A and wrote "Well done" next to the grade.

Suddenly I was acing seventh-grade science. For my second science report I did exactly the same thing: walked over to the library the day before it was due, pulled out the various science-related encyclopedias, and skimmed through them, quickly looking for an entry to copy. This time I settled on the topic of drugs, specifically illegal drugs—something I would end up devoting much attention to in my academic research decades later. Once again, I copied down the text in the encyclopedia, word for word. The encyclopedia entry included an eye-catching illustration of a poppy plant with a syringe stuck into it, showing that the poppy plant was used to make heroin. I copied that picture for the cover of my report, which I titled "The Dangers of Drugs."

This time Mr. Qualteri was ecstatic, waving my report in the air and announcing to the whole class that "Peter here has written a *very* impressive science report. It shows how destructive and deadly illegal drugs are." My heart swelled to see the huge "A+—Excellent!" he'd scrawled at the top of the page. Unexpectedly, I had become the model antidrug student.

But then laughter broke out in the back row. Robert Vega clearly had something to say about this; I immediately suspected it had to do with my having smoked pot with him. Mr. Qualteri asked Robert to stay after class. I walked out as calmly as I could, trying not to appear nervous. The next day after class, Mr. Qualteri asked me to stay for an extra minute.

"Peter, you know how much I liked your science report on the dangers of drugs," he said. "But Robert tells me that you smoked marijuana at his house last week. Is this true?"

It was true. I had been at Robert's house, and he and his brothers were smoking dope, and I had tried it, for the first time in my life, only a toke or two, when they passed me the joint. But Mr. Qualteri didn't want it to be true, and at that moment, neither did I.

"No, Mr. Qualteri, that's not true. It's true that Robert and his brothers were smoking marijuana at their house last week, and it's true that I was there with them, but I said no."

He sighed with relief and patted my shoulder. "I thought so. Robert's just a troublemaker. You should hang out with other kids."

Before I left the room, I said, "Thank you, Mr. Qualteri. See you tomorrow."

"No, Peter," he replied. "Thank *you* for that wonderful report. I have very high hopes for you, young man." And then he actually smiled, just a flicker.

Late that spring, the principal called me into his office one Friday afternoon. I was anxious. Maybe Mr. Qualteri had finally figured out I had lied to him.

"Please, have a seat," Mr. Salazar said as he closed the door behind me. As I nervously wiped my sweaty palms down the front of my pants, he smiled at me. "Mr. Qualteri tells me what a terrific student you've been in his class this year, really exceptional. I'm always glad to hear such good things about a student. You've also been doing well in your other classes; your teachers speak highly of you. In fact, Mr. Qualteri has recommended that we skip you to the ninth grade, that way you'll catch up to your age group. How would you like that?" Without waiting for a reply, he continued: "Oh, and I'm happy to tell you that you'll be receiving the Trailblazer Award this year, given to the top student in the class. Congratulations!" Mr. Salazar reached out to shake my hand and flashed a warm smile. "You should be proud of yourself." As I slowly got up and walked out of Mr. Salazar's office he gave me a pat on my back. "Keep up the good work."

"Thank you, Mr. Salazar. I will." The words came easily, automatically, but I could not look Mr. Salazar in the eye. I walked slowly down the hall, not quite believing what had just happened. But one thing had become clear: doing well in school was one way I could control my fate and take care of myself—and get others to care about me.

Later, when I received the Trailblazer Award—a small, round, gold-colored medal, hanging on a red, white, and blue ribbon—I showed it to my mother, hoping she might be impressed. I knew not to make too big of a deal about it, though, so that she didn't think I was becoming a conformist. When I explained what it was for, she said, "Oh, that's nice. Too bad it has a red, white, and blue ribbon—looks too patriotic. I didn't realize you were doing so well in school." She then added, "Just don't let it go to your head. We wouldn't want you to start thinking you're better than the other students."

That fall I moved on to the ninth grade. Everyone reassured me that eighth grade was a bad year anyway and that I wouldn't miss it. I never did shake my guilt that I had lied to Mr. Qualteri about the few puffs of pot, but at least I didn't try pot again for years. And I remained oblivious about the plagiarism.

My friendship with Robert Vega died out after seventh grade. We barely even saw each other in the halls. Some years later, while my mother was clipping stories from the *Rocky Mountain News*, she came across a small news item reporting that a Robert Vega had been busted for robbing a convenience store on South Broadway. That was Robert's neighborhood, and it sounded like the sort of trouble he'd always courted, but I hoped it wasn't him.

Tourists

FOR MONTHS I had been pestering my mother about taking some sort of trip, just for fun, but never actually expected her to agree. A vacation was something that other families did. We simply couldn't afford it, and even if we could, my mother would rather spend the time and money on political things. When she finally said yes to a vacation, at first I thought she must be joking. My mother saw the look of disbelief on my face and said, "Really, let's do it."

This would not be just any vacation. It would be a trip to Europe. For once in my life, there would be no ideological debates, no rallies or demonstrations, no boycott campaigns, no leafleting, no consciousness-raising meetings, no slums, no revolution to chase. We would do it on the cheap, but it would still be a real vacation.

The idea began when my mother wrecked her car. I was thirteen. She was never a very good driver, and during rush hour one afternoon she took a left turn with the sun in her eyes and plowed right into another car. Our little yellow Datsun station wagon was totaled. My mother was lucky that she only broke her leg. She called me from Denver General Hospital. When I picked up the phone she said, "Peter, I'm okay, but I'm at the hospital. I had a car accident." I rushed to see her. Her right leg, all swollen and black-and-blue, was strung up in traction, a metal rod inserted to hold the bones together. It would take months to fully heal, but I was relieved that it hadn't been worse. My mother's poor driving posed a greater danger to her than any right-wing government or corporation.

For several months, while she was in a cast and on crutches, I did all the cleaning, cooking, and chores around the house. I even emptied my mother's chamber pot. I had attended to my mother like this back in Peru when she got sick, and I enjoyed feeling needed. My reward was that we would use the few thousand dollars in insurance money for a trip to Europe early the following summer. Back in 1969, my mother had taken my brothers and their friends on a six-week trip to Yugoslavia, chosen because at that time it was the only communist country where U.S. citizens could easily travel. My mother had wanted to take me, but we were still in Detroit at that time and my father balked; I was only five and he said I was too young to go. So, as she explained to me, she figured she owed me a Europe trip, and this was the right time to finally do it.

My mother took me out of school in late May, a couple of weeks before seventh-grade classes ended, because plane tickets to Europe were cheaper then. "Your teachers will understand," she assured me. "It happens all the time." I was not as eager to skip school these days, but I was not going to complain about leaving.

Off we went with our sleeping bags and duffels, hitchhiking to New York to catch our plane across the Atlantic. I was thrilled; I'd finally be traveling with my mother again, just the two of us, but instead of roughing it in South America and living in slums and remote villages, we'd be normal tourists in Europe.

During the two or three days we were in London, we were like all the other tourists, except for my mother's political commentary. We saw the British Museum and Buckingham Palace. My mother was our political tour guide. "Before American imperialism," she explained, "there was British imperialism. Look at all this, it was built on the backs of the poor." Standing in front of Egyptian statues at the British Museum, she mused, "Look at what the British stole from the world."

We hitchhiked to Dover to catch the ferry across the English Channel to Calais, and from there caught a ride to Paris. The plan was to track down and stay with my mother's old boyfriend, Jean-

Pierre, with whom we had lived in Buenos Aires and traveled to Peru five years earlier. I'd liked him well enough, but hoped he and my mother would not get back together. I wanted to visit Paris, not move there.

The problem was, my mother didn't tell Jean-Pierre we were coming, and so we simply showed up at his house, late at night, only to find out he was out of town. It was a big sprawling home in a Paris suburb, shared by three youngish families—seven adults and five small children. Somehow, although they spoke very little English and we spoke even less French, my mother convinced them to let us stay in Jean-Pierre's room. She always had a knack for making quick friends and gaining their trust, which saved us at midnight in Paris without a hotel room. The walls in Jean-Pierre's room were covered with dozens of black-and-white photographs, many of them taken in South America, including a few of me and my mother.

Jean-Pierre showed up a few days later, startled but happy to see us. "Carol, is that you? When did you get here?"

"Oh, a couple of days ago. We've been staying in your room," my mother said with a smile, and then gave him a long hug. "Hope you don't mind."

Jean-Pierre looked exactly like I remembered him, but since we saw him last he'd come out as homosexual instead of bisexual. My mother tried not to act surprised, while I tried to hide my relief. Jean-Pierre took an extra day off work to be our Parisian tour guide, leading us along the Left Bank, showing us the Louvre, the Eiffel Tower, and the Basilica. In the evenings, everyone in Jean-Pierre's house cooked a huge feast and ate together at a long table in the backyard; these dinners went on for hours and hours, helped by the fact that it didn't get dark until after 10:00 p.m. The lively chatter was all in French, but there was so much laughter that I couldn't help but join in. These evenings reminded me of the communal dinners at the old Berkeley commune, but with more kids, better food, and more happiness.

We traveled on by train, south to Spain. We were happy to finally be in a country where we spoke the language. I was rusty, having given up my Spanish as soon as we moved to Denver. But now that we were in Spain I was glad to have an excuse to use it again, and proud of how good my accent was. Our first stop was the northern Basque region; my mother wanted to see where the ETA—Basque Homeland and Liberty, the armed separatist organization—was from. We stayed several days at a hostel in San Sebastián, a scenic coastal city not far from the French border. ETA attacks over the years had scared a lot of the tourists away, but it didn't bother us.

From there, we hitched a ride to Madrid and then on to Córdoba. We rode with a bullfighter-singer, who told us all sorts of bullfighting tales but wouldn't sing when I asked him to, and traveled the rest of the way with a caravan of truckers hauling huge loads of wheat. The truck drivers insisted on paying for our meals that day, as if we were their guests, and they were equally insistent that a civil war was coming soon. But the more intellectual types we met were sure the country was headed for social democracy. "Spain had a civil war once before," my mother informed me. "The fascists won, just like Pinochet and the fascists in Chile." We spent a couple of days strolling around Córdoba and visiting its famous mosque that had been converted into a church. We were relieved to find a bed for only $5 a night. At nearly fourteen, I was too big to share a bed with my mother, but it was worth it to help stretch what little money we had.

We hitchhiked on to the southern coastal city of Málaga, and then waited in the hot sun for hours before we caught a ride to the port city of Algeciras to take the ferry across the Strait of Gibraltar to Morocco. My mother and I kept getting lost in the narrow, winding, ancient alleyways of the Moroccan towns of Tangier, Tétouan, and Chaouen, which was both exhilarating and unnerving. What I remember most about Morocco were the swarms of children surrounding us everywhere, tugging at our clothes, hawking trinkets. As annoying as they were, I felt empathy for these little kids—only five years earlier I had been hanging out with street kids in Jauja, pestering tourists in the same way that these kids were now pestering me.

Back in Spain a few days later, we splurged on a plane ticket to Barcelona, where we stayed at a cheap *pension* in the touristy Las Ramblas area. Barcelona was hot and sticky, but it was easy to enjoy the city without spending any money; we just strolled all day up and down the busy pedestrian walkways of Las Ramblas.

"Why don't we have nice places like this to walk in American cities?" I asked my mother. "Where it's just for people and not cars?"

"Because the big American automobile companies would never allow it," she replied.

We then traveled north to Belgium by train, where we visited Roberto, my mother's Uruguayan ex-lover from Santiago, and his Belgian wife. My mother and Roberto had reconnected a couple of years earlier, and when he heard we were coming to Europe he invited us to stay with him. Roberto had moved to Brussels after escaping the military coup in Chile. He worked painting houses during the day and at a restaurant at night. He showed us around the city's grand main square—including my favorite attraction, the *Manneken Pis*, a statue of a little boy pissing water in a fountain. Carlos, the other Uruguayan we had lived with in Santiago, had been given asylum in Sweden, and he came down to visit us in Brussels. It was familiar and comfortable being around Roberto and Carlos again, especially for my mother, who was eager to talk about their time in Chile together.

The end of our trip was nearing, and I was determined to make it to Amsterdam. "I'd really like to see the Anne Frank House," I told my mother, hoping she would be sufficiently impressed by my appreciation of history to say yes. But she didn't want to go; said she wanted to rest up and spend more time with Roberto in Brussels. I persisted. "Please, it's so close, only a short train ride. I could even go by myself."

And so I did. The next morning my mother put me on an early train with a return ticket for the last train back that night. After walking right past the Anne Frank House, I spent much of the rest of the day wandering aimlessly around the city's famous red light district, gawking at the scantily dressed women sitting on display in their softly lit windows; walking through the Sex Museum; and trying to make sense of the strange toys and other contraptions in the adult shops. No one seemed to mind or even notice that I was there alone; I was just one more wide-eyed tourist in the crowd.

I kept thinking to myself how much my mother would disapprove, even be horrified. I remembered her campaign against Denver's porn shops, marching down East Colfax Avenue during a "take back the night" feminist demonstration she'd helped organize the year before. She also protested outside the Crazy Horse strip club bar, handing out anti-pornography leaflets. The photo of my mother in the *Rocky Mountain News* story about the protest identified her as "a woman who refused to give her name." And for Halloween one year she had put on a costume and mask and dashed in and out of the porn shops on South Broadway not far from where we lived, screaming at the employees and customers that they were sexist pigs exploiting women.

My mother met me at the Brussels train station late that night. "Did you have a nice time?" she asked.

"Oh, it was great. I really liked the Anne Frank House."

I was reluctant to board the plane home. I had never had a happier time with my mother than during those five weeks of traveling around, carefree and (mostly) politics-free, living for the moment rather than trying to find or make a revolution.

I asked my mother, "Can we do this again?" I knew it wouldn't be anytime soon. We had used up all the car insurance money, and we were now too broke to afford to buy another car. We would go without a car for the next couple of years.

"Sure, Peter," my mother replied. "We'll take another trip like this someday."

We never did.

Baker's Dozen

I SANG MY way through junior high. It turned out my voice was my ticket out of the west side. School was my salvation, and my choir teacher was my savior. I had the deepest voice in the seventh-grade choir class. It didn't matter that I couldn't read music—I could wing it by following along, singing bass, belting out tunes with gusto, and making my choir teacher proud. And it was an easy A, with no homework.

By ninth grade, I was ready for the big league: the Baker's Dozen jazz choir, with the boys sporting tight black polyester pants, puffy shirts, and red velvet vests. We sang at school events, at Cinderella City Mall and other shopping centers, and in fancy hotel lobbies. We were treated as though we were special; we felt special; we *were* special. We were the only school group featured in a full-page photo spread in the 1980 Baker Junior High School yearbook.

I adored Mrs. Kates, the energetic, freckle-faced choir teacher with glowing shoulder-length red hair. One late-spring day, she asked me to stay after a Baker's Dozen rehearsal.

"Peter, where are you going to high school next year?" she asked.

"West High," I replied.

"Yeah, I figured." Then, after a long pause, Mrs. Kates said, "How would you like to go to East High instead? My son went there; he loved it. I think you would, too. It's a *much* better school than West." She added, "Maybe you could even be in the jazz choir, one of the best in the state. They're called the Angelaires."

I loved the sound of that word.

"But how?" I asked. "I don't live in the East school district."

Mrs. Kates flashed me a knowing smile. "I have an idea."

When I got home that afternoon, I announced to my mother that I would be going to East High School, as if somehow that would make it true.

"But why?" she asked. "What's wrong with going to West High?"

I knew my mother well enough not to explain that West High was probably the worst school in the city and East was one of the best. That was the last thing my mother would want to hear. Students who went to East often went on to college; students who went to West usually didn't, and often had trouble even graduating. Unlike any other parent in America, this would convince her I had to stay at West. Instead, I said, "There's this special voice class that's only offered at East. Mrs. Kates, my choir teacher, really wants me to go to East so I can take that class and be an Angelaire. She knows some higher-ups in the school system and thinks she can get me a special transfer."

My mother wasn't convinced. "Peter, I'm really concerned that if you go to a place like East you could become an elitist. And if you became ambitious you're more likely to sell out to the system instead of fighting it."

"No, don't worry, that would never happen," I protested. "Come on, have a little faith in me."

"But wouldn't West High be good enough? Maybe even better in some ways, since it's a Chicano working-class school." She added: "And there would also be less pressure to succeed; more like Baker. You like Baker, right?"

I nodded.

I kept pushing. "Look, it's not as if I'm asking to go to some rich white suburban school, like Cherry Creek High, or live with my father and go to school there. So what's the big deal if I go to East?"

"I don't know, Peter, this whole thing makes me uneasy, makes me question whether you really want to be with me instead of with your father. Your father would have no problem agreeing with what you're asking for."

"Don't worry, I don't want to live with my father, but I really, really want to go to East. Okay? It's not like I'm selling out or anything."

"Maybe we should talk about what you're going to do with your life."

"I don't know what I'm going to do with my life," I replied impatiently. "But I probably want to go to college. I'm probably not going to be a factory worker like Joel."

My mother nodded.

"And I don't want to spend my life filling gas tanks at a filling station."

She nodded again.

"And I'm not going to be just like you. You're too negative about everything, thinking everything in the world is a problem that needs to be fixed."

"Well, Peter, I suppose I do want you to do something about the world's problems. But I don't want you to do it just for me, I want you to do it because it's sick not to."

"Mom, I'm *only* fourteen."

After more prodding and pleading, my mother finally, reluctantly, agreed.

The transfer request was approved a few weeks later. When I arrived at East in the fall, I joined the choir, and later got into the Angelaires, but never actually took that voice class. No one noticed when I didn't sign up for it, even though it was the excuse for the transfer.

Denounced

FOR ALL THE ups and downs in my relationship with my mother, I never doubted that I needed her and that she needed me. I'd chosen her over my father, if reluctantly. However, not all of her sons saw her that way. Ronald also lived in Denver, but we almost never saw him, and he was growing increasingly estranged from her, as slights imagined and real built to a breaking point.

One day, when I was fifteen, Ronald suddenly announced that he wanted nothing to do with our mother. Now in his early twenties, he told her that she had been a bad mother and that he planned to move as far away as possible because there was "not enough room in Denver" for the two of them. Her unforgivable betrayal, apparently, was my mother's kindness to Ronald's girlfriend, Dawn, during a tumultuous moment when he and Dawn had temporarily broken up. Now that they were back together, Ronald announced, they were moving to the other side of the world: New Zealand. After years of conciliatory efforts by my mother, Ronald finally began communicating with her again, and she spent the rest of her life tiptoeing around him. Her diaries during this period are littered with self-tortured entries about what went wrong between her and Ronald: "I do feel guilt, lots of it, and for what I don't know, except that he probably needed an extra measure of love."

It wasn't only her, though. We all tiptoed around Ronald on the rare occasion that we saw him. No one could hold a grudge quite like he did: he had cut off contact with Grandpa Rich after Grandpa chastised him for not finding a job; he had a falling-out with Greg, his best friend and roommate in Denver, because of a perceived slight; he suddenly stopped talking to our cousin Alan, and this later continued even as Alan was dying of cancer. Ronald never cut ties with our father, but he was always critical and kept his distance.

I hadn't been close to him, either; had barely seen him since we lived together at the commune in Berkeley. In Denver, he did take me skiing a few times. He always insisted on racing down the slopes to see who could ski the fastest. The year I was fourteen, he gave me a lift ticket for Christmas. Joel came with us, though he'd never even been on skis before, and I myself had only skied a handful of times. As soon as we got to the ski area, Ronald took off on his own, leaving me to introduce Joel to skiing, though I was almost a beginner myself. As Ronald got on the lift, I shouted at him as loud as I could, "You asshole!" We didn't see Ronald again until the lifts closed for the day.

Joel was hopeless; the ski patrol ended up banning him from the slopes for recklessness. He didn't mind—it was a "bourgeois sport" anyway—so he spent the afternoon watching football on the TV in the ski lodge. Hours later, Joel's jeans were still soaked from falling—neither one of us owned snow pants.

When Ronald finally showed up, he was fuming that I had called him an asshole in public. "How dare you insult me like that? How dare you! I should just leave you here." On the two-hour drive back to Denver on I-70, Ronald kept threatening to pull over and leave me by the side of the road. "That would teach you a lesson," he yelled at me as I slunk down in the backseat of his white Subaru. "You should be grateful I brought you skiing, but no, you insult me." Joel stayed out of it. Ronald had never been much of a big brother to me, but this was the end of any pretense.

Before he and Dawn moved to New Zealand, Ronald had a big yard sale. I told him our mother wanted a few small items they were getting rid of and asked if we could come pick them up in a borrowed car. Sure, Ronald said, as long as our mother stayed in the car.

She did, parking in front of the house with the engine running. Ronald did not even glance toward the car. As bad as I felt for her, there was no point in confronting Ronald. It wasn't going to change his mind. I quickly found the things my mother wanted and ran back to the car. As we drove off, my mother asked how Ronald was doing, whether he had asked about her, whether he had said anything at all about her. I didn't reply—which was a reply of sorts—and her disappointment was visible.

My mother took Ronald's rejection hard, telling everyone that her son had "denounced" her. It tormented her. The more depressed she grew, the angrier I became at Ronald. Sure, he had grievances, I thought to myself. But didn't we all? Well, yes, Ronald would say— he had urged me to cut her off, too. Maybe he blamed our mother for not being around to get him out of juvenile detention when he was arrested after fighting with his girlfriend. Or maybe he resented her for giving me more attention and letting him bum around South America by himself when he was only fourteen. Perhaps something else happened that I didn't know about. Whatever had happened to Ronald, the middle child who got lost in the divorce and had basically been on his own since his early teens, I still thought he was being cruel.

I did my best to console my mother. "Peter doesn't like me wringing my hands over the situation with Ronald," she wrote in her diary, "or to blame myself at all." One day when my mother was especially down, I wrote her a letter to try to describe the person I thought she was, and to assure her that her youngest son still loved her, understood her, and would never give up on her:

> Mami, mom, mum, mama, Carol, Andrea . . . She is
> many people at different times of her life trying to figure
> out which person she wants. A mother, a housewife, a
> swinging single, an adventurer, a lover, a feminist, a
> runner, a saver, a peacemaker, a revolutionary. She likes

*a little of each person so she switches and adds and takes
away from the various persons to make the next day
a challenge and exciting experience. She survives day
by day on hope and without this hope she would have
no will to survive in the world. She fights for what she
believes in but she slowly changes these beliefs over the
years.*

*She's not attracted to older men because they have in
them some of the things she rejected, so she is satisfied
with her brief but sweet excitement with the younger
men she falls in love with, a new challenge to change
these men into the sculptures she wants until they go
on to other adventures and new experiences leaving her
behind or she leaving them behind while she heals her
broken heart with new problems. It would be a dead
world for her without problems.*

*She sits back and watches her sons grow up, none
of them the way she planned, and she wonders and
watches her youngest son grow out of phases and clothes.
She wonders at how he will turn out because he's gone
through so much with her, she hopes some good has
rubbed off on him from her, she learns from him, he
learns from her. She realizes that he's started going his
separate way and that he's started to have a few ideas
that are different from hers. She realizes she hasn't kept
him totally isolated from the evil American society, yet at
the same time she's glad he experiences everything because
she wants him to be his own person for better or worse.
She sees things in him, the good and the bad that will be
with him whether or not he's a revolutionary or a fink.
She knows that her son will probably be somewhere in
between, some good and some bad, but she also knows he
loves her very much and that no matter what happens*

she'll love him, too, just like she loves her other two sons,
but he'll never denounce her like his older brother has
done.

She is a strong woman with many weaknesses who
is critical of everything whether good or evil. She is
confused because she doesn't understand life, but no one
else understands it either.

After reading it, my mother didn't say anything but just gave me
a warm hug, holding me tightly for longer than I ever remember her
doing. More than two decades later, right after my mother's sudden
death, I was sorting through her belongings and came across a sealed
envelope with the words *For Peter* handwritten across the front. Inside, I found that letter, with a photo of the two of us stapled to it.

Saving Raul

THOUGH WE HAD left Raul for good in Peru five years earlier, he and my mother were still legally married, and part of my mother's heart was still with him. They wrote to each other constantly, starting as soon as we moved back to the United States. One of Raul's letters was some fifty pages long, a heroic recap of his entire life history of political struggles—handwritten using a quill dipped in lemon so that only my mother could read it. He sent a separate letter with instructions on how to decipher it above a fire, with the heat turning the invisible lettering brown. When she wrote him back, asking how much of that long letter, which she had labored hard to read, was actually true, he replied, "At least 90 percent."

My mother insisted on updating me on Raul's life, even as I rolled my eyes and told her she should forget about him. At times I secretly feared that my mother might even try to take me out of school again and move back to Peru, but I knew that this time I would not have gone with her.

"I know you think Raul is crazy, and maybe he is," my mother said to me. "But he's the only man who ever really loved me. Your father never even told me he loved me. He never even gave me an orgasm!"

"Mom, I didn't need to hear that."

"I know, but I really want you to understand."

As I was getting older, it seemed like my mother was trying harder and harder to explain and justify certain things to me. Maybe she worried that I would grow to resent her like Ronald did. She especially wanted me to understand why she had left my father. The truth was, it was difficult for me to imagine that the two of them had ever been together in the first place. Now that I was a teenager myself it was even more clear to me that twenty-one-year-old men should not be dating fourteen-year-old girls, and no one should marry at age seventeen.

Raul's first letter after we moved back from Peru claimed that he had gone into hiding because the authorities had ransacked our place in Huertas a few days after we left, taking documents and books, and even shooting bullet holes into the cloth portrait of Lenin. Raul mailed my mother the Lenin portrait pockmarked with holes, though with Raul it was hard to know what was true. My mother never put that portrait back on the wall.

Raul also wrote that he had been arrested while leading a demonstration during a national strike and charged with "attacking the armed forces." He spent more than three months in prison until he was released after a hunger strike. My mother sent him money while he was scraping by in Huancayo selling and distributing the radical newspaper *El Diario Marka*; the next year, when Raul became a father, he named his daughter after my mother and asked her to be the godmother—and so my mother sent more money.

"What did Raul do this time?" I asked my mother when she told me he was in jail again. "Did he join Sendero?" My mother was currently working on a book about the role of women in Sendero Luminoso, the rapidly expanding guerrilla insurgency that began in the Peruvian highlands. She was delighted that so many of the guerrilla commanders were female.

"No," my mother said, "Raul's not disciplined enough or committed enough for Sendero; they would never take him."

Sendero did take Raul's younger brother Lucho, who had lived with us in Comas and was killed in prison a few years later. Fearing Raul might meet a similar fate, my mother was determined to save him. She saw to it that hundreds of letters and petitions addressed to the Peruvian authorities were sent from the United States calling for Raul's release. As always, there was no response. She made dozens of copies of a leaflet with Raul's name and picture on it; in the image, he was holding up his clenched fist. The leaflet called him a "prisoner of conscience" and demanded his release. She became even more concerned about Raul when she learned from friends in Huancayo and Jauja that local authorities were threatening to send him to El Frontón, Lima's island prison.

For months, my mother wrote tirelessly to U.S. congressmen, telling them that Raul was her husband and pleading with them to make inquiries. She kept showing up at the office of Colorado senator Gary Hart until eventually she gained his support. She finally received a letter from the Presidencia de la República in Peru informing her that Raul was being held pending investigations of accusations of terrorism, but never specifying exactly what that meant. She then turned to Amnesty International. An Amnesty chapter officially adopted Raul's case, and Amnesty representatives in Peru were able to visit Raul in prison. They reported that Raul was in good health and good spirits—indeed, he had apparently fathered his second child while in prison, but not with the mother of his first child, who visited him regularly.

Raul was soon let out of prison; it was never entirely clear whether he had been convicted of anything. It also wasn't at all clear whether my mother's lobbying effort had anything to do with his release. It didn't matter. "Raul is free, he's finally free!" my mother said to me triumphantly one afternoon when I got home from school.

"What's he going to do now?" I asked.

"He says he's going to stop doing political stuff and open up a restaurant in Huancayo. I told him the revolution still needs him, that he shouldn't give up on that."

Meanwhile, though my mother was still officially married to Raul, she was never too lonely in Colorado—far less lonely, in fact, than I believed at the time, given how many men she wrote about in her diaries. There was skinny Chris, who liked to dance barefoot and designed and carved tombstones for a living; there was Seyed, the Iranian student she seduced, who smiled at my mother from the front row of her Sex Roles class (thanks to her, he decided to switch his major to sociology from chemical engineering); there was Josh, the Canadian who took my mother around town on his motorcycle and played improvisational piano just like Keith Jarrett; there was her fling with another Iranian, Houshang, who did free oil changes for us after we finally got a car again; there was Enoch, the black security guard she met at the bank a few blocks from our house; and there was Viviano, the Peruvian who was even younger than Raul. Many years later, long after I had left home, my mother married Viviano—when he was in his early thirties and she was in her early sixties—so that he could live and work legally in the United States, but she then immediately divorced him after finding out he had a girlfriend and a child back in Lima.

My mother's assorted men since Raul had two things in common: they were all in their twenties or thirties, several decades younger than her, and their relationships with my mother were short-lived, lasting from weeks to months. Whenever my mother mentioned her latest love interest, the first thing I asked her was "How old is he?" hoping that the response would be at least within a decade of my mother's age. "Oh, Mom," I would tease her, "when are you going to find someone at least close to your own age?" Her only response was the sparkle in her eye.

My mother's various love interests over the years were a recurring topic in her diary, often overshadowing her preoccupation with revolutionary politics. In one entry in late 1980, when she was in her late forties and having a secret affair with one of her students who was in his twenties, she wrote:

I'm tired of chasing the man who shows some interest in me.
I should be more like Inca [our dog]. She'll go chasing off to

smell out a dog, and she'll lead anyone who's interested on a merry chase and play hard, shake them out of their lethargy if she can, but she never goes off moping if they're not interested. Her self-esteem isn't dependent on their response. Peter says, "She just knows she's better than them if they're not interested." Of course, Peter sees my situation differently. He says I have to expect problems if I like young men because it's not reasonable to expect them to be satisfied with me as a sexual mate. Can I accept such an assessment graciously? Is it even true? There are plenty of young women who are very loyal to older men lovers. Am I homely just because I have wrinkles and spots on my skin?

The next day, my mother's affair with her student ended. As she explained the breakup in her diary:

He was able to tell me that he always had the recurring sense that our relationship was wrong because of the big age difference. I asked him if he thought something was wrong with me for ending up so often with young lovers and he said, "No, I'd like to have young lovers, too." But he advised me, more or less, to seek someone my own age.

My mother never took his advice, or mine. She kept chasing younger men, usually much younger. But no matter how many came in and out of my mother's life, nothing made her happier than receiving another poetic, pages-long letter or collect call from Raul. As much as I never wanted to believe it, he was, indeed, the only true love of her life.

Fitting In

ON MARCH 30, 1981, I was sitting in Mr. Miller's tenth-grade Medieval History class at East High, learning about the crusades, when another teacher burst into the classroom and whispered into Mr. Miller's ear. He stopped scribbling on the chalkboard and turned to the class with a solemn look. His voice was heavy and slow. "There's been a terrible tragedy. President Reagan has been shot."

The entire class fell silent—except for me. "Yes!" I blurted out spontaneously, almost instinctively, raising both my fists high.

Everyone looked at me in horror. Mr. Miller, my favorite teacher that year, turned bright red, his thick neck bulging more than usual. And then the bell rang. Realizing what I'd done, I thought I could sneak away quietly, as if nothing had happened, but Mr. Miller quickly walked to my desk and hovered over me, twisting the tip of his wavy white mustache as I put my notebook away. "You should not disrespect our president like that, young man. That is *not* appropriate behavior." I mumbled an apology without looking up at Mr. Miller and left quickly. How could I explain it? I felt embarrassed for having caused a scene, though it did not make me feel more sympathy for Reagan.

For my mother and pretty much everyone else we hung out with, Ronald Reagan was evil personified, what my mother called an "evilmonger." For someone who never used foul language, "evilmonger" was a top-shelf insult, worse than "sellout," "fink," "reactionary," or even "pig." And Reagan embodied the most evil of all evils— American imperialism.

When I got home that day, my mother was listening to NPR news on the radio. The media was reporting that shooter John Hinckley was psychologically disturbed, and obsessed with the teen movie star Jodie Foster. "I can't believe they are trying to portray this guy as some sort of psycho case," my mother complained while adjusting the antenna. "They act as if there could not be obvious political motives." She then added with a sigh, "It's just too bad Reagan managed to survive." I'm not sure my mother could have pulled the trigger herself if given the chance, but she admired those who could and certainly was not going to join the loud chorus of condemnations.

Mr. Miller seemed to forgive me, and I eventually took every class he taught. He loved the Medieval History term paper I wrote about the origins of Oxford University, and even encouraged me to consider going to college somewhere like that. My outburst in class notwithstanding, I was doing everything I could to fit in at East. That was also true, of course, at the dozen or so other schools I had attended up till then, but in this case I was better at it and enjoying it more.

I was not only fitting in, I even felt kind of cool. East High was a magnificent old school, one of the oldest in the state. At lunchtime, the students hung out together on the sprawling grassy esplanade. The school had an open-campus policy, meaning we could spend the lunch hour wandering up and down East Colfax Avenue. East was full of school pride; it had graced the cover of *Life* magazine decades earlier as one of the top public schools in the country, and was now celebrated as a model of successful busing: a socially and racially diverse inner-city school with a majority of students who went on to college. We proudly thumbed our noses at all the boring generic white schools in the rapidly expanding suburbs.

To really be accepted at East I thought I needed to play a sport. Running around kicking a soccer ball in the dirt streets of Peru didn't really prepare me to try out for the soccer team; most of those kids had been playing soccer together on organized teams with real coaching for years. Besides, what I really wanted to play was American football. So I showed up for the first day of football practice tryouts. The coach took one look at me and said, "Maybe tight end." The next day I was so sore I could not even get out of bed. That marked the end of my football career.

As a last resort, I tried tennis. I had swung a racket a few times in junior high gym class, so I knew the rules and some of the basics. I had picked up a metal Wilson T2000 tennis racket at a garage sale; it looked exactly like the one Jimmy Connors played with. I was not very good, but neither was the East High tennis team. I'm not sure our coach, Mr. Rasmussen, even knew how to play tennis. And so I made the cut, barely, and was matched with a doubles partner who fortunately was much better.

To fit in even more, I started doing all sorts of extracurricular activities. Besides choir and the Angelaires, I joined the speech team, and kept at it even though I never did all that well at the weekend speech tournaments. My father sent me some of his old polyester ties and sport jackets. The jackets didn't quite fit me and the ties were too fat, but at least I had the proper attire. My mother, though she frowned on ambition and didn't seem to care if I won or lost, was always supportive of my performances. In a diary entry she wrote, "Peter was chosen to represent East High in the citywide 'extempora-neous speech' contest—will be accompanied by the school principal. I told him I couldn't imagine anyone choosing to put himself under that much pressure, and he said, 'it's ego.' Also said he's 'getting to be a good B.S.'er.'"

My mother especially liked my involvement in school plays be-cause they reminded her of Raul and me doing street theater back in Huancayo. Performing with the mime troupe, I wondered what Raul would think of me now, putting on the face paint again just like he taught me, but on a school stage rather than on the streets with him. Those were my best memories of Raul.

I also started working for the student newspaper, the *Spotlight*. When I interviewed teachers, coaches, or staff for a story, I felt like a journalist rather than a lowly student. I always enjoyed the challenge of coming up with catchy headlines; best of all, my reporter status entitled me to a highly coveted hall pass. I'd simply flash my *Spotlight* card at the faculty hall monitors and they'd leave me alone, assuming I must be working on some story for the paper. By senior year I was editor in chief and had my own column, "Pete's Point," though no one ever called me "Pete." I also often struggled to come up with a point—one column was a blow-by-blow, middle-of-the-night account of procrastinating about writing the column, which was due the next morning—and I'm not sure anyone ever actually read it.

I proudly sent a copy of the newspaper to my brother Joel (who had moved a few years earlier from Oakland to Birmingham, Alabama, to join another Marxist-Leninist group), but he wrote me back saying he was disappointed I wasn't using the paper as a "platform to mobilize students to challenge the system" like he had done at Berkeley High with the alternative student paper, *The Rag*, before he dropped out. It was then that I realized that the only thing that would ever truly impress my brother was if I also dropped out of school—or, even better, got kicked out of school—for some radical political cause. That was the last time I tried to impress him; I finally accepted that I never would.

Part of fitting in meant avoiding having many friends over to our tiny one-bedroom duplex on East Second Avenue. A few months into tenth grade, my mother and I moved from the west side to a better neighborhood on the east side of Broadway so that I could be close to a school-bus stop and not have to take public buses. I could then walk a few blocks to catch the bus in front of Sherman Elementary School, where I worked for a while mopping floors for an hour or so early each morning before my bus arrived. After a couple of years without a car, my mother bought a 1977 light blue VW Rabbit, which meant that we no longer had to borrow wheels from my mother's friends. She let me drive it to school once I turned sixteen and got a driver's license.

My mother gave me the bedroom. Her bed was in the living room, right inside the front entrance, and doubled as the couch; a bookcase full of her radical books served as a backrest. We had no dining room; the kitchen in the back accommodated a round, four-person table. The bathroom, which at least we had to ourselves, housed a small tub, but no shower. Our roof leaked, every faucet in the house dripped, the paint was peeling badly inside and out, and the patch of grass in front was half bare and overgrown with weeds. Big cracks around the doors let cold air in, and when we added weather stripping, the doors wouldn't shut. My mother did all she could to make the place nice and homey, with framed pictures on the wall, lots of plants, colorful tablecloths and throw rugs, but it remained a cramped and poorly maintained one-bedroom rental. We paid $200 per month plus utilities—much more than double what we had been paying on the west side.

It's not as though my friends were rich. But I know that none of

With Inca in front of our home in Denver, 1982

With my mother behind our home in Denver, 1982

their mothers slept in the living room on a bed that also served as a couch. They mostly lived in nice family neighborhoods like Park Hill or in the better parts of Capitol Hill. Everyone had a shower. A couple of friends had parents who owned ski condos. My friend Matt even had a swimming pool in his backyard, which we turned into a party scene on a few occasions when his folks were out of town. And no one had a mother who spent most of her time protesting and plotting the revolution and who cheered when the president was shot. I didn't tell my mother I was embarrassed by our modest place, but I think she noticed I wasn't inviting many friends over.

I spent more and more of my time out of the house, coming home whenever I felt like it. As always, there were no rules. It got to the point where it almost seemed as if my mother and I competed over who came home the latest. She noted in her diary: "Peter says I'm too old to stay out so late, that he's in the prime of his life and is the one that should be coming home in the middle of the night."

My mother and I still had our old favorite routines together, though, including early-morning weekend waffles. We both liked our breakfasts together, despite the fact that I wasn't very sociable at that hour: "Breakfast with Peter is both a turn-off and a treat at the same time. He's reading the sports section of the newspaper and I'm trying to tell him about my dreams." And we still loved going to the movies, our movie tastes having become more compatible. One December afternoon we watched the movie *Reds*, about the Russian Revolution, starring Warren Beatty and Diane Keaton. When my mother asked me what I considered to be the meaning of the movie, I told her it was obvious:

"Nothing works, the real revolution will never happen."

My mother didn't like that answer. "Well, I thought the movie was great. Not dismissive of revolution at all. It was pro-revolutionary and tried to be realistic and nondogmatic. It tried to give a critical but sympathetic view of the U.S. revolutionaries as well as of the Russians."

When Joel came to visit a few weeks later, the debate about *Reds* continued, the first time I could remember getting into a political argument with him. Joel said he hadn't liked it that a woman (Diane Keaton) was holding a man (Warren Beatty) back from his political work; I countered that the woman's pleas were justified because the man thought he was the only one making the revolution, and he didn't take love seriously. My mother said nothing and seemed amused by our back and forth. As she described it in her diary, "I'd love to sit back and hear all three of my sons making meaningful conversation like that, and not have to get involved at all, because each one of them represents a little of me."

When I needed her to, my mother could play the supportive mother role at school events and even seemed to like it, coming to my plays and choir performances and clapping and cheering with the other proud parents—though rarely interacting with them. She even agreed to type up my papers during the first year of high school as long as I promised to take a typing class the next summer. I watched intently over my mother's shoulder as she typed up my first term paper, about the history of the samurai sword in Japan, written for my Asian Studies class. I bought a red and white plastic folder to put it in—the East High colors. My mother noticed how engrossed I was in the whole process. She wrote in her diary, "If Peter doesn't get an 'A' for this, it will be a major test of his strength of character."

My mother never asked what grade I got on that paper; as had always been true, grades were the last thing in the world she cared about. But she did care what I wrote about, often nudging me to choose a political topic, and wanted to see my papers and have the chance to critique or praise them. And as I discovered later, my mother would also comment on them in her diary. An entry about one of my English papers in early 1982 read:

> Peter wrote an essay about "These Things Have I Loved," for his English class, and I'm asking him for a copy. It's one of his gems—contrasting the joy of being dirty and playing hard in South America with the things that turn him on now, and seeing his life as a process of sharp changes and adjustments, valuable experiences leading up to his present seriousness and concerns for achievement.

But most of the time, I did everything I could to make sure to keep my mother's world and my school world as far apart from each other as possible. They seemed irreconcilable. The more I fit in at school, the less I felt like I fit with my mother.

Mixing those two worlds sometimes created awkward moments, such as when my friend Rene would come over. He lived with his mother in a high-rise apartment complex just a few blocks away from where we lived. Their place wasn't that large, but he and his mother each had a bedroom, and they even had cable TV with HBO. Rene and I were on the tennis team together and we both got lead roles in the school musical, but he was far more popular than I was, and girls flocked to him. He was handsome, with short, dark wavy hair, and he had a certain worldly charisma that made his flirting seem effortless. Hanging out with Rene made me feel cool, even as it made me intensely aware that I was far less cool than he was.

My mother was one of the many who seemed charmed by Rene when he came over after tennis practice or theater rehearsals.

One day when he was hanging out in my room, Rene asked me, "Is your mother some sort of communist?"

I hesitated. "What gives you that impression?" I had never told Rene much about my childhood, only that I had spent some time in South America. And I certainly never said anything about my mother's radical politics.

"Well, all those books in your living room. Marx, Lenin, Engels, Mao, Che—aren't they all communists?"

"Well, yes, I suppose they are."

"So is *she* a communist?"

"Yeah," I said, shrugging, "but she hates the Soviet Union—she says they aren't communist enough, that they're actually capitalist."

"Wow," Rene said, grinning. "I've never met a real communist before."

I laughed awkwardly. "I know it might be hard to believe, but she says it's just a matter of time, that the revolution is inevitable, that history is on her side."

"Let's Put a Pencil to It"

ONE LATE FALL day during my senior year, I got home from school, checked the mail pile on the kitchen table, and found a fat envelope addressed to me. I ripped it open before I even took off my coat.

"Dear Peter, We are pleased to inform you . . ."

I didn't have to read any further. I was in. I pressed the paper to my face and kissed it. The next year I would be going to Tufts University. It was the only school I had applied to, early decision.

The problem was that I had decided to apply to Tufts without consulting either my mother, who had never encouraged college, or my father and Rosalind, who had made it clear that they hoped I'd choose a school in the Midwest. Years earlier, my father had set up college trust funds for all three of his sons. I had no idea if that money would cover Tufts' tuition. I assumed everything would work out somehow, now that I had gotten in. And besides, I thought, my father should be happy I was actually going to college—my older brothers had simply cashed in their college trust funds when they turned eighteen; they didn't see the point in going to college. I knew they would scoff at my dream of attending this fancy private school back east (two decades later, Joel would start a late academic career teaching sociology and writing about Mao's China at the type of elite private East Coast school he had frowned on me attending).

I called my father right away. "I've got some good news, I got into Tufts! I'm going to Tufts next year."

There was a long pause on the other end of the line. "Tufts? Isn't that a rich kids' school? Where exactly is Tufts, Peter?"

"It's near Boston."

"Ah, Boston. East Coast. That's pretty far away. Well, let's talk about it when we see you at Christmas, okay?"

"Yeah, sure, but I'm going to Tufts," I insisted, annoyed that my father didn't even congratulate me.

"How much is the tuition?"

"I'm not exactly sure. They sent me a thick envelope; it's probably in there."

"Well, bring what they sent you and we'll put a pencil to it."

Going over my college trust fund had become a father-son ritual, which he seemed to enjoy more than I did. Whenever I visited him during the holidays he always brought out a manila folder with my name on it, checked the spreadsheets, and showed me how much the fund had changed in value since my last visit. I could never remember exactly how much was in there, but I always assumed it must be enough to pay for college.

When my mother came home, I told her my news. But from her I was not expecting any big congratulations. "Guess what? I got into Tufts—Tufts University, near Boston."

"Oh, wow. I didn't know you had applied there. So I suppose this means it's official; you really *are* going to college next year."

I just nodded and smiled.

"Well, I guess that's it then," she said with a sigh. "I hope you'll be happy." And then she added: "Carl's paying for it out of your college trust fund, right?"

"Yeah, don't worry about that."

She looked relieved and gave me a hug. "I'll have to come out and visit you there sometime. I think I have some old friends in the area I can stay with." My mother projected complete calm about this sea change in our lives, but that night she confessed to her diary: "I am *really* freaking out at the prospect of seeing Peter go off on his own," adding, "Peter is nervous about growing up and being alone. So am I."

The day after getting the acceptance letter from Tufts, I was eager to get to school. Even if my parents weren't thrilled for me, I knew that my friends and teachers, especially Mr. Nelson, my English teacher and the faculty sponsor of the student paper, would be impressed that I was going to an East Coast school. For months, all anyone could talk about was who was applying where and what their first choice school was, and it was clear that many of the top students hoped to go to the East Coast. And the college mecca of the East Coast, by all accounts, was a magical-sounding place called Boston.

I did all the research. I was captivated by the glossy pictures in the college brochures of old brick buildings covered in ivy, graceful rowers on the Charles River, and the picturesque bridges that linked Cambridge and Boston. But I didn't think I would get into Harvard (I had good grades but mediocre test scores) or fit in at MIT. Tufts was the next logical choice, at least according to the college guidebooks I had studied so carefully; it even had a strong international relations program. I had told my mother years earlier that I wanted to study international relations so I could be a diplomat. "Why on earth would you want to be a diplomat?" she'd asked, laughing.

"I like the word 'diplomat,' I like how it sounds," I replied, and she laughed even harder.

I had never been to Tufts, or to Boston, or anywhere else in that part of the country, so I had no idea that being "outside of Boston" in Medford was not quite the same thing as being in Cambridge. Unlike so many of my friends, I'd had no East Coast college tour with my parents. My father, Rosalind, and Grandma Andreas had all hoped that I'd at least consider Bethel College in Kansas, the Mennonite school that almost all of my relatives had attended. My father had also suggested that I could try to use his home address to get in-state tuition at a public university in Michigan. My father was always looking for the best deal—he'd drive to multiple grocery stores to save a few cents on a gallon of milk, or drive out of his way to fill up his tank at the least expensive gas station. He'd surely want to try for the best deal when it came to college for me.

That Christmas, I sat down next to my father in his home office as he took the manila folder from his gray metal filing cabinet. Nothing made my father happier than to sit down with a pencil, calculator, spreadsheet, and a pad of paper, and work out a financial problem—"Let's put a pencil to it," he always liked to say. It satisfied him to juggle all the numbers and figure out finances like some sort of math puzzle. My father was an accountant at heart. He was never without his checkbook in his front shirt pocket, even when at home, and boasted that he had saved every check he'd ever written in his entire life. He proudly framed the check (check number 8, January 27, 1944) for the first car he bought: a used 1931 Ford Model A coupe, for $175.

Looking over all the figures in the trust fund spreadsheet and expertly tapping away on his calculator, my father had that quiet confidence of an expert accountant. His desk was covered in neatly stacked papers, leaving just enough room for a few small framed family photos—a color portrait of him and Rosalind taken around the time they were married; a black-and-white portrait of my older brothers and me together when we were little.

Though we'd been going over this spreadsheet together every Christmas for the past several years, my father seemed much less pleased by what he was finding on the page this time.

"That's a *very* expensive school," my father remarked.

"Maybe I can apply for financial aid?" I suggested.

"Absolutely not," he shot back, as if offended that I would even think of such a thing. "Financial aid is for truly needy families."

"But it sounds like we *are* needy," I persisted, pointing to the spreadsheet.

"No," he insisted. "Not like other families. We shouldn't abuse the system like some people do."

My father was proudly self-reliant, never taking a handout, never even taking a loan from a bank. He hated to use credit cards, always preferring to write a check. "Well, let's put a pencil to it again," he said. By the end of the afternoon, with a little extra encouragement from Rosalind, he somehow figured out how to stretch the college funds to cover the tuition.

I was ecstatic. Back at school in Denver after the winter break, I took out the light blue Tufts University sticker that had come with the acceptance letter and proudly pasted it on the back windshield of our light blue VW Rabbit. It was a perfect color match. Somehow that rusting car with balding tires and fading dull paint suddenly seemed a lot fancier.

Some six months later, my father and Rosalind drove out from Michigan for my high school graduation. I would be driving back with them for the summer, and they would take me to Tufts for the start of the fall semester, like all the other parents.

The day before the graduation ceremony, I went home earlier than my mother had expected and found her in bed with Enoch, a thirty-something security guard from the bank up the street. She introduced me to him awkwardly.

I nodded, and he mumbled a hello, hurriedly got up, put his clothes and holster belt back on, and disappeared out the back door.

"Well, at least you'll have your own bedroom when I'm gone," I said to my mother with a grin.

She chuckled. "Yeah, I obviously need it."

The East High School class of 1983 graduation was held at the Denver Coliseum on a warm June day—a vast space that meant my parents could easily give each other a wide berth. I was just glad they were there. There were no celebratory family pictures taken that day. My mother didn't own a camera, and my father and Rosalind just gave me a quick hug before leaving the coliseum. I'm sure my father was immensely relieved that he didn't run into my mother at the ceremony. But avoiding her entirely would not be so easy.

When my father and Rosalind arrived at the house to pick me up and load their red Buick Skyhawk for the long drive east, my mother invited them in for a cup of herbal tea. My parents had not seen each other in eight years, not since the bitter court custody battle. Now, standing at our front door, my father didn't shake hands with my mother. He didn't speak to her or even look at her. But following Rosalind's lead, he reluctantly came inside. We all crammed in around our tiny round kitchen table covered in an olive-green tablecloth, my father sitting as far away from my mother as possible and staring into his teacup. I felt his discomfort, and could not help but feel bad for him. I also felt bad that these two people, who had spent two decades together and produced three children, could not get along well enough to even shake hands or say a word to each other. My mother and Rosalind did all the talking, smiling and making chitchat.

"What a lovely place you have," Rosalind said, sugarcoating her observations. "It's so cozy. Is that picture from Pakistan?" she asked.

"It's so nice that you could come to Peter's graduation," my mother said. "It means a lot to him."

I had wanted this gathering—for all of us to be together in the same place, getting along normally, even for only a few minutes, exchanging superficial pleasantries—but now I wanted it to end as soon as possible. I was impressed that my father had come in and was sitting there politely, in my mother's kitchen, only a couple of feet away from the woman who, in his view, had stolen his children and wrecked his family. This was surely the last place in the world he wanted to be.

After we stuffed my belongings into the car trunk and backseat, leaving just enough room for me, my father and Rosalind waited in the car while I said good-bye to my mother.

"We'll go to Europe again sometime," she said confidently into my ear during our long farewell hug on the front porch, as if to say our adventures together were not over.

I pulled away from her, tears rolling down my cheeks. "I guess you'll now have to find the revolution all on your own," I said to her with a smile. But behind the smile, I was overcome with the most devastating feeling of grief and loss that I had ever experienced. Throughout all the moving around, family crises, and political upheavals over the years, my mother and I had stuck by each other—so much so that I had colluded in her kidnapping of me, fleeing the country, and hiding for years. She was not always the most nurturing and protective mother, in the traditional sense, but she was still my most dependable life companion. I was suddenly terrifyingly aware that I was on my own. The mourning began the instant I walked off that porch.

As we drove away, I looked at my mother out the back window. We waved until we couldn't see each other anymore—just like we had in my first memory, when out the back window of my father's car I had waved to my mother until she couldn't keep up and eventually disappeared into the distance.

EPILOGUE

Defection

THOUGH I COULDN'T have known it at the time, that day I left for college marked the end of my lifelong allegiance with my mother. She would live for another twenty-one years, past her seventy-first birthday, but much of the rest of her life we would spend struggling to understand and accept each other.

At first, during my time at Tufts, it looked like we would maintain that bridge, that closeness we'd always felt. I did my work under the large, colorful world map she'd mailed me, which hung above my desk. We had long phone conversations about everything from the syllabus for my Intro to International Relations class (my mother was concerned that Edward Hallett Carr, my favorite author on the reading list, "doesn't show a very profound understanding of class struggle") to my frustrations with my rowdy, all-male freshman dorm mates.

I had felt instantly out of place at Tufts despite—or because of—all my initial expectations. I transferred to Swarthmore my sophomore year. As soon as I got off the train at the bottom of the Swarthmore campus, I knew I'd made the right decision. I hadn't consulted any of my parents, but none of them seemed to mind: my father and Rosalind considered peace-loving Quakers the next best thing to Mennonites, and my mother must have been pleased about the school's political activist history—in the 1960s Swarthmore was known as the "Kremlin on the Crum," though that reputation had certainly faded by the 1980s.

It was at Swarthmore that I discovered I enjoyed studying politics, especially international politics, and thought maybe I'd even like to be a professor like my mother. But that's where the commonalities ended: I had little interest in using my role to promote radical political activism. I barely participated in any activism at all, beyond spending one winter break in Sandinista Nicaragua and listening to a long fiery speech by Fidel Castro in Managua, which I then described in proud detail to my mother. Despite my upbringing, after leaving home I attended only one demonstration—a pro-choice march in Washington in the late 1980s, carrying a sign that read GEORGE BUSH'S MOTHER DIDN'T HAVE A CHOICE! (I was trying to impress a girl.)

The fact was that, as a lot of my college classmates were going through their political awakenings, I was already burned out on activism. Raised by a rebel mother, childhood rebellion meant not becoming too much of a rebel. I had politically overdosed on a childhood full of marches and heated, late-night arguments about Lenin and the "correct political line"; college was my detox. While politics to my mother meant high-intensity ideological combat, at Swarthmore it was more about asking probing questions than having all the answers. And the more questions I asked, the more I began to question my mother's politics.

Right after graduation I moved to Washington, D.C., and shamelessly used my mother's personal contacts to get internships in the policy world. First I served as a part-time research assistant for Richard Feinberg, one of my mother's old lovers from Berkeley, now an economist and Washington insider who worked at an international development think tank. He chuckled when I contacted him and immediately offered to hire me for the summer. My mother felt uneasy about this. She wrote in her diary: "I worry that Peter is dazzled by Feinberg (a defender of capitalism with a little morality thrown in to keep the masses in line)." I also lined up a part-time internship at National Public Radio with John Dinges, the foreign desk editor, who my mother and I had lived with for a few months in Santiago when he was in the early years of his career as a journalist.

To my mother, the mere fact that I was "in Washington" meant that I was failing to fight the system. I tried to tell myself that I was fighting it from the inside, but the truth was, she was right. The more fluent I became in muted "policy speak," the less I spoke my mother's language. In the D.C. world, it was all about "U.S. interests" and "policy choices" and "improving diplomatic relations" and "strengthening ties" and "enhancing cooperation"; it was not about promoting revolution, exposing U.S. imperialism, and subverting capitalism. The long phone chats we had enjoyed in college now became less frequent and more tense. Much to my mother's dismay, I also had no interest in hearing about her latest love affairs. "Pèter," she noted sadly, "is baffled by my promiscuity." We were losing patience with each other: "I feel like being with Peter, but if he were here he'd be insufferable."

It didn't help that the intellectual community within which I was trying to prove myself couldn't speak my mother's language either, and vice versa. I winced at dinner parties at the inevitable exclamations of "That's *your* mother?" My mother had published her controversial book sympathetic to Sendero Luminoso in 1986, *When Women Rebel: The Rise of Popular Feminism in Peru.* Part of the book was about why the radical Maoist group was so attractive to rural women in Peru, including having a striking number of women as its top commanders. In Washington, to sound even remotely "pro Sendero" was like saying you supported the Khmer Rouge. As a kid just out of college trying to be taken seriously in Washington policy circles, I did my best to defend my mother when people asked, but more and more I just changed the subject.

At first I tried to argue with my mother, pleading for her to tone down her message and to distance herself from Sendero for the sake of her own credibility, but she resented it when she felt I was "preaching" at her about her extremism. I tried to get her to read the latest Americas Watch human rights report about Peru, which condemned atrocities committed by both Sendero and the government, but she scoffed that Americas Watch wasn't a real defender of human rights because "they do not defend the right to revolution."

It got harder to have long, honest phone conversations together the way we used to, and I didn't see her in person much, either, though we did rendezvous in Peru in early 1988. My girlfriend, Robyn, came with me on a four-month trip across Colombia, Peru, and Bolivia. I had long wanted to revisit some of the places I had lived as a kid. I had not been back to South America since I was eleven, more than a decade earlier. We connected with my mother for a few weeks in Cuzco, the old Inca capital, where she was taking Quechua lessons, the native language of Peru's indigenous population. My mother went with us to visit Machu Picchu and hike the last part of the Inca Trail, tourist activities she had never done with me when we lived in Peru.

But she hadn't changed most of her habits: when she insisted that we squeeze into the crowded public bus in Cuzco like the locals, by the time we got to our hotel my wallet had been stolen right out of my front pocket. She laughed at my anger. "Oh well, maybe the problem is you're too much of a soft gringo now. When you were

With my mother at Machu Picchu, January 1988

living here you would never have allowed your wallet to be stolen so easily. Maybe this is a good lesson for you, you know?"

I just gritted my teeth and rolled my eyes. Robyn thought I was overreacting. She liked my mother.

In Lima, Robyn and I visited Comas and Villa El Salvador, which had developed and grown dramatically. Familiar as they were, I could never imagine living there again. We also took the train from Lima over the Andes to the Mantaro Valley, the same train that had derailed the first time I took it with my mother back in December of 1973, some fourteen years earlier. In Jauja, we found the family that my mother and I had stayed with shortly after we arrived in Peru. They still lived on Junin Street, not far from the main plaza. Angelica remembered when I was an eight-year-old street kid following her to weekend movies and helping her pass secret notes to her boyfriend.

Robyn and I found Raul in Huancayo, where he was running the little hole-in-the-wall downtown restaurant he had opened after getting out of prison. My mother had told me how to find him, since they had always kept in touch. She said Raul was now known in Huancayo—either affectionately or disdainfully—as *El Loco* (the Crazy One). We sat at a table near the door, where I quietly sipped my soup, watching Raul intently and wondering if he'd recognize me on his own. We must have stuck out, since it was not the type of place that attracted foreigners. Raul hurried around the restaurant with authority, barking at his employees; it seemed like he enjoyed being the boss. I motioned for him to come over to our table.

"Do you know who I am?"

Raul looked at me, his expression blank.

"It's me, Peter, Carol's son," I said, getting up from the table and extending my hand.

Raul's eyes grew wide behind the cracks in his glasses and his jaw dropped. He flashed a huge smile and gave me one of his old familiar backslapping bear hugs. He sat down with us, and couldn't stop beaming and smiling, hands folded across his potbelly, still not quite believing that I was actually sitting there. He ordered beers for the table and lit a cigarette. He saw my surprise; I had never seen him smoke or drink before.

Raul wouldn't let us pay for our meal, and he insisted we visit the next day to meet his young daughter, Andrea, and her mother, who was a revolutionary herself. Raul had sworn off radical politics, so he teased and laughed at his girlfriend when she proudly brought out the red-colored homemade bombs with string fuses that she had made as a member of Peru's MRTA guerrilla group, a Cuba-inspired Marxist insurgency. In many ways she was the opposite of my mother: she talked very little but put her life much more at risk.

"Silly woman," Raul teased her, "she still thinks there will be a revolution."

She also showed us the red bandana that she used to disguise her face, like other MRTA guerrillas. It was an uncomfortable moment for me, being handed homemade bombs to admire, but I was also impressed that she trusted us enough to show us. I wondered how she felt about her daughter being named after my mother, and I also wondered, perhaps cynically, if Raul had chosen the name simply to encourage my mother to keep sending money. After that visit I never saw Raul again.

Beyond being the last time my mother and I would be in South America together, and a sharpening of so many of my childhood memories, that trip would shape my life in another way, in the form of an encounter with an elderly woman on a bus. As we crossed the border from Peru to Bolivia, a friendly old lady sheepishly asked me to store a bag full of toilet paper under my seat. I didn't understand until the border guards arrived and began confiscating smuggled toilet paper from the passengers. The toilet paper demand came from the Bolivian cocaine industry, where it was commonly used to dry and filter coca paste, which was then transported to remote jungle laboratories to be refined into powder cocaine. Most of this would eventually end up in the noses of American consumers.

A few weeks later, Robyn and I caught a ride on a cargo boat traveling down the Amazon River from Iquitos, Peru, to Leticia, Colombia, a bustling jungle town at the convergence of Peru, Colombia, and Brazil, which owed much of its existence to smuggling. Some of our fellow passengers were *pisadores* (coca stompers) with distinctive scars on their feet from exposure to the chemicals used to make coca paste. In Iquitos, late at night before our departure, I watched as several dozen drums of chemicals were quietly loaded onto our boat, and then off-loaded in the middle of nowhere before we reached Leticia.

I would later find out that many of the chemicals used by the Andean cocaine industry were actually imported from the United States and ended up on the black market. America's rapidly escalating "war on drugs" was so focused on stopping the northward flow of cocaine that it had largely overlooked the equally important southbound flow of U.S. chemicals needed to cook the coke.

This turned into a lifelong interest in studying cross-border smuggling and the politics of policing it. Though the story of the old woman and her toilet paper is the one I've always told myself was where this interest came from, it's possible those roots are deeper, reaching back to the days in which my mother used me to smuggle money and propaganda across borders, or my own kidnapping and clandestine border crossings, or maybe that seventh-grade paper about illegal drugs that my science teacher was so impressed by.

After that trip to South America, I took a series of jobs in the Washington policy world. I worked at a foreign policy journal and a liberal think tank, and helped draft a report on U.S. antidrug initiatives in South America for a congressional committee. I convinced myself that I was doing my part, however small, to challenge the Washington establishment, yet, all that time, in the back of my mind I could hear my mother telling me I'd *become* the establishment. She chastised me for not critiquing the drug war through the lens of capitalism and imperialism.

My mother also kept trying to get me to discuss Peru politics and Sendero with her, but I'd had enough. In the spring of 1991, I wrote to tell her that we had too many "philosophical differences," and that we should "call a moratorium on talking with each other about Peru." I ended the letter pleading with her not to "join the revolution" in Peru. As had been true since I was a child, I still worried she'd end up getting herself killed for a radical political cause. Long gone were the days of my childhood where I would have blindly followed my mother anywhere. Finding the revolution no longer sounded "fun." But I still worried about her safety, as I always had.

Not long after that, it became clear that we should avoid talking about politics altogether. The idea that I no longer shared my mother's political beliefs was devastating for her, and she took my political rejection as a personal one: "Peter's defection, which I've been trying to deny for years, means I've lost a big battle that I should have known could never be won. For him, it's not defection, it's who he is, caught irrevocably between two worlds (or 3 or 4 worlds?), and determined above all else not to be a 'loser.' Unfortunately, he now has to define me as a 'loser,' and that hurts." My mother felt that I had not only turned my back on her but also on the cause for which she had spent her life fighting. In a late-night diary entry in April 1991, she wrote that she was having trouble sleeping because of "Peter's betrayal of class struggle."

She also assumed that as my bond with her grew less pronounced I was becoming closer to my father. But if she had understood my father better it would have been clear that he had a hard time getting close to anyone. He was stable as a rock, but just as difficult to penetrate. It often seemed as if Rosalind was the only thing standing between him and an isolated life in the woods. After he retired, it became harder and harder to even get him out of the house.

I had never doubted that my father cared about his sons: when we were growing up, he had offered each of us comfort and security, even long-distance. And he had kept fighting to get me back all those years, against my stubborn whirlwind of a mother. But there's no denying how deeply that fight scarred him, in ways that also scarred our relationship. A week before my twenty-sixth birthday, when my girlfriend of two years left me for the suave NPR producer who I had introduced her to at a party on the roof of our Washington apartment building, my father's only response was "Well, Peter, that's what you get for shacking up and playing house before getting married. It's no surprise another man raided your bedroom." Shocked and hurt, especially given the history of his own marriage to my mother, I tried to explain to him that I'd been looking for more sympathy and support. What I got back was a long, typed letter expressing his lament that I had been raised by my mother and had therefore adopted her "loose morals" and "alternative lifestyle," in which there is no respect for marriage, family, and commitment. He pointed to the superiority of his own morals, evident in his lasting relationship with Rosalind.

"Where Are the Students Studying Mao and Lenin?"

I MOVED TO Ithaca, New York, in the fall of 1992 to enter Cornell's PhD program in government. I had wanted to be a political science professor ever since Swarthmore. I hoped that getting away from Washington would help ease the political tensions with my mother, but the fact that I had chosen academia as my career path created new heartache because I was not, and would never be, the kind of radical activist academic she had hoped. A few months before I began my graduate studies, my mother wrote in her diary:

> Part of me thinks that when he [Peter] studies more theory, becomes a student again, he will become "enlightened," take a revolutionary point of view, but that's not logical, because it's just as likely he will take the "practical" approach to graduate school (i.e. become an opportunist, go with the flow, please his professors, and get published). Exactly where are the students studying Mao and Lenin, for instance? Never mind that they led the most successful struggles against capitalism and imperialism.

By my second year in grad school, my mother's worst worries were confirmed. An August 1993 diary entry read: "Peter is not merely misinformed. He is consciously misinformed and I have to accept that he is no revolutionary. I do need to deal with my grief over this." Another entry a month later: "He [Peter] says I'm simply grounded in faith and conviction, incapable of carrying on rational discourse. I said I would like to read the papers he's writing, but I'm not sure he will send them to me."

I didn't realize then the extent to which my mother felt personally wounded by my mainstream academic career. In early August 1993, as she waited for me at the airport, she wrote: "I am nervous about our meeting. Maybe he is, too. I feel as if he's hostile to me because of his own career trajectory, that he feels he has to either change me or disown me in order to be accepted by his peers. This is immensely painful."

Although I would certainly never disown her, and had long given up trying to change her, I was tired of always feeling politically judged that I was never radical enough. As I gained more political self-confidence in graduate school, I pushed back more and more. I wanted a lot more security, comfort, and stability than she had ever provided for me when I was a child—in that sense, I was more like my father than my mother. But it's hard to have your own mother consider you a sellout.

My mother became even more alarmed when my dissertation research took me back to Washington for a year to be based at the Brookings Institution, the quintessential establishment "think tank" inside the beltway. I had hoped my mother would be impressed that I had been offered a fellowship to facilitate the D.C.-based part of my research, but on the phone she said, "Brookings? Really? Isn't that right wing?"

"They define themselves as centrist," I replied. "And it's probably more liberal leaning."

My mother quickly shot back, "Centrist in Washington means right wing. You know that, Peter. And the so-called center has been moving to the right for years now. Do you really want to even be affiliated with such a reactionary place?" I would have settled for a simple "Congratulations."

Every once in a while, though, I could still make her proud.

When my first book, *Drug War Politics*, which I wrote with my Swarthmore thesis advisor and two others, came out in 1996, she ordered copies to send to all of her closest relatives and friends. In 1998, after reading a draft of my dissertation, she confessed to her diary that "I am burning up inside with pride." She also eagerly told her friends when I was awarded a fellowship at Harvard to turn my dissertation into a book, and again later when I was offered a faculty position at Brown. Even so, she couldn't help wishing that I were following more closely in her footsteps:

> *I am realizing that he [Peter] has avoided using Marxism (not to mention Lenin and Mao) in his thesis. He will eventually pay a price for that. Most likely he is beginning to realize that already and knows he's under-educated but is fighting doing anything about it. I have warned him all the way along that he should be prepared to be blacklisted if he becomes a conscientious scholar. He did not want to hear it. So he took a safe path and now he's stumped and has to trash the whole Marxist thesis to save face.*

In retrospect, for as important as our political differences seemed at the time, it came at too high a price. During my childhood, I had hated my mother's endless, intense battles with Raul, Joel, and others, but now we were doing exactly the same thing, and it prevented us from being able to enjoy each other at the end of her life.

Chasing Rainbows

EVEN AS HER years of hard living began to catch up to her, my mother refused to slow down. She surprised everyone—herself included—by getting a tenure-track job at the University of Northern Colorado in Greeley. The sociology department's only demand was that she give up her "honor system" of letting students decide their own grades.

For the first time since I could remember, my mother, now in her mid-fifties, had job security, benefits, and a real salary. But as it turned out, she hated grading, and felt disillusioned by the lack of revolutionary fervor among the students of the 1990s in northern Colorado. She wrote in her diary that she dreaded "teaching Social Change when the TV is full of the 'triumph of democracy and free enterprise.' " She did have a few cheerful moments, however: in the fall of 1990, she wrote, "Classes are going really well . . . a bunch of students are ready to make a revolution or something, crying in my office, wanting to do something that will make a difference. So I will certainly get in trouble. It will be a miracle if I get tenure." She did get tenure, but soon after that decided to retire early.

Right before my mother retired she wrote her fourth book, *Meatpackers and Beef Barons: Company Town in a Global Economy*, an exposé of the meatpacking industry, based on an account of the exploitative working conditions in the local slaughterhouse owned by the Monfort family. But larger presses rejected the book manuscript as too ideological, which fed into her general disillusionment: "I'm being made to feel like a pariah for being politically radical, for having principles, for taking a clear class position. This is really infuriating." She was terribly upset when the University Press of Colorado declined to keep the book in print once the limited initial print run ran out, always suspecting that pressure from the Monfort family was responsible.

Retired or not, my mother resisted any push to "act her age." Her romantic interests continued to focus exclusively on much younger men. At age sixty-six she struggled with how to tell one potential suitor she wasn't interested in him because of his age: "I do have a problem with accepting OLD MEN into my life"—by which she meant anyone her own age.

At the same time, my mother was frustrated that her body was starting to slow her down: "At present I am fighting 'plantar fasciitis,' which has nothing to do with fascism, though I'm suffering from that, too. It has to do with *dancing too much.*" She had never been allowed to dance in public growing up as a Mennonite and spent much of her life making up for it.

My mother was also increasingly worried about her high blood pressure, but avoided doctors because she was convinced she'd be forced to take expensive meds pushed by pharmaceutical companies. She also started to lose more and more of her hair, which had been thin to start with, and took to covering her head with colorful scarves, her only sign of vanity. My mother always said she wondered if her hair loss came from a curse by Mama Juana, Raul's grandmother, whom we had all suspected of being a witch.

As always, my mother was spending all of her time with younger people, usually much younger, but for the first time she had begun to feel old, and was terrified of becoming dependent on others: "I am mortified that my body is so vulnerable . . . *I do not want to be hospitalized, ever.*"

She had imagined that she might write a memoir, but instead turned to "visual memoir"—creating dozens of torn-paper collages, many of which recalled moments in her life. One was a collage of the two of us, heading off to South America, walking hand in hand toward the sun. She called it *Chasing Rainbows*.

Through it all, though, my mother never let go of her political activism. One of the last times I saw her, at a dinner with Joel to celebrate her seventieth birthday, she was fuming about the U.S. invasion of Iraq the previous spring. My mother had been going to marches and demonstrations, signing petitions, writing letters to the editor, and firing off protest letters to politicians in Washington. I should have been proud and happy that she still felt so passionate about

My mother's torn-paper collage *Chasing Rainbows*, depicting the two of us traveling to South America together in 1972

being an activist, but instead I let myself overreact when, between bites, she blurted out, "You know, Bush is more evil than Hitler."

"That's a crazy thing to say," I snapped, embarrassed to be having this conversation in the middle of an Afghan restaurant. I was certainly no fan of Bush or the war, but I also no longer had the stomach for the kind of over-the-top hyperbole she had raised me on.

My mother persisted. "No, I'm serious. Who is going to stop him? Bush has far more power than Hitler ever had. It's scary."

As both she and Joel began to insist that I was in denial about the unprecedented existential threat that U.S. militarism posed to the world, I lost patience, called for the check, and took an earlier than planned plane back to Providence the next morning. Despite all our history and the love we shared, politics still held the power to break us apart.

I would not see my mother again until the following August, more than nine months later, at Joel's wedding. He married a woman he had met at an antiwar demonstration in San Francisco. During their wedding ceremony, they proudly wore matching T-shirts with the words "NO WAR!" in bold letters on the front. In my wedding toast I joked, with a smile and a wink at my mother, that we should thank George W. Bush for bringing Joel and his bride together—and that this certainly made Bush less evil than Hitler. My mother laughed and rolled her eyes. That was the last time I would ever see her.

"Uh oh, I think I'm having a heart attack, what to do."

When I first read that scribbled line, the last line in my mother's diary, I froze. The notebook lay next to my mother's bed, where she had died alone the day before, on December 7, 2004, less than a month after her seventy-first birthday. Only an hour earlier, my brothers and I had emailed family and friends to say that our mother had died "peacefully in her sleep," the same language that would be used in her *Denver Post* obituary.

I tried to re-create in my mind my mother's final living moment. How did she write that last line at night if the lights were out? Or perhaps it was already morning and it was light enough out to not need the lights on to write in her diary? Did the sudden intense pain in her chest wake her up? Or was she already awake early, as she often was, writing in her diary before getting out of bed? Was she scared? Calm? Comforted by having her diary by her side, even if her sons were not? This was what I'd been afraid of my whole life—suddenly losing my mother—and now it had finally happened.

My brothers and I hastily organized a small memorial service. A local Iranian friend of my mother's volunteered her house for the event, and several dozen activist friends, most of whom I had not seen since I was a teenager, gathered to pay their respects. There were the feminist lesbians from Denver, activists from RIP Bookstore and the Coors strike from the late seventies, and a handful of her closest former students. Even though my mother had died alone, there was no doubt that these passionate allies had been an extended family of sorts. One person read a Pablo Neruda poem, *"Alturas de Machu Picchu,"* and we all sang the Communist "The Internationale," reminding me of our days together in Chile. In between the planned eulogies, people stood spontaneously to say kind things. Joel and I struggled to talk coherently through the tears. Ronald sat stone-faced the entire time; he didn't say a word and didn't shed a tear, but I was glad that at least he was there. Years earlier, he and my mother had reconciled enough to be in regular contact again, and it pleased her enormously that he and Dawn and their ten-year-old son, Derek—the only grandchild my mother would ever know—had recently moved to Colorado.

Back in Providence, I unpacked the duffel bags filled with my mother's diaries that I had brought home, and put them in neat stacks in chronological order. I began reliving her life, reading backward in time from the very moment she died. At first I wondered if she'd disapprove; years earlier, she had written:

*I've been thinking about protecting my diary and correspon-
dence from getting robbed or misappropriated or misused.
Safest, of course, is to get rid of them, and I wouldn't do that.
Could put a sign on it saying it should be destroyed when I
die—that's what I'm thinking about, but that seems a little
drastic, too. . . . Could make them off limits to anyone but my
sons (who wouldn't be interested in them anyways).*

But for me, my mother was still alive in these pages—so preserv-
ing the diaries was my way of keeping her alive. I couldn't stop reading. It felt like one last chance to talk to her about our life together,
to say good-bye.

Hard as the passages were for me to read, my mother seemed, in
some ways, ready to let go during those final years: "I am, and have
been, fixated on how to make myself disappear with no fuss and
bother; it is not depression. It's just a sense of completion and a kind
of boredom that can only come from having lived to the max."

She might even have been able to predict how it would happen:
she had been struggling with chest pains for some time, yet kept
them hidden from her children. In one diary entry, she noted, "I
started having angina earlier when I was reading, and now it's returned. This is why I keep wanting to be with my sons. I have not
told anyone about these attacks." Three years later, she wrote: "I had
a short bout of angina in the middle of the night. Realizing 'I might
wake up dead,' I had an extraordinary feeling of wanting *not to leave
my children*—it was a powerful surreal experience that is hard to describe (impossible to describe)."

I did not fully realize how much she longed for her children,
nor how concerned she was that we, or the world at large, might
judge her to be a "bad mother." This was one of her biggest worries
at the end of her life, despite all the years of flaunting parental con-
ventions. "When they don't call me I think they are unhappy, then
I feel I've been a BAD MOTHER and need to ask for 'forgiveness'

for something. Yet I know (even if they don't) that I was not a BAD MOTHER. Stuck again. This is a perpetual problem."

To some degree, she was able to acknowledge, privately, that in her younger years she had to choose between her children and her political goals: "I really feel terrible sometimes when I think what I've put my kids through. I guess I'm trying to make it up to them by letting them go a bit now while still being there (or here) for them when they need me, which I wasn't always able to do when I felt I was carrying all the burdens of the world on my shoulders."

Instead of discussing any of this with me, however, she waited for me to tell her how good a mother she had been, how heroic—but I didn't. And she certainly didn't hear those words from Ronald, with whom things had never fully healed: "July 18, 2001: 3:24 a.m.— awake again, though I've been sleeping. I am needing a balm, and wondering if I've done all I can to heal the wounds of those teenage tensions with Ronald. Can I ask him for FORGIVENESS? I need help with this."

As for me, I wish I could explain to my mother what I feel now. In some ways, she did fall into some "bad mothering." A child should not feel that he must let his mother kidnap him in order to secure her love, or be a nightly witness to his mother's political screaming matches and marital passions, or bear the weight of her suicidal thoughts. A child should not be allowed to play with a loaded gun because it is "good training for the revolution," nor should he see his mother arrested as she shoplifts his birthday present. He should not have to defy his mother's ideological insistence that he attend a bad high school because it is more "working class." All in all, a child needs more stability than to live in three states and five countries in more than a dozen different homes and schools between the ages of five and eleven. Certainly, I hope to protect my own daughters from all of this.

And yet—and yet. There is so much she gave me, too, so much I would never trade for a thousand "normal" childhoods. My mother was absolutely convinced she was doing the right thing, unconventional as it was. She wanted to share with me her deepest convictions and passions for justice, to raise me according to her own highest beliefs. Some would say that the way she chose to do so was selfish and self-absorbed, yet if she had left me with my father from the very beginning, as some of her relatives urged, her own life would have been far easier. But she could not bear to leave her little boy behind. In the last years of her life she was nostalgic about our time together, realizing our bond had been as important as the ones she always sought in the arms of younger lovers: "I watched a mom and her 8–9 year old son while at the coffeehouse and remembered what a privilege it was to spend all those years trekking around the world with Peter. Better than having a 'partner' in some ways, but I suppose I didn't realize that at the time?"

What I do know is that I always felt my mother loved me and wanted me. She was sometimes negligent, even recklessly so, but I never felt neglected. In the end, my mother kept that promise she made to me when we headed off to South America in 1972. She promised that I would someday understand and be glad that we had gone on this adventure together, that I would even feel lucky. She was right. I do feel lucky—though I also feel lucky my life didn't get completely derailed along the way. And even though I don't share my mother's brand of radical politics or faith in the coming revolution, without her I would have led a more narrow, insular life, less aware of other peoples and cultures and less concerned about the world's great injustices and inequalities. I wish I shared her trust in the benevolent power of the masses to rise up and correct the wrongs of the world, but her fiery idealism and passion for social justice is inspiring all the same.

Acknowledgments

This is not the sort of book that a political science professor typically writes, though it is certainly about politics. When I wear my more scholarly hat I write more standard academic stuff. Maybe that's why, when I first started to write this book, I kept it to myself, just as I had long kept the details of my childhood to myself. I also disliked the pretentious-sounding word *memoir*, and was uncomfortable using it. So I'm happy that, rather than scratching their heads and raising their eyebrows, many friends, relatives, and colleagues not only encouraged me to write this story but some of them took the time to read drafts. I especially thank Rosalind Andreas, Corey Brettschneider, Anne Button, Zairo Cheibub, Nitsan Chorev, Phoebe Damrosch, John Dinges, Matt Gutmann, Clair Kaplan, Wendy Lavallee, Paul Lavallee, Rick Locke, Cathy Lutz, Jim Morone, Suzanne Rich, Jim Ron, Jason Salzman, and Deb Taylor. My brother Joel read the manuscript multiple times, and while not always sharing my perspective, was supportive from start to finish. I'm also grateful that my father was such a meticulous keeper of letters and documents, which he kindly shared with me to help fill in important gaps. We've long lost touch, but I want to thank Jean-Pierre for having a camera during our time together in South America. Jane Rosenman, Suzanne Strempek Shea, and Diana Spechler provided terrific feedback. Melani Cammett and Angelo Manioudakis gave me the perfect secluded place to go through the final revisions without distraction. At Simon & Schuster, Millicent Bennett embraced this book when it was still a rough draft and helped me polish it into something much better, and Jonathan Cox expertly carried it across the finish line. I am deeply indebted to both of them. Jonathan Karp came up with the title (and wisely rejected my alternatives). Tamara Arellano shepherded the book through the production editorial process. My agent, Rafe Sagalyn, was encouraging from the beginning and smartly advised me to take my time. Kristen Lavallee made sure that I enjoyed the here and now even as my mind was often on faraway places in my distant past. I dedicate this book to Stella and to Annika, who arrived in this world while I was in the midst of writing and who did everything they could to keep me from finishing. Hopefully someday they'll enjoy reading about their father's childhood years with their radical grandmother, whom I wish they could have met.

PETER ANDREAS is the John Hay Professor of International Studies at Brown University, where he holds a joint appointment between the Department of Political Science and the Watson Institute for International and Public Affairs. Andreas has published ten books, including *Smuggler Nation: How Illicit Trade Made America*, which was selected by Amazon and by *Foreign Affairs* as one of the best books of the year. He has also written for a wide range of publications, including *Foreign Affairs*, *Foreign Policy*, the *Guardian*, *Harper's*, *The Nation*, the *New Republic*, the *New York Times*, *Slate*, and the *Washington Post*.